D0986849

WITHDRAWN

The Neutralization
of Southeast Asia

Dick Wilson
foreword by
Gene T. Hsiao

Published in cooperation with
the Asian Studies Program of
Southern Illinois University
at Edwardsville

The Praeger Special Studies program—
utilizing the most modern and efficient book
production techniques and a selective
worldwide distribution network—makes
available to the academic, government, and
business communities significant, timely
research in U.S. and international economic, social, and political development.

The Neutralization of Southeast Asia

PRAEGER SPECIAL STUDIES IN INTERNATIONAL POLITICS AND GOVERNMENT

Praeger Publishers   New York   Washington   London

Library of Congress Cataloging in Publication Data

Wilson, Richard Garratt.
    The neutralization of Southeast Asia.

    (Praeger special studies in international politics and government)
    Includes bibliographical references and index.
    1. Asia, Southeastern—Foreign relations.   2. Asia,
Southeastern—Neutrality.   I.   Title.
DS518.1.W47   327'.0959   74-3516
ISBN 0-275-09110-4

PRAEGER PUBLISHERS
111 Fourth Avenue, New York, N.Y. 10003, U.S.A.
5, Cromwell Place, London SW7 2JL, England

Published in the United States of America in 1975
by Praeger Publishers, Inc.

Printed in the United States of America

The idea of neutralizing Southeast Asia—a historical battlefield
of both indigenous and external forces—is a subject that has attracted
the attention of many statesmen and scholars alike for many years.
However, it did not take shape until the issuance of the Kuala Lumpur
Declaration of November 27, 1971 by the five member states of the
Association of Southeast Asian Nations. Due to the deep complexity
and wide ramification of the problem, realization of the idea is still
not in sight. Nevertheless, if peace is to be maintained in this nuclear age where a process of political and economic multipolariza-
tion is rapidly unfolding, some form of neutralization for the whole
region is not only desirable but may be necessary.

This volume is the first systematic presentation of the problem in a scholarly fashion. Thorough in research, comprehensive
in scope, solid in content, intelligent in approach, smooth in organization, and lucid in writing, the work opens with a survey of the origins and development of the neutralization idea, its advantages and
disadvantages to the Southeast Asian nations and to the big powers
involved. Then it discusses the relative positions of the individual
Southeast Asian nations on the issue, the attitudes of the major external powers, and the prospects for a regional unity based on the
common security and economic interests of all the parties concerned.

The author, Dick Wilson, is a seasoned observer of Southeast
Asia. Graduated from Oxford University with a First Class Honors
Degree in Law and a Baccalaureate in Civil Law, he attended the
University of California Law School at Berkeley as a Fulbright
Scholar and earned an LL. M. degree in 1953. Then he traveled
and worked in many parts of Asia before teaching law at the University of Dacca in 1954. In the succeeding years, he was a correspondent of The Financial Times (London) in Poland and editor of
the Far Eastern Economic Review (1958-64) in Hong Kong. He won
the Ramon Magsaysay Award for Journalism in 1964 for his work in
economic journalism in Asia. During that same period, he was also
a correspondent in Hong Kong for The Financial Times and The
Guardian (of Manchester). Among the top Asian political leaders he
interviewed were Chinese Premier Chou En-lai and Japanese Prime
Minister Eisaku Sato.

From 1964 to 1969, Mr. Wilson lectured in London on Asian
affairs while serving as a freelance writer for The Times, The Financial Times, The Spectator, the BBC, and a wide range of other
periodicals. In 1969 he became a special advisor to the Straits

Times group of newspapers in Malaysia and Singapore. Since 1972 he has resumed his freelance work in London while traveling and lecturing throughout the world.

Among his numerous publications are: A Quarter of Mankind (1966; published in the United States in 1968 under the title Anatomy of China); Asia Awakes: A Continent in Transition (1970); The Long March 1935 (London, 1971; New York, 1972); East Meets West: Singapore (Singapore, 1971); and The Future Role of Singapore (Oxford University Press, for Royal Institute of International Affairs, London, 1972).

The Asian Studies Program of Southern Illinois University at Edwardsville is glad to have the opportunity of cosponsoring the publication of Mr. Wilson's present work. I personally believe that this volume is a meaningful contribution to Southeast Asian studies and a very useful reference to all those who are interested in international affairs.

ACKNOWLEDGMENTS

I wish to express gratitude to the many Ministers and officials of the Southeast Asian governments who explained their views on neutralization to me, and to many friends who helped me to locate material and develop ideas--especially S. M. Ali, M. Pathmanathan, and Arun Senkuttuvan.

CONTENTS

LIST OF ABBREVIATIONS

The following books or periodicals are so frequently cited that abbreviations are used:

ARB   Asia Research Bulletin, Singapore

BP   Bangkok Post

FAM   Foreign Affairs Malaysia

FEER   Far Eastern Economic Review

MD   Malaysian Digest

ND   New Directions in the International Relations of Southeast Asia: The Great Powers and South East Asia. Lau Teik Soon, ed., Singapore University Press for Institute of Southeast Asian Studies, 1973.

NDE   New Directions in the International Relations of Southeast Asia: Economic Relations. Lee Soo Ann, ed., Singapore University Press for Institute of Southeast Asian Studies, 1973.

STK   Straits Times, Kuala Lumpur edition.

STS   Straits Times, Singapore edition.

SWB   British Broadcasting Corporation, Summary of World Broadcasts.

SWB-FE   British Broadcasting Corporation, Summary of World Broadcasts, Far East

THE NEUTRALIZATION PLAN

In 1970 the government of Malaysia proposed that the entire region of Southeast Asia, embracing at least 10 sovereign states all too small or too weak to be individually effective in world affairs, be neutralized under big power guarantee. The overt purpose of this arrangement would be to free a region that has the reputation of being the Balkans of the Asian continent, full of quarrels and conflicts, from the interference and intervention of the big powers for their own purposes. In 1971 the proposal was endorsed, though in an ambiguous form, by Malaysia's four partners in ASEAN, the Association of Southeast Asian Nations—Indonesia, the Philippines, Singapore, and Thailand. The five Foreign Ministers of these states pledged to work toward, not a neutralized Southeast Asia, but the recognition of Southeast Asia as "a zone of peace, freedom, and neutrality." (Strictly speaking the Thai signatory, Dr. Thanat Khoman, was a Special Envoy of his government at that time though he had formerly been Foreign Minister and continued to supervise foreign affairs under his new title.) The five governments proceeded to spend several years discussing and arguing how to implement this, and how much of the original Malaysian proposal to incorporate.

This was not the first suggestion of neutrality in a region that had produced, in U Nu's and Ne Win's Burma and in Prince Norodom Sihanouk's Cambodia, two of the most convincing and authentic examples of neutralism or neutrality in an Asian context. Nor was it even the first suggestion for the more complex and demanding concept of neutralization, since that had already been canvassed as a solution to the problems of Indochina by such statesmen as Anthony Eden and Charles de Gaulle. But in the southern or oceanic part of Southeast Asia, where pro-Western attitudes have predominated throughout the postwar era (in Indonesia only since 1965), neutrality was in 1970 something novel, intriguing, and even daring. The Malaysian government's proposal constituted the first serious and thought-out diplomatic initiative to come from within the region (and hence to be distinguished from suggestions by such foreign statesmen as Eden or de Gaulle) for a collective solution to the international security problems of this troubled region.

In that sense it was a milestone, certainly in Southeast Asia's and arguably in Asia's history, and it is in that sense that it is discussed in this book, the purpose of which is to set out the Malaysian proposal in all its ramifications, to place it against its spatial and chronological background, to set down the lines of discussion and argument it provoked within Southeast Asia, and to explain the varying attitudes of the Southeast Asian states themselves and of the larger powers beyond. While multiple neutralization in the strictest sense (it should be noted that the only European precedents are for simple neutralization) is probably not suitable for the joint needs of Southeast Asia in the circumstances of today, it does provide a desirable and satisfactory long-term goal for which Southeast Asian opinion could successfully be aroused, and in the course of discussing it in all its detail the five governments of ASEAN have certainly clarified their own ideas about their several and collective diplomatic futures.

IMPORTANCE OF SOUTHEAST ASIA

For all its "Balkan" image the region whose future is at stake is actually, and especially potentially, more important than many others on the globe. Including its "mediterranean" or intervening seas, it covers an area larger than the United States. Its frontiers embrace more people than either the United States, the Soviet Union, or the European Community. Its collective gross national product now stands at around U.S. $60 billion. It represents a vast market for both consumer and capital goods and is abundantly rich in the raw materials needed for modern industrial life—particularly petroleum, mineral ores, and tropical agricultural products.

Strategically it is placed at the crossroads of the modern world. It is a bridge between Asia and Australia. It is a compulsory passage between China and Europe, between Japan and the Middle East, between the easternmost parts of the USSR and its western half, between Europe and Japan, and between China and Australia. The city that stands in the center of it, Singapore, is the third busiest port and third largest oil refining center in the entire world. About 80 percent of the world's rubber and 60 percent of its tin are derived from this region.

All these facts help to explain why so many nations outside Southeast Asia have developed a strong interest in the region, and why the large powers in particular have in modern times been tempted to compete with each other in order to defend or extend their interests there. They explain why it was possible for a senior Southeast Asian scholar and diplomat to declare to an international conference in the region at the beginning of the 1970s that because of very recent developments, "it is perhaps not our fate to have to bow our heads in the direction of Moscow, Peking, or Washington in the way that most of our fathers bowed to Tokyo just three decades ago."

CHALLENGE OF THE 1970s

In the early postwar years, most of Southeast Asia was engrossed in its struggle for national independence from the colonial rule of the French, Americans, British, and Dutch. Many of the states that succeeded in establishing their independence in the 1940s or 1950s were almost immediately confronted by the challenge of armed rebellion on the part of their Communist compatriots, eagerly supported from Moscow and Peking. When the threat was deflected, they had to face the triple challenge of nation-building (often in circumstances where no important "national" history existed, or where the line of descent from earlier glories was muddied by migration, the passage of centuries, and the absence of authentic history), national unity (constantly threatened by secessionist tendencies in the more outlying regions as well as by ethnic or religious minorities), and economic modernization (thwarted by the inexorable growth of population and the neglect of industrialization during the colonial phase). It was only by the late 1960s that the new nations of Southeast Asia were ready and able to consider what policies they should pursue in common in the jungle of the latter-day twentieth-century world of multipolar capitalism.

Their need to consider this was accelerated by the sudden change in the international influences at work on the area, a change that began as the 1960s came to a close. One of the first small signals of change was the decision by the British government of Harold Wilson in 1968 to withdraw, for economic reasons, Britain's military presence "east of Suez," which included the historic naval base at Singapore and other facilities that had only a few years before been instrumental in assisting Malaysia and Singapore to resist the armed confrontation of an indignant and bellicose Sukarnoist Indonesia. Later this policy was slowed down by the successor government of Edward Heath, and the British presence was replaced in both Singapore and Malaysia by a Commonwealth five-power arrangement involving not only British but also Australian and New Zealand as well as local Malaysian and Singaporean forces. But this in turn was threatened in 1973-74 by the decision of the Whitlam government in Canberra to withdraw the Australian participation in this arrangement and by the return of Wilson to power in London, and by the mid-1970s the future of the Australian, New Zealand and United Kingdom (ANZUK) presence in Singapore and Malaysia seemed very limited.

Meanwhile the Nixon administration in Washington had decided to secure a negotiated withdrawal of American forces from the bitter and protracted war in Vietnam, accompanied by the so-called Guam or Nixon Doctrine by which America proposed henceforth to attempt to encourage a satisfactory resolution of Asian problems through the use of indigenous Asian forces, without the assistance of U.S. ground troops. The significant shift of American policy toward Southeast Asia was accompanied by the entry of China into the United Nations in 1971, closely followed by the accolade of a presidential visit to Peking by Mr. Nixon with all the publicity and prestige that this entailed. China had been the sleeping giant beyond Southeast Asia's horizon for so many years that it was a shock for most Southeast Asians to realize one October night that a Chinese voice was now to speak in the United Nations and exercise a permanent veto power in the Security Council, and that China would inevitably extend its influence in the world and need to be dealt with on "normal" diplomatic terms by the governments of the region. Since there were such grave apprehensions about the possibility of future Chinese designs on the region, extending from the somewhat unrealistic nightmare of Chinese military conquest to the less highly colored fears of heightened Chinese support for national liberation movements seeking to bring left-wing governments to power in Southeast Asia, this development was an extremely worrying one.

For good measure, another new factor was entering into the complex equation of Southeast Asian politics, namely the resurgence of Japan to become not merely the third wealthiest country in the entire world (and the wealthiest in Asia) but a power increasingly under pressure to acquire the political and military role in the region which it had so steadfastly refused under the U.S. umbrella before Mr. Nixon began to remove it. Meanwhile, from the other side of the world, the Soviet Union had begun to intrude not only into the Indian Ocean but also into Southeast Asian waters, apparently out of a desire to minimize the possible control of these strategic areas by its two enemies, China and the United States. As a result of the abdication of the British in the late 1960s, the Indian Ocean was, in the words of Singapore's Foreign Minister, S. Rajaratnam, "put up for auction." And then, at the beginning of 1973, a cease-fire of a kind was negotiated in Indochina, and American forces were gradually withdrawn from the battle areas of that troubled country. It was clear to realists in the region that in the future no American soldiers would be sent to fight in Indochina or in any other mainland state of Asia.

The combination of all these circumstances set the scene for the neutralization debate inaugurated by the Malaysian Prime Minister, Tun Abdul Razak. Small wonder that a leading Singaporean intellectual, invited in 1972 to paint a picture of the region's future, suggested that the relevant analogy was actually "not that of a painting but of a used canvas on which several artists are working all at once." It was impossible to tell what the picture would become, and all one could do was to describe what could be seen of the original painting and of the rough, tentative outline that the various artists were filling in.

1

THE NEUTRALIZATION
IDEA

When Tun Abdul Razak became Prime Minister of Malaysia in September 1970, he began a new initiative that was to prove of immense importance in crystallizing Southeast Asian opinion about that region's long-term international future. He proposed that the region be neutralized under big power guarantee. In his first major policy statement to an international audience, at the Non-Aligned Summit Conference in Lusaka, Zambia, the Prime Minister-designate declared:

> Nowhere are the principles of self-determination and
> noninterference more in need of urgent application than
> in the Indochina region where for more than twenty years
> the people have been tortured by the nightmares of war.
> It is my hope that in reaffirming the right of self-
> determination and noninterference in the Indochina area,
> the Non-Aligned Group would at the same time take a
> positive stand in endorsing the neutralization of the
> area and possibly of the entire region of Southeast Asia,
> guaranteed by the three major powers, the People's Re-
> public of China, the Soviet Union, and the United States.
> I mention the need to extend the area of peace and neu-
> tralization to include all of Southeast Asia because it
> is obviously easier and wiser to strengthen the fabric
> of peace before it is ruptured rather than attempt to
> eliminate disorder and conflict once they have pene-
> trated into the region.[1]

Razak's argument was based on the state of flux in which the region then found itself. The dismantling of the British naval and military base in Singapore, the gradual U.S. disengagement from the Vietnam War, the growing strength of Japan, and the emergence of

China into the regional scene—all these developments at the beginning of the 1970s promised a sea change in the power balance of Southeast Asia which its governments would do well to anticipate and guard against. Razak told the Malaysian Parliament in a later speech:

> When we look at the area around us we cannot fail to note that Southeast Asia has not enjoyed peace and security for more than two decades. This region has been convulsed by war essentially because of the involvement of major powers in our affairs. It is clear from this therefore that peace and stability can only be safeguarded by a policy of neutralization which will ensure that this region will no longer be a theater of conflict for the competing interests of the major powers.
>
> It is also clear that this policy of neutralization can only be successful if it receives the understanding and support—or, more specifically, the guarantee—of the great powers themselves, namely China, the Soviet Union, and the United States. This requires first of all that the States in the region should work to bring about the conditions which are necessary for the realization of the neutralization proposed and show that a neutralized Southeast Asia meets with the basic legitimate interests of the great powers themselves. . . . We are naturally aware that this is a long-term solution and it requires to be accepted by the superpowers as well as by the countries of the region themselves. It requires that we should first of all keep our own houses in order, that we should resolve sources of tension and conflict within the region, and that we should develop stronger ties of cooperation and solidarity among countries of Southeast Asia. It also requires, as I have already explained, the support of the superpowers which can only be secured when we can demonstrate that this arrangement provides a guarantee that their respective interests will not be adversely affected. . . .
>
> In considering questions on foreign policy we must not be too taken up with immediate and transient issues. We must have a sense of history and we must be guided by a vision of the future. We must be conscious of the past—and by this I mean not just the immediate past of the last one or two decades. We must have a broad sweep of the historical processes and impulses affecting the area round us. In this way we develop a correct and coherent view of the future so that we will then work

towards a clear and specific objective within which all our other decisions can be framed. For us in Malaysia our vision for the future is that of a Community of Southeast Asia. . . . When we look at the map of Asia, it is possible to see that Southeast Asia is a clear and coherent unit which through the vicissitudes of history has not been able to play its proper role in the world. As this Government works to strengthen our links with other Southeast Asian countries to promote greater regional cooperation and understanding and to evolve new relationships with the emerging power centers of the 70s, we shall be guided by this vision of a community of nations in Southeast Asia which will finally fulfill its proper destiny in the world.[2]

THE RATIONALE

The rationale of the new proposal was most effectively spelled out in an article by Ghazali bin Shafie, one of Razak's key Ministers and the most articulate exponent of the new mood in a country which in the first thirteen years of its independence from British rule had seemed unable to shake itself free from its colonial cocoon and had followed a broadly pro-Western line in foreign policy.

Ghazali argued, in an article published in the Japanese quarterly Pacific Community in October 1971, that the new factors in the regional scene were potentially dangerous unless new ground rules were established. "In the interest of peace in the area, and very likely of the world, the entire Southeast Asian region should be neutralized. The countries in the region should get together and, as a group, serve notice to the world that the region should no longer serve as a theater for international power struggle. Major powers should be given the assurance that each power's withdrawal and non-involvement will not result in any advantage to other powers."

The first phase in the neutralization process, Ghazali went on, should be for each state within the region to respect the others' sovereignty and territorial integrity and "not participate in activities likely to directly or indirectly threaten the security of another." To the contrary, the regional states should promote regional cooperation, devise methods of ensuring peace among themselves (and accept the full responsibility for peace), and present a collective view to the outside powers on vital security issues. Following this, "all foreign powers should be excluded from the region." The second phase would be for the major external powers—the United States, the USSR, and China—to accept Southeast Asia as an area of neutrality, exclude it from their own power struggles, guarantee that neutrality, and work out ways of making that guarantee effective. In other words, the insiders would be responsible for maintaining peace among themselves, and the outsiders would be responsible for preventing externally inspired conflict in the region.

Ghazali conceded that "all this will require monumental efforts in diplomacy." The big powers would be reluctant to step back unless they were sure that the losses would be mutual, shared equally among them. The creation of "a supervisory body capable of enforcing the neutralization arrangement" would be most difficult. Furthermore, the exercise would have to await an Indochina settlement. "There can be no neutralization for the region so long as the war in Vietnam continues." Indeed, Ghazali declared that it was time the Southeast Asians themselves took an initiative in this matter. "For too long the diplomatic fate of Southeast Asia has been in the hands of powers external to the region. . . . It is time surely that Southeast Asian countries must be the primary actors in the settlement of what is after all their own future." Tun Razak later welcomed the Paris Agreement on a Vietnam cease-fire in January 1973 with the words: "So far as Malaysia is concerned, this negotiated settlement of the Vietnam conflict is an important step forward in the realization of our proposal for the neutralization of Southeast Asia."[3]

Earlier Schemes

This was not the first advocacy of some kind of neutralization for the region. Curiously enough, it had fallen to a Malayan delegate at the Asian Relations Conference in New Delhi in March 1947, John Thivy, to suggest a "neutrality bloc" in Asia. This was rejected by the Indians and others, and it was not in any case meant to be confined to Southeast Asia—indeed, it could be regarded as the forerunner of the eventual nonalignment policy developed by Nehru.[4] De Gaulle's pronouncements on the Indochina situation of his day implicitly rested on a similar idea, and Eden had declared in 1966, in the same context, that "our duty is to prepare plans providing international guarantees for the security of a neutral belt" in Southeast Asia.[5] In the same year a group of Princeton scholars, headed by Klaus Knorr, prepared a study of the problems and prospects of neutralization in Southeast Asia for the U.S. Senate Committee on Foreign Relations, headed by Senator William Fulbright.[6] In 1969 Leonid Brezhnev launched the Soviet proposal for a collective security system embracing all Asia, predicated on the desire of the Asians to be insulated from big power conflict. Maurice Schumann of France canvassed in 1970 for the establishment for a zone of neutrality and peace in Indochina, and such figures as George F. Kennan and Governor George W. Romney have also lent their names to the idea.

But the Razak proposal of 1970 was the first initiative to originate from within the Southeast Asian region, exclusively for the region, and the first to be sustained with solid argument against a battery of critics. As Dr. Ismail, Razak's deputy in his early years of premiership, later claimed, the neutralization proposal could be regarded

> as the extension or concomitant of the determination by the peoples of the region to shape their own destiny by themselves. This surely is the crucial difference between our neutralization policy, which is based on self-reliance, and the neutralization schemes of the past which however well-intentioned were the fruit of the diplomatic ingenuity of outsiders. Such schemes were doomed to collapse since they were not rooted in national sentiments and aspirations of the people most directly concerned. In very simple words, ASEAN's call for a neutral Southeast Asia is genuine because it is native-based. It is the product of independent Southeast Asian initiative and judgement.[7]

Malaysian Authorship

Why Malaysia? In many respects Malaysia must have appeared the least likely candidate for such a role. Under its first Premier and father of the nation, Tunkun Abdul Rahman, Malaysia had acquired a reputation for following the Western camp. His close personal links with Britain, set against a background where independence (in 1957) had come later than anywhere else in the region,* and more at Britain's urging than Malaysia's, encouraged the Tunku to take what was then an unfashionably sympathetic attitude towards the West, its political institutions, and its economic systems. Only on the question of racial discrimination did the Malaysian Premier do battle with his fellow premiers in the "white" Commonwealth, and it remains one of the Tunku's proudest boasts that it was he who drummed South Africa out of the Commonwealth. On other issues, however, the Malaysia of 1957-70 seemed almost "more English than the English." British military bases were retained in the country, and the economic dominance of British companies was not challenged.

---

*Save for Singapore, which was a special case, becoming free of Britain only in 1963.

When the time came, therefore, for the Tunku's deputy, Tun Razak, to take the chair in 1970, it was understandable that he sought ways of distinguishing his regime from his predecessor's. The neutralization proposal has been seen, "perhaps cynically, as an attempt to mark the coming-of-age of Tun Razak from under the banyan tree of the enduring Tunku Abdul Rahman."[8] In fact the original authorship of the idea was claimed by Dr. Ismail, Razak's deputy after 1970, who had previously advocated the declaration of the neutralization of Southeast Asia, to be followed by a nonaggression pact between the countries within the region.[9] This suggestion was made as a parliamentary back-bencher in 1968, and no notice was taken of it at the time; ironically, it was Razak who had to reply, on behalf of the Tunku Abdul Rahman's government, pouring some cold water on Ismail's idea. Outside parliament, however, Razak spoke less cavalierly of the concept. Two years later he thankfully picked it up and took it as the principal foreign policy pillar of his new government. It is, however, not quite correct to say that the international advocacy of the proposal began only after Tunku Razak assumed the premiership. Ghazali had told the preparatory group which met in Dar-es-Salaam early in 1970 to prepare the arrangement for the nonaligned summit in Lusaka later that year: "It is Malaysia's hope that nonaligned countries will be able to endorse the neutralization not only of the Indochina area but of the entire region of Southeast Asia, guaranteed by the three major powers, the People's Republic of China, the Soviet Union, and the United States, against any form of external interference, threat or pressure."[10] That was in April 1970, a full five months before the Tunku stood down.

It would seem that the idea was a combination of Ismail's suggestion of 1968, Razak's determination to find new directions in foreign policy, and Ghazali's favorable reactions to the 1966 U.S. Senate study, fortified by the failure of the Djakarta Conference on Cambodia in the spring of 1970 to obtain U.S. approval for the neutralization of Cambodia.[11] It is quite likely that Razak's desire to get away from the pro-American aura of his predecessor meant that he was looking for a policy known to be not fully acceptable in Washington. If by this he hoped to improve Malaysia's prestige in the Third World, he was fully vindicated.

The neutralization proposal, superficially simple, proved highly complex when it came to be discussed seriously by the governments of the region and by outsiders. The history of that debate will be rehearsed in the following chapter; here we shall set out the principal problems created by the proposal. They fall into three categories: technical issues of definition, machinery, and geographical coverage; disadvantages accruing to the big powers asked to guarantee the region's neutrality; and disadvantages accruing to the regional states asking for it.

DISADVANTAGES TO SOUTHEAST ASIA

The price that the regional states of Southeast Asia would pay for guaranteed neutralization could be expressed in this way: They would have to opt out of the power struggle in the wider international arena, and they would by the same token have to renounce any recourse to the big powers. Neutralization would mean, in the words of Ghazali bin Shafie, "that countries in the region of Southeast Asia will take no further part in the world power game."[12] It was all very well for Dr. Ismail to deny that the neutralization formula would enforce a permanent powerlessness on the part of the region, with psychologically unacceptable "connotations of weakness."[13] The fact is that Indonesia in particular interpreted the conditions of neutralization as imposing on Southeast Asia, because of the obligations that the Southeast Asian states would incur towards the great powers, a new form of collective colonialism.[14]

Specifically, neutralization would require all the Southeast Asian states to "undertake to maintain their impartiality and . . . refrain from involvement directly or indirectly in ideological, political, economic, armed, or other forms of conflict, particularly between powers outside the zone."[15] The obligations accepted by Laos when it was neutralized in 1962 included the following:

It will not resort to the use or threat of force in any way which might impair the peace of other countries, and will not interfere in the internal affairs of other countries;

It will not enter into any military alliance or into any agreement, whether military or otherwise, which is inconsistent with the neutrality of the Kingdom of Laos; it will not allow the establishment of any foreign military base on Laotian territory for military purposes or for the purpose of interference in the internal affairs of other countries, nor recognize the protection of any alliance or military coalition including SEATO;

It will not allow any foreign interference in the internal affairs of the Kingdom of Laos in any form whatsoever;

It will require the withdrawal from Laos of all foreign troops and military personnel, and will not allow any foreign troops or military personnel to be introduced into Laos;

It will accept direct and unconditional aid from all countries that wish to help the Kingdom of Laos build up an independent and autonomous national economy on the basis of respect for the sovereignty of Laos.[16]

But, as David Mozingo has observed, "The historical record
. . . is unambiguous. Most Southeast Asian governments facing domestic crisis turn quickly to foreign powers, and the latter have almost never resisted the temptation to intervene."[17] Any regime that
feels itself under threat of destruction will resort to outside help,
and that help will more often be sought from outside the region than
within—partly because the other regional states cannot compete with
the big powers in wealth and military strength and partly because
the more distant powers have fewer axes to grind in Southeast Asian
politics (whereas help from within the region would have to be paid
for by conceding some area of national interest to a neighbor: Indonesia might help the Philippines on condition that the Muslim inhabitants of Mindanao were better treated, Malaysia if Manila sur-
rendered its claims to Sabah). Genuine independence of the kind that
neutralization presupposes would involve some sacrifices by the
Southeast Asians. It can be argued that "only Burma and North Vietnam have shown that they are prepared to pay the price, economically
in the first case, militarily in the second, of independence."[18]

A "critique" prepared by one government for the Kuala Lumpur
meeting of Foreign Ministers of ASEAN in November 1971 was the
first regionally produced document to spell out the pros and cons of
neutralization under big-power guarantee from the point of view of
the neutralizers and the neutralizees. It listed two rights to be gained
by the neutralized states and two duties that would have to be undertaken by them. The rights were:

1. The obligation of the guarantor state to forego any act or
policy of coercion against the neutralized state. "A guarantor state
must, for example, refrain from supporting domestic revolutionaries
against the governments of the neutralized state." This would apply
to Chinese or Soviet support for Communist insurgents as well as to
Western help for right-wing or separatist revolutionaries. The partial
American assistance given to the Darul Islam and Revolutionary
Government of the Republic of Indonesia (PRRI) rebels of Sulawesi
and North Sumatra against the Indonesian government in 1958 might
have been argued as a case of this kind of coercion.

2. The right to demand of the guarantor states that they come
to the aid of the neutralized state in the event that its status is violated. It is this "right" that leads the critics of the neutralization
proposal to complain that, far from insulating Southeast Asia from
big-power intervention, it would actually invite big-power interference.[19] It would mean that China or the USSR would have an excuse
(even an obligation) to send troops to prop up a left-wing regime
under threat from internal or external forces or from a combination

10

of both, and that the United States would equally be able or required to send its army to sustain a right-wing government under attack from the left. Hence the importance of an effective internal peace-keeping machinery within the region, and the need for the regional states to act in concert when invoking the assistance of the guarantor states. Even this would not save the region from involvement in big-power conflict if the violation that prompts the recourse to the as-sistance of the guarantors is itself an act of one of the guarantors. If China were to attack Thailand, for example, then the invocation of this part of the neutralization agreement could oblige the United States, the USSR, or both, to step in against China, thus escalating the conflict from a regional to a global level. The same could apply in reverse if the United States were to attack Burma. It would, of course, be possible for the guarantors to agree to act only collectively, if the neutralizees so wanted. But that would have the effect of giving each guarantor a power of veto over big-power intervention to help a government in the neutralized zone.

But on the other side of the coin are the obligations imposed on the neutralizee, and the "critique" set these out under three headings:

1. "First, it is obligated to refrain from using its military forces for any purpose except self-defense and the maintenance of internal order." Neutralization would be wrecked if one of the pro-tected states were to become involved in any overseas military action. It may be argued that Japan also labors under a similar self-denying ordinance in the shape of Article 9 of its U.S.-inspired Constitution renouncing war as an instrument of policy. This has obliged post-occupation Japanese governments to build up armed forces only under a "Self-Defense Force" label. The Southeast Asian neutralizees would not have to go so far as to remain unarmed, but they would have to abandon any intention of intervening militarily—or of threaten-ing to intervene militarily—beyond their own national borders. This could presumably include a permanent inability to respond to any United Nations call for units to be assigned to international peace-keeping duties. "A neutralized state," in the words of the "critique," "must give up any aspirations to great or middle power status." It can be imagined how unpopular this aspect of neutralization appears to many Indonesian leaders who see their country as a prospective middle or even great power.[20]

2. "Second, it is obliged not to enter into any military alliances with other states, and to withdraw from any such preexisting alli-ances." Obviously neutralization would be incompatible with Thailand's

11

and the Philippines' membership in the Southeast Asian Treaty Organization (SEATO) or with Malaysia's and Singapore's membership in the Five-Power Commonwealth Defense Arrangement. Military ties with allies would have to be broken—Thailand's and the Philippines' ties with the United States, Malaysia's and Singapore's with Britain, Australia, and New Zealand. But further than this, it is possible to say that neutralization would best be secured by a refusal of the protected states to accept membership in any international body involving political commitments. The critics of Malaysia's proposal have pointed out that Switzerland has refrained from joining even the United Nations itself for fear of an incompatibility between such membership and its own neutralized status, and that Soviet pressure was placed on Austria to curb its aspirations to seek membership in the European Economic Community (although Austria did join the European Free Trade Area (EFTA) and has negotiated, along with other EFTA members, a special associate-status relationship with the EEC).

The "critique" posed the question in relation to Southeast Asia by asking whether membership in the United Nations, in ECAFE (the U.N. regional commission in Asia), in the Asian-Pacific Council (ASPAC), and even in ASEAN itself, would be compatible with the status of a neutralized state. If and when neutralization does become realizable, it would probably be agreed, as an integral part of the arrangements, that ASEAN would continue and would subsume into itself the role of the collective body that would speak for the protected states in the world arena—but it would presumably have to close its doors to new members outside the neutral zone, such as Sri Lanka and Bangladesh.

It would doubtless also be agreed that the protected states could continue their membership in the United Nations and in its regional commission (ECAFE) and agencies without jeopardizing their neutralized status—with the possible rider that they would not take part in any peace-keeping activities. The team of Princeton scholars whose 1966 study of neutralization in Southeast Asia was such a milestone suggested later that Article 2 of the United Nations Charter (which in Paragraph 5 requires member states to support it in its actions against wrongdoing nations, and not to help the latter) be amended, or that informal agreement be reached to the same effect.[21] It must, however, be noted that neither Austria nor Laos have deemed it necessary to leave the United Nations after their neutralization in 1955 and 1962 respectively, and there is one school of thought in Switzerland that Swiss neutrality would not these days be sufficiently threatened by U.N. membership to justify the inconvenience of non-membership.[22] But membership in ASPAC (the Asian Pacific Council), in any Islamic body with international political overtones, and in similar groupings (including possibly the Commonwealth) would surely be found incompatible. The neutralized states in Southeast Asia might well find themselves prevented from joining any Asian Common Market that may emerge, although the latter is so unlikely that this renunication must appear highly academic.

3. "Third, it is under a duty not to allow other states to use its territory for military purposes." The American military air and naval bases in Thailand and the Philippines would have to be closed as would the more limited British, Australian, and New Zealand facilities in Singapore and Malaysia. A fortiori, one regional state could not allow another regional state to use its soil for military purposes, so that Laos and Cambodia would be required to cease acquiescing in North Vietnamese use of the "Ho Chi Minh trail" to ferry troops and materiel to the insurgents in the South via Cambodian and Laotian territory (assuming that the two Vietnams were to enter the neutralization arrangement, as the Malaysians hopefully envisage, as separate states). The arrangements for the pacific settlement of intraregional disputes would presumably fall short of collective military enforcement, but if they were to be made more credible by being given teeth, then the movement of armed forces within the region in conformity with such arrangements would have to be exempted from the requirement that regional states not allow foreign troops on their soil. The upshot of this part of the discussion regarding the disadvantages of neutralization to the neutralized states is that a Southeast Asian state would not find neutralization attractive unless it genuinely regarded its independence and national welfare as being in jeopardy. "Neutralization," according to the "critique," "is an attractive proposal only for states which find themselves to be bones of contention between outside actors for control."[23] Indonesia and Vietnam are certainly not in that position, and most Filipinos and Malaysians would surely feel that such a description of their predicament was exaggerated.

DISADVANTAGES TO THE BIG POWERS

If Southeast Asia were neutralized under big-power guarantee, the big powers would undertake two duties, which may be defined as follows:

1. The obligation to respect the status and integrity of the neutralized states

2. The obligation (which may also be viewed as a right) to come to the assistance of a neutralized state in the event of the latter's status and integrity being violated by another power

The first of these requirements constitutes an obvious limitation on the big powers' freedom of action. A big power might be willing to deny itself this freedom only if it had no direct national interest at stake in the area, or at least a small enough interest for its inability to intervene unilaterally not to matter very much, and if it were assured that no competing big power would take advantage of this self-restraint by intervening to its own benefit.

It becomes necessary to measure the interest, or perceived interest, of each big power in the region, and this will be attempted in chapters 11 to 16 below. It must suffice here to observe that no single big power reckons now to have a predominant interest in Southeast Asia that, if it were quantifiable, would be larger than that of all the other big powers put together—not even, since the Guam Doctrine, the United States. As the American and West European interest has waned in recent years, the Russian, Chinese, and Japanese interest has grown. A very rough quantification might allocate big-power interest in Southeast Asia in the proportions 40 to 50 percent American, 15 to 25 percent Russian, 10 to 20 percent Chinese, and 10 to 20 percent Japanese. The larger American share results from the still considerable U.S. military presence in Southeast Asia, added to business investments and political friendships. The Soviet Union has also attempted a military presence, but confined to its navy, while China and Japan have so far refrained from acquiring direct military stakes in the region.

All the big powers share an interest in the use of the sea lanes that cut through the region, especially the Strait of Malacca, the Strait of Singapore, and the Sunda Strait, which form the principal routes for merchant shipping as well as naval vessels plying between the Indian Ocean on the one hand and the South China Sea and Pacific Ocean on the other. It is in the big powers' interest to keep these lanes open and free for international use, and hence the opposition by the United States, USSR, and Japan to the de-internationalization by the coastal states of Malaysia and Indonesia (China's support for internationalization is more a reaction against the Soviet position, more a tactical ploy than an expression of considered national interest at a time when China still lacks the naval power to compete with Russia and America in these waters). For Russia in particular these straits represent the only maritime link in winter between its European and Siberian ports, since passage through the Arctic Ocean is blocked by ice. The Straits of Malacca issue is another reason why the big powers might be willing to guarantee neutralization.

In terms of political interest, all the big powers have their preferred friends in the region, but no one Southeast Asian State is a completely dependent protégé, and in the days of detente following President Nixon's visit to Peking, all of them have relations of some sort with each of the four big powers. Obviously North Vietnam and Burma, along with the leftist groups struggling for power in Cambodia, Laos, and South Vietnam, are close to the USSR and China (and there is a struggle for primacy between these two Communist big powers). But they also enjoy diplomatic and economic relationships with the United States and Japan. Similarly the basically pro-Western Philippines, Malaysia, Singapore, and Thailand have for some time abandoned their earlier total boycott of the Communist powers. In economic terms the United States and Japan have the largest stakes both in investment and trade, but China and Russia are diligently building up theirs.

One can concede, therefore, the proposition that since no one of the big powers has a preponderant stake in Southeast Asia, and since each big power has some stake in the region, it is theoretically possible to put it to them that no one of them would lose if they were all voluntarily to renounce their right to intervene. One could try to find here, in Ghazali bin Shafie's phraseology, "a solid and well-founded assurance to each of the three superpowers that their positions will not suffer disproportionately in comparison to the positions of the other two." For they must, if neutralization is to work, "be given a well-founded assurance that, if one superpower withdraws from its quest for suzerainty or influence, the other two will do likewise.24

But this is the negative side of the proposition so far as the big powers are concerned. The positive attraction of a neutralized Southeast Asia would vary in each case. For one big power a neutralization agreement might be seen as a means of preserving the existing balance of power in the region. For another it might offer a face-saving device for reducing costly commitments in the region without appearing to abandon its ideological objectives, or alternatively for squaring those objectives with a rising wave of isolationist public opinion at home. For yet another, neutralization might appeal as a useful temporary arrangement that would give it time to prepare its own further advance in the region in terms of diplomatic and economic influence.

DEFINITION AND MACHINERY

A host of problems is created by the desire to impose upon the complex and evolving sets of relationships that the Southeast Asian

15

states enjoy a structure of neutralization rigid enough to stand up before the bar of international diplomacy and opinion. The term "neutralization" itself must first be defined. Cyril E. Black, Richard A. Falk, Klaus Knorr, and Oran R. Young in a recent scholarly work give the following as the conventional definition: "A neutralized state is one whose political independence and territorial integrity are guaranteed permanently by a collective agreement of great powers, subject to the conditions that the neutralized state will not take up arms against another state, except to defend itself, and will not assume treaty obligations which may compromise its neutralized status." But the same authors go on to give the following as their preferred broad and comprehensive, though necessarily abstract, definition: "Neutralization is a special international status designed to restrict the intrusion of specified state actions in a specified area."[25] In the view of these authors, neutralization is a far more flexible concept than was imagined in the nineteenth century.

The neutralizers and neutralizees must be closely identified. For the time being the proposal envisages the five Southeast Asian states of Indonesia, Malaysia, Philippines, Singapore, and Thailand being guaranteed by the three big powers—the United States, the Soviet Union, and China. But the Southeast Asian group is seen as eventually embracing Burma and the Indochina states—North Vietnam and South Vietnam (or any unified Vietnam that might eventually be formed), Cambodia, and Laos. It may be noted that the 1966 U.S. Senate study assumed that the neutralized area would certainly embrace South Vietnam, possibly North Vietnam, Cambodia, and Laos as well, and could be extended to other mainland states if they wished—a formulation excluding Indonesia, Singapore, Malaysia, and the Philippines.[26] And the Indonesians at one stage suggested that Great Britain, France, West Germany, and Japan be added to the list of big-power guarantors, presumably in order to make it less easy for the superpowers to influence events in the region by secret understandings among themselves.[27] Malaysia has publicly welcomed Japan as a possible fourth guarantor,[28] and Holland, Australia, New Zealand, India, and Iran have been unofficially suggested as additional candidates for the role.[29]

The neutralizees must undertake, in the words of the ASEAN officials charged with formulating the details of the proposal, to "maintain their impartiality and refrain from involvement directly or indirectly in ideological, political, economic, armed, or other forms of conflict, particularly between powers outside the zone." Outside powers, for their part, "shall not interfere in the domestic or regional affairs of the zonal states."[30] But how should "interfere" and "involvement" be defined? It seems clear from the intra-ASEAN debate that foreign military bases on Southeast Asian soil, even if

16

they are there at the explicit request of the host government (as is the case with the U.S. and Commonwealth forces in Thailand, Philippines, Malaysia, and Singapore), would be regarded as "interference" and therefore disallowed. But what about nonmilitary activity? Suppose an outside power placed massive economic investment into one of the Southeast Asian states, enough to give it a considerable voice in that state and influence over its government, would that be "interference?"

These questions relate to the links between any one regional state and an outside power. Another set of problems is posed by the need to regulate relationships between the states within the neutralized zone. They also must undertake not to interfere with each other, not to intervene in each other's internal affairs—but they must also establish some machinery by which they can police the zone themselves without resort to outside powers. If Malaysia and the Philippines were to go to war over the disputed sovereignty of Sabah, both (or at least the one that took the first step) would clearly be in breach of the neutralization agreement, and the big-power guarantors might expect, or be expected, to intervene. There ought to be an obligation, therefore, on the part of Indonesia, Singapore, and Thailand to seek actively to prevent the conflict from reaching a state of war, and possibly to seek to stop it by joint military operations if they failed to prevent its outbreak. The preconditions and procedures for this machinery for intraregional settlement of disputes would have to be very clearly defined, and even then its chances of success would be modest when stock is taken of the incidence of such conflicts (see Chapter 19). An internationally agreed to code of action is required by which, in the event of an armed clash between two neutralized states, the facts of the case must be verified by a control body (possibly comprising nationals of nonneutralized states) with full access to the sites of conflict. A predefined machinery for mediation and conflict resolution must then speedily be put into effect by the control body or other "neutral" neutralizees. If this fails, then the aggrieved neutralizee (or the neutralizee named by the control body or mediation machinery as the innocent, or less guilty, party) may (must?) invite the guarantors to intercede. Finally each guarantor must consult with the aggrieved neutralizee and with the other guarantors to decide on a swift concrete program of action against the "aggressor."[31]

All this sounds quite utopian, given the utter failure of the far more modest Laos Accord of 1962. Small wonder that Dr. Ismail eventually lowered the Malaysian sights to the extent of professing satisfaction with an open guarantee by the Big Three to respect the region's neutrality: "This guarantee in its simplest form need only take the form of an oral pronouncement at the United Nations."[32] Another unofficial Malaysian commentator has argued that "soft" or

17

informal guarantees would suffice for the time being, pending the negotiation of something more binding.[33]

Even if the settlement machinery were perfect, it would not, of course, solve the problem of peaceful change. The machinery would help to defuse any violent clash in the region; to the extent that the clashes are imposed from the outside this is desirable, but to the extent that they reflect the development of indigenous forces of change within the region, the desirability is less obvious. Any machinery of law and order benefits the status quo at the expense of the reformers and revolutionaries, and Southeast Asian neutralization would be no exception. One scholar goes so far as to argue that, by freezing the status quo, neutralization "may make peaceful change more difficult to achieve and may even divert the forces of change into armed conflict."[34] The strong reaction of the rebel radio station, the Voice of Malayan Revolution, to the neutralization scheme as a plot to destroy liberation movements shows that the left agrees with this analysis.[35]

A particular difficulty in Southeast Asia is that the relative power of the states within the region is not balanced: Indonesia is a potential middle power, and a united Vietnam would aim at a very much more influential role in regional and world affairs than is dreamed of by the Philippines or Malaysia, whereas Singapore, Cambodia, and Laos can merely hope to be left alone by their immediate neighbors. When to this is added the fact that the big-power interest is not balanced, and that internal forces in the region are still in ferment, the prospects for neutralization do not appear too bright. It has been pointed out that in the Balkans, where there was some equilibrium—international, regional, and domestic—neutralization in an earlier age was not effective; how much more difficult it would be for Southeast Asia.

SKEPTICAL RECEPTION

Skepticism about the neutralization proposal has been expressed in many quarters. Neutralization, these critics argue, did not save Belgium in two successive world wars. Neutral Norway and Denmark were occupied by Nazi Germany, and both Sweden and Switzerland were forced to make concessions to Germany in order to escape Hitler's invasion. Neutrality did not save Thailand from Japan in the Second World War, and the international neutralization of Laos in 1962 was stillborn. Against all this, one could say that Switzerland and Sweden did succeed, though with difficulty, in staying out of the two world wars, if for no other reason than that they were both heavily armed. The Swedes still spend more per head on defense than any other country. This is one reason why neither the Swiss

nor the Swedes feel unmanly about their neutrality, and it would be
open to Southeast Asia also to maintain a high level of defensive
armament and military preparedness. Tun Razak came back from
a visit to Switzerland full of praise and envy of the Swiss military
draft system. One difference, however, is the fact that what has to
be neutralized in Southeast Asia is a number of nations each of which
will insist on maintaining its own army (often in a state of rivalry
with its neighbors) and its own level of militarization.

The skeptics go on to point out that a joint Sino-Soviet-American
guarantee is unthinkable, if only because of the Sino-Soviet dispute,
not to mention the ideological realities behind the Soviet-American
and Sino-American detentes. Furthermore, if North Vietnam is
intent, as so many believe, on expansion, then the prospects of neutralization are indeed remote. "One hopes," wrote Brian Crozier
in the Daily Telegraph in 1972, "that the countries of ASEAN will not
lightly abandon such guarantees as they have for the illusory insurance
of a scrap of paper."[36]

Dr. Ismail, the late Deputy Prime Minister of Malaysia, conceded many of these doubts when he said of neutralization in 1970,
when the idea was just being canvassed for the first time in the region,

> My Government is aware that we are still a long way
> away from attaining that desirable objective which we
> believe should be high in the priorities of the regional
> agenda. There is a need for each of the countries of
> the region to set its own house in order. There is also
> need to promote the closest contacts and cooperation on
> a bilateral as well as multilateral basis among the coun-
> tries of the region and thereby develop a greater sense
> of regional consciousness and solidarity. There is
> finally the need to demonstrate that our activities and
> policies do not adversely affect the basic legitimate
> interests of the major powers. It is only then that the
> countries of the region would be in a position to seek
> an undertaking from the three superpowers to guarantee
> their independence, integrity, and neutrality.[37]

Yet the Malaysians pressed very firmly with their proposal and
eventually, through their determination and diplomacy, forced the
entire region to come to terms with it.

NOTES

1. FAM vol. 3, no. 2, December 1970, p. 16 (speech of 9 September 1970).

2. Malaysia's Foreign Policy, Malaysian Government, 1971 (speech of 26 July 1971).

3. MD vol. 5, no. 2, 31 January 1973. See also Zainal Abidin A. Wahid, "The Problem of Security in Southeast Asia: Is Neutralization the Answer?". Paper presented at Korea University, Asiatic Research Center, August 1970.

4. G. H. Jansen, Afro-Asian and Non-Alignment (London: Faber and Faber, 1966), pp. 57-61.

5. Anthony Eden, Towards Peace in Indochina (London: Oxford University Press, 1966), p. 12. See generally for early discussions of neutralization Peter Lyon, War and Peace in South East Asia (London: Oxford University Press, 1969), pp. 169-76; A. W. Stargardt, "Neutrality within the Asian System of Powers," in ND, pp. 104; and Philippe Devillers, "A Neutralized South East Asia," in ND, pp. 114.

6. Klaus Knorr et al., "Neutralization in Southeast Asia: Problems and Prospects," (Washington, D.C.: Government Printing Office, 10 October 1966).

7. FAM vol. 4, no. 4, December 1971, pp. 82-83 (speech in Bonn, 9 December 1971).

8. T. J. S. George in FEER, 11 December 1971.

9. STK, 14 June 1968.

10. FAM vol. 13, no. 1, June 1970, p. 37.

11. A Malaysian commentator has identified four factors in the adoption of the neutralization policy—(1) disenchantment with traditional allies and the realization that they were not dependable, (2) a desire to learn from the Vietnam experience, (3) the new spirit of self-dependence, and (4) the absence of any conventional military threat to Malaysia. See Noordin Sopiee, "The Neutralisation of Southeast Asia," a paper presented at a Conference on Asia and the West Pacific of the Australian Institute of International Affairs, Canberra, 14-17 April 1973.

12. STK, 16 March 1971.

13. Sunday Times, Singapore, 16 April 1972.

14. STK, 25 June 1973 (editorial).

15. Current Notes on International Affairs (Canberra, October 1972), pp. 501-2.

16. Cyril E. Black, Richard A. Falk, Klaus Knorr, and Oran R. Young, Neutralization and World Politics (Princeton: Princeton University Press, 1968), p. 170.

17. ND, p. 51.

18. J. L. S. Girling, "A Neutral South East Asia?" in Australian Outlook, vol. 27, no. 2, August 1973, p. 131 (a most penetrating critique

19. Japan Times 22 June 1973.

20. Black et al. (op. cit., p. 64) actually cite as an example of the potential enhancement of the burden on big powers by the neutralization of other countries the possible case of Indonesia's becoming neutralized and thus prevented from contributing to a U.N. peacekeeping role—so that the latter obligation is left to be undertaken by the bigger nonneutralized powers. (If all states were neutralized, there would be no one left to guarantee them!)

21. Black et al., op. cit., p. 165-66.

22. Ibid., p. 51-56.

23. Black et al., op. cit., pp. v-vi: "Neutralization seems potentially attractive only for relatively minor states, that by reason of strategic position or symbolic political value, have become or threaten to become the focal point of contest for control or dominant influence between principal regional or global rivals."

24. STK, 24 March 1971.

25. Black et al., op. cit., p. xi.

26. Knorr et al., op. cit., p. 13.

27. See S. M. Ali and V. K. Chin in New Nation (Singapore, 26 November 1971).

28. Japan Times, 15 October 1971.

29. M. Pathmanathan of the University of Malaya, in an unpublished paper.

30. Current Notes on International Affairs, op. cit., pp. 501-2.

31. See Knorr et al., op. cit., p. 12.

32. FAM, vol. 4, no. 4, December 1971, pp. 82-83 (Bonn speech, 9 December 1971).

33. Sopiee, op. cit.

34. Girling, op. cit., p. 123.

35. 17 April 1971. A similar comment was broadcast on the Voice of the People of Burma on 20 February 1972.

36. "Neutral Dreams in South East Asia," Daily Telegraph, London, 5 July 1972.

37. FAM, vol. 3, no. 2, December 1970, p. 58 (speech at the United Nations, 15 October 1970).

CHAPTER

2

**THE ASEAN
DEBATE**

     Having launched his neutralization proposal before an initially
receptive world, Tun Razak proceeded systematically to lobby and
gain support for it at four distinct levels of diplomacy. He and his
ministers and officials raised the subject and invited approval or
discussion at the widest universal level, which is to say in the United
Nations; at the narrowest regional level, within ASEAN; at such inter-
mediate levels as the Commonwealth Heads of Government Conference
and the Conference of Non-Aligned States; and finally, of course, bilat-
erally with the individual governments of Southeast Asia and the big
powers. The Malaysian Prime Minister undertook a series of overseas journeys in which he pressed his idea, not only on his neighbors
in Southeast Asia, but on the big and medium powers as well. He also
made a point of visiting countries like Switzerland and Austria where
he was able to get a first-hand impression of how various forms of
neutrality or neutralization had worked in recent practice.

     The neutralization proposal was explained at the U.N. General
Assembly in New York in the fall of 1971, but its reception was not
a happy one. The Malaysian delegation directed its diplomatic efforts
to the consultative meeting of 53 nonaligned states represented at the
Assembly, with a view to getting Southeast Asian neutralization em-
bodied in a declaration that the latter was preparing to present to the
General Assembly. Eventually this was done in Article 19 of the
Declaration, which called for urgent implementation of the Malaysian
proposal in order to free Southeast Asia from big power rivalries
and interference. Neutralization, the Declaration stated, would fully
guarantee the peace and security of the area, as well as the independence and territorial integrity of its states. But the value of this endorsement was ruined, from Malaysia's point of view, by another
section of the Declaration, which urged the United Nations to give
material and moral support to liberation movements. In the United

Nations and among the nonaligned the phrase "liberation movements" is taken to refer chiefly to the forces, with which there is a great deal of sympathy, fighting against white rule in Southern Africa. For Tun Razak and his counterparts in the rest of Southeast Asia, the phrase carries a more sinister ring, evocative of the Communist-led insurgencies against which all the Southeast Asian governments have had to defend themselves, with considerable bloodshed, during the postwar period. Understandably, after this episode Malaysia lost interest in the nonaligned declaration in New York.[1]

The specter behind the Asian liberation movements was, of course, China, whose government supported them in various ways, and the ASEAN group's credibility in convincing the rest of the Third World to treat "liberation" in Asia differently from "liberation" in Africa was fatally weakened by its own disharmony on the China question. It was in this same General Assembly session in the fall of 1971 that Peking was welcomed into the United Nations, and yet the ASEAN quintet managed to split three ways on this vital vote. Malaysia and Singapore voted for the admission of the People's Republic of China, the Philippines voted against, and Indonesia and Thailand both abstained. However, the five ASEAN Foreign Ministers did agree in New York to meet again in Kuala Lumpur that November to consider the possibility of an ASEAN declaration on neutralization.

Meanwhile the Malaysian proposal had been given an airing at a number of international forums. It was first deployed before the Non-Aligned Heads of Government at Lusaka, in September 1970, in a speech that represented Razak's international debut on the eve of his becoming the new Prime Minister of Malaysia. It was here at Lusaka, however, that the Southeast Asians began to shed some of their illusions about the Non-Aligned group and about the solidarity and seriousness of the Third World as a whole. President Suharto of Indonesia was privately appalled by the ill-informed and unsympathetic attitude of so many Africans, Arabs, and Latin Americans towards Southeast Asian problems. The honeymoon was finally ended at the later Conference of Non-Aligned Nations held at Georgetown in August 1972. When the meeting admitted a delegation from the Provisional Revolutionary Government of South Vietnam, Malaysia's Ghazali bin Shafie and Indonesia's Adam Malik walked out in protest.[2] Since then no particular effort has been made to deepen Non-Aligned support for neutralization, although the Malaysians continue to portray their proposal as conforming to the ideals of nonalignment. In his speech at the 4th Non-Aligned Summit Conference in Algiers in September 1973, Razak did not attempt to explain neutralization all over again, preferring to spell it out that while he supported the liberation movements in their struggle against colonialism, imperialism, and racism, "this basic principle of the nonaligned movement should not be used to countenance interference in the internal affairs of sovereign states."[3]

There was less embarrassment at the Commonwealth Heads of Government meetings where the neutralization proposal was not controversial and where Malaysia was able to get somewhat vague support for it. It was disappointing, perhaps, that the Singapore Commonwealth Summit in 1971 merely stated, in its final communique, that the proposal had been discussed,[4] and even at the subsequent conference in Ottawa in 1973 the formal support given to neutralization was highly noncommittal.[5] But at both conferences (as with the Non-Aligned) Razak was able to expound his ideas privately to other heads of government and try to overcome their skepticism.

Within Southeast Asia there were a number of international forums at which Malaysia could, and did, argue the neutralization idea. One was the Japanese-sponsored Ministerial Conference on Economic Development of Southeast Asia held annually in different capitals. At the sixth of these conferences in Kuala Lumpur in May 1971, the Malaysians took the opportunity to proselytize for their proposal.

But the most important arena was the Association of South East Asian Nations, which alone brought together the principal countries of the region without any outsiders present. From the start Malaysia regarded ASEAN as the crucial constituency by whose vote neutralization would succeed or fail, and the biggest effort of diplomacy was directed, separately and collectively, to the other four partners in ASEAN.

The fundamental goal of the neutralization proposal, namely to prevent big-power interference in Southeast Asia, was widely accepted in ASEAN. "The continuing tragedy of our time," said Philippine Foreign Secretary Carlos P. Romulo, "is that our affairs are very much shaped by the ill-considered actions of the superpowers."[6] Razak once went even further, declaring: "The massive foreign intervention to which Southeast Asia has been subjected has been unparalleled in any other region of the globe."[7] But the neutralization idea needed strenuous pushing by Malaysia as an acceptable or practicable means of realizing this aim, and there were critics who felt that the aim itself was out of date. Premier Lee Kuan Yew of Singapore recently noted that the big powers were ceasing to compete for the support of the smaller nations and were settling such world issues as the Vietnam War among themselves. "For small countries," he told the visiting Yugoslavian Prime Minister in 1973, "the question now is not how to avoid being sucked into the warring camps of the two big powers, but how to have their interests taken into consideration when the great powers reach their compromises."[8] His analysis was endorsed by the largest-circulation newspaper in Indonesia.[9]

The campaign to convince the four ASEAN partners began in earnest in the fall of 1971, when the five ASEAN Foreign Ministers found themselves together in New York for the annual session of the United Nations General Assembly. President Nixon had announced his historic decision to visit Peking, and it was anticipated that China was at long last on the point of replacing Taiwan in the United Nations. The five Foreign Ministers agreed on 2 October to meet again in Kuala Lumpur in November to consider the consequences of these dramatic developments and also to consider the Malayan suggestion for a declaration of neutrality.

THE KUALA LUMPUR CONFERENCE

They duly came together in the Malaysian capital for a two-day meeting on 26 and 27 November. Razak and Ismail elaborated their ideas and faced a barrage of questions. How was neutralization to be defined? What would it mean for the existing bilateral and multi-lateral defense arrangements, especially SEATO? What precise geographical area would be covered? Why not bring in Japan and the West European states as big power guarantors? The Singapore delegation, always closest to the Malaysian, was the first to present a detailed preliminary evaluation of the neutralization idea which raised innumerable questions about it and exposed many of its demerits.

The first thing, the "critique"[10] referred to in Chapter 1 insisted, was to make sure what was meant by neutralization and how it was to be distinguished from neutrality, neutralism, and demilitarization. Neutralization can only be a process whereby in international law a state assumes the status of a permanent or perpetual neutrality, both in times of peace and war, and is so recognized and guaranteed by other states. The neutralized states (neutralizees) are legally bound to the guarantor states (neutralizors) by a network of reciprocal rights and obligations. Switzerland offers an example of this.

Neutrality, of the kind that Sweden has traditionally professed, is something quite different. First, neutrality can be the product of a unilateral declaration by the neutral state, without the need for an international agreement. Second, neutrality can be ended at any time by the unilateral decision of the state concerned, whereas the status of a neutralized state is permanent and can only be terminated by the agreement of all the guarantor states as well as of the neutralized state. Thirdly, neutrality is a policy adopted by a state only during a time of war and applied only to specific conflicts, while neutralization is a generalized position that prevails in time of peace as well as of war.

Neutralism is merely the practice of a foreign policy by which a state does not ally itself to either of the rival superpowers as part of their competing collective security systems. It is a policy adopted by many smaller states since the end of the Second World War, and especially in the Third World, but it does not necessarily entail a strict neutrality in wars between other states. Nehru's India was the pioneer of this concept.

Demilitarization means the renunciation of arms, and it is sometimes linked with neutralization. Luxembourg was demilitarized during the period of its neutralization, whereas Switzerland and Austria are not.

The "critique" went on to set out the respective rights and duties of neutralizors and neutralizees, together with the disadvantages accruing to each side (see Chapter 1) and then elaborated the three possible paths to neutralization—what could be termed the Swiss, Laotian, and Austrian models.

The Swiss model means neutralization guaranteed by the great powers of the day in the form of a binding multilateral treaty between them and the neutralized state. The Laotian model means an enlargement of the number of guarantor states to include not only the great powers but also some medium powers as well as the states that neighbor on the state to be neutralized. The Austrian model means a unilateral declaration recognized by the great powers and by other states but not in the form of a binding treaty. On 26 October 1955 a constitutional federal statute was enacted by the Austrian parliament by which "Austria, of its own free will, declares herewith its permanent neutrality and will never in the future accede to any multilateral alliances nor permit the establishment of military bases of foreign states on its territory." Such an act of self-declaration would be futile if it were not recognized by the great powers and other states. At least one delegation reminded its ASEAN colleagues that when the Kingdom of Cambodia under Prince Sihanouk wrote into its constitution that neutrality was a law of the land and that Cambodia renounced its freedom to enter into military or ideological alliances, this was never recognized by all the big powers and other outside actors, and was therefore abortive.

The Southeast Asian case differs from all these models in one important respect, namely that a number of neighboring states would be involved as neutralizees. Malaysia preferred the Austrian model, but it was suggested in the early discussions that a self-declaration by five or ten small states all neighboring one another and constituting an entire region of the world would command more weight than a unilateral declaration on the part of one single state. To this it was pointed out that without the support of the big powers outside the region even a collective self-declaration could prove to be a dead letter.

The "critique" closed with a tightly argued passage posing very concretely the different problems the Malaysian proposal presented:

The success of neutralization does not end merely with the conclusion of an international neutralization agreement, but continues with its subsequent stability and maintenance. The essential preconditions for neutralization are that compromises or the appearance of compromise must be an acceptable diplomatic outcome to all actors concerned, and that there exists a sufficiently converging state of perceived interest to terminate, avoid, or postpone military forms of competition for the control of the neutralized unit. The acceptability of neutralization depends on the comparative merits of other diplomatic alternatives. The stability of neutralization depends on the congruence of the objectives of the guarantor powers inter se and vis-a-vis the neutralized state itself. The maintenance of neutralization rests on an accompaniment of many factors including the good faith of the guarantors, the capacity of the neutralized state for autonomy, the will and capability of the guarantor powers to take action if the terms of neutralization are brought into jeopardy, and the effectiveness of any machinery set up to preserve neutralization.

Seven questions were then listed, as follows:

1. Does each of the States of Southeast Asia regard its independence and welfare to be in jeopardy?

2. Does each of the States of Southeast Asia perceive itself as a present or future bone of contention between or among outside actors for control?

3. Will each of the States of Southeast Asia be able to identify the outside actors which are competing or likely to be competing for control over it?

4. Is there a convergence of interests among these outside actors to make neutralization possible, and to ensure its stability and maintenance?

5. Does each of the States of Southeast Asia regard neutralization as a more effective means of its independence and national welfare than the alternatives, i.e. unilateral or collective military force, alliance arrangements, quasi-parliamentary diplomacy at the regional and global levels?

6. What does each of the States of Southeast Asia understand by the concept of neutralization?

27

7. Is membership in the U.N., ECAFE, SEATO, ASPAC, ASEAN, the Five-Power Defense Arrangement, compatible with the status of a neutralized state?

The Kuala Lumpur meeting was unusual in many ways. The Thai government had just changed its constitutional status and had moved into the final phase of the Thanom-Praphas regime, so that Thanat Khoman, the former Thai Foreign Minister and cofounder of ASEAN, had to attend with the new designation of Special Envoy of the National Executive Council of Thailand, speaking with less authority and more inhibition than before. Adam Malik of Indonesia flew in with a posse of generals in his delegation, apparently determined to prevent any swing towards the recognition of Peking. China had been admitted to the United Nations only a month before, and this was the first occasion for a joint appraisal of what that meant for the region. As president for that year of the U.N. General Assembly, Malik had had to welcome the Chinese entry, although his government at home, convinced of China's ambition to promote left-wing regimes in Southeast Asia by backing "wars of liberation," was openly disappointed at the U.N. decision. His military escort, explained diplomatically as a body of advisers for when the security aspects of neutralization came to be discussed, was more likely a warning and reminder that the Foreign Minister's evident instinct for nonalignment and for detente with China did not represent the army's views and could not therefore represent Indonesia's views. Foreign Secretary Romulo of the Philippines went to the Kuala Lumpur meeting with a brief to get support for President Marcos' pet scheme for an Asian Summit in Manila.

THE KUALA LUMPUR DECLARATION

After three days of discussion the Kuala Lumpur Declaration was adopted; it was extremely wordy and full of worthy generalities to satisfy all parties and all sides. The five Foreign Ministers concluded the Declaration as follows:

Agreeing that the neutralization of Southeast Asia is a desirable objective and that we should explore ways and means of bringing about its realization, and convinced that the time is propitious for joint action to give effective expression to the deeply felt desire of the peoples of Southeast Asia to ensure the conditions of peace and stability indispensable to their independence and their economic and social well-being, [The Foreign Ministers] do hereby state:

(1) that Indonesia, Malaysia, the Philippines, Singapore, and Thailand are determined to exert initially necessary efforts to secure the recognition of, and respect for, Southeast Asia as a Zone of Peace, Freedom, and Neutrality, free from any form or manner of interference by outside powers;

(2) That Southeast Asian countries should make concerted efforts to broaden the area of cooperation which would contribute to their strength, solidarity, and closer relationship.[11]

The harsh words of a Thai newspaper, The Nation, were echoed by many observers: "In the longest sentence the staff of this newspaper has ever read, the joint communique issued on Saturday by the ASEAN said nothing."* In spite of the lip service paid to neutralization, none of the governments wanted to give up the protection they derived from their defense pacts with outside powers, with the sole exception of Indonesia. Merdeka, the Indonesian newspaper, commented that the Declaration showed up the differences within ASEAN: as long as unanimity eluded the five partners, the great powers would hardly respect their aspirations.[12] One factor that worked against the Malaysians was the American diplomatic message that an excessively neutralistic declaration would play into the hands of the neo-isolationists in the United States and would make it more difficult for Washington to maintain the American military presence in the region,[13] a point that gained force in the context of the double about-face of Nixon's visit to Peking and the United Nations' admission of China. The Indonesians, Thais, Filipinos, and Singaporeans were all anxious not to accelerate a United States withdrawal from the region, though some of them would not care to say so in so many words.

Comments on the Declaration were mostly skeptical. T. J. S. George of the Far Eastern Economic Review conceded that it sounded like a good piece of horse-trading if it meant that China might agree to a "hands off" policy towards the region if in compensation Russian and American influence were to be effectively expelled. But how was the United States presence to be completely thrown off? Would not its economic presence replace the military presence? How could Southeast Asia accept China's sincerity? And, finally, how was Southeast Asia to conduct the concerted and skilled diplomacy towards the

---

*By communique, the Declaration is meant; there was also a joint communique covering the other matters discussed by the Ministers apart from neutralization.

big powers which neutralization demanded while they were still squabbling among themselves on other issues? [14]

But Razak insisted that the Kuala Lumpur Declaration was a "commitment to neutralization." The timetable for it would be in four stages: (1) a show of determination by the five ASEAN governments; (2) an approach to the other Southeast Asians in Burma and Indochina to commit themselves; (3) an approach to the big powers to secure their guarantee; (4) the phasing out of foreign bases and defense pacts. "If we can get outside powers to respect us," he said, "then we don't need any security arrangements." [15]

COMMITTEE OF ASEAN OFFICIALS

In the Joint Communique issued after their Kuala Lumpur meeting the Foreign Ministers "agreed to establish a Committee of Senior Officials initially of the ASEAN countries to study and consider what further necessary steps should be taken to bring about the realization of their objectives" in the Declaration, to be convened in Malaysia. The Committee was to be the principal forum in which the detailed argument over neutralization was thrashed out. [16] Soon afterwards a rumor to the effect that the "Committee" idea had been dropped [17] stimulated the Malaysian government to confirm that its Ministry of Foreign Affairs was taking the initiative in getting the Committee started and also to insist that the Kuala Lumpur meeting of Foreign Ministers and the Committee on Neutralization had nothing to do with ASEAN. [18] Mr. John Ng of the Malaysian Foreign Ministry wrote to the Far Eastern Economic Review that "ASEAN is a purely economic and cultural organisation." [19] This was splitting hairs, since Malik, Thanat, the Singapore Mirror, and Malaysian Digest (both official publications) had referred to the meeting as an ASEAN meeting, [20] though admittedly it was not one of the regular series of annual meetings held in different capitals every spring. Obviously an attempt was being made to dissociate the two concepts, presumably to enable one of them to survive the failure or discrediting of the other. The dissociation from ASEAN was doubtless the price extracted from Malaysia by her four partners for their grudging lip-service to neutralization.

A Zone of Peace

A neutralization division was soon set up in Wisma Putra, the Malaysian Foreign Ministry, headed by Albert Talalla, and the first meeting of the ASEAN Committee of Officials on Neutralization, as it was termed, was held in Kuala Lumpur from 11 to 13 May 1972 (following endorsement of the preliminary arrangements by the Foreign Ministers during their regular annual conference at Singapore on 13 to 14 April), with a further session on 6 to 8 July.[21] Four definitions were agreed upon by the Committee as follows:

(a) Zone of Peace, Freedom, and Neutrality: "A zone of peace, freedom, and neutrality exists where the national identity, independence, and integrity of the individual States within such a zone can be preserved and maintained, so that they can achieve national development and well-being and promote regional cooperation and solidarity, in accordance with the ideals and aspirations of their peoples and the purposes and principles of the United Nations Charter, free from any form or manner of interference by outside powers."

(b) Peace: "Peace is a condition where the prevalence of harmonious and orderly relations exists between and among States. No reference is hereby made to the internal state of affairs in each of the zonal States. A situation of ideological, political, economic, armed, or other forms of conflict, either among the zonal States themselves, between one or more of the zonal States and outside powers, or between outside powers affecting the region, is not a condition of peace."

(c) Freedom: "Freedom means the freedom of States from control, domination, or interference by other States in the conduct of their national and external affairs. This means the right of zonal States to solve their domestic problems in terms of their own conditions and aspirations, to assume primary responsibility for the security and well-being of the region and their regional and international relations on the basis of sovereign equality and mutual benefit."

(d) Neutrality: "Neutrality means the maintenance of a state of impartiality in any war between other States as understood in international law and in the light of the United Nations Charter. Taken in the context of the Kuala Lumpur Declaration, however, it means that zonal States shall undertake to maintain their impartiality and shall refrain from involvement directly or indirectly in ideological, political, economic, armed, or other forms of conflict, particularly between powers outside the zone, and that outside powers shall not interfere in the domestic or regional affairs of the zonal States. "[22]

The Committee recognized that alternative means for achieving a "zone of peace, freedom, and neutrality" should be considered. At the next meeting of ASEAN Foreign Ministers in Manila on 13 and 14 July, a press statement was issued which stated that the Ministers "reiterated the view that neutralization of Southeast Asia is a desirable objective and also noted that the Committee [of Officials meeting in Kuala Lumpur] at its next meeting will continue its study of neutralization as a means of establishing Southeast Asia as a 'zone of peace, freedom, and neutrality' and that other means will also be considered. " The statement also declared that the Ministers "noted with satisfaction that the Committee had reached a common understanding of the interpretation of a 'zone of peace, freedom, and neutrality' in the context of Southeast Asia. "[23]

A third session of the Committee was held in Djakarta, a fourth in Baguio City (in June 1973), and a fifth in Singapore in March 1974. These meetings were evidently attended at a high level of government, conducted in admirable secrecy, and marked by a thorough examination of the Malaysian proposal, its merits, demerits, and alternatives.[24]

The Vietnam Ceasefire

At the end of 1972, just a year after the Kuala Lumpur Declaration, the prospect opened up, with the Paris Peace talks, of a military disengagement in Indochina. This was obviously an opportunity for the ASEAN nations to stake their claim, if they were serious about neutralization. Observers were beginning to make the link. Dennis Healey, the British Labour Party leader, for example, in an article in the New York Times in 1971 headlined "Neutralize Southeast Asia Now," had urged a political settlement in Indochina within the context of the neutralization of Southeast Asia as a whole.[25] But the chance was lost because of ASEAN's inability to agree on a strategy for Indochina. Ghazali bin Shafie elaborated on the neutralization proposal and its role for peace in the region in an address to international businessmen in London in November 1972:

What we are trying to do is to work out an accommodation of the interests of the major powers in Malaysia and in Southeast Asia in such a way that these interests are restricted, regulated, and balanced, in return for our

pledge of noninvolvement and neutrality in their conflicts and rivalries.

We envisage this as a permanent arrangement to
bring about long-term security and stability to the region.
Of course, in the short term it is possible to rely on multilateral or bilateral defence arrangements. But we must
recognize them for what they are: namely short-term ex-
pedients which give us time in Southeast Asia to organize
and strengthen ourselves and which will last only for so
long as it serves the interests of the parties involved or
which is perceived by their respective electorates to
serve such interests.

We must, therefore, think ahead, in anticipation of
future developments, lest we find ourselves caught up in
situations about which we can do precious little.

What we are trying to do in Malaysia and in Southeast
Asia, therefore, is the creation of an environment which is
safe and stable because the major powers are satisfied that
a situation exists where their legitimate interests are met
and where there is no preponderant influence of any particular power which would then be regarded as a threat
to the others, who would necessarily take countermeas-
ures.[26]

But when the five Foreign Ministers of ASEAN next met, in
Kuala Lumpur in February 1973, they could offer nothing towards
an Indochina settlement, despite the membership of Indonesia in the
International Control Commission. They merely saw the Vietnam
ceasefire as in line with their Kuala Lumpur Declaration, and the
Thai plan to hold a further conference of all ten Southeast Asian
states—including Burma and Indochina—was resisted by the others.
It was agreed to convene such a conference when it seemed appropriate, and the appropriate moment never arrived.[27] ASEAN's views
on Indochina were neither sought by nor pressed on the combatants
and their big-power patrons who eventually negotiated the cease-fire
agreement.

In part ASEAN's negativism could be attributed to the sheer
novelty of the situation. Philippine Foreign Secretary Romulo voiced
the feeling that peace made him and his colleagues uneasy: "Perhaps . . . we are unaccustomed to the idea of peace, having lived for
so long in the tense atmosphere of war." The cease-fire, he added,
"binds us in a paradox—we anticipate stability yet we fear for our
security." But whatever the reasons, the feebleness of the ASEAN
response to the challenge of Paris was a great disappointment. Goh
Cheng Teik of the University of Malaysia's History Department

commented: "When governments from within the region who can and ought to be . . . active agents of change adopt this passive posture of philosophical aloofness, one cannot help but be amazed."[28]

The Committee of Officials on Neutralization labored on despite these doubts. Its second session in Djakarta drew up "guidelines for relations among states within and without the zone of peace," and these were endorsed by the Foreign Ministers at their next annual meeting, in Pattaya, Thailand, in April 1973. They expressed "confidence that a favorable climate was being created for the progressive realization of Southeast Asia as a zone of peace, freedom, and neutrality."[29] At the Committee's third session in Baguio City the debate concentrated on the two separate questions of the measures required to establish a regional machinery for the pacific settlement of disputes and of "certain expectations" the Southeast Asian states would have of the countries asked to recognize and respect the zone of peace.[30] The Foreign Ministers at their Djakarta conference in May 1974 merely commended the Committee's progress toward a "blueprint" for realizing the Kuala Lumpur Declaration, and urged priority consideration of action proposals designed to establish a zone of peace, freedom, and neutrality.[31]

It will be noted how the emphasis was in fact shifting away from neutralization under big power guarantee. The Kuala Lumpur Declaration does not speak of "neutralization" as such but only of a "zone of . . . neutrality." The idea of big-power guarantee gained less and less favor as its possible ramifications were argued out. And for all Razak's bravura in calling the Declaration an endorsement of neutralization, the Malaysians found that the other delegates to the Committee of Officials insisted from the beginning on discussing the alternatives to neutralization as a way of securing the goal of a "zone of peace, freedom, and neutrality." Even Ghazali bin Shafie, one of the plan's authors, conceded by the summer of 1974, "The old 19th-century concept of neutralization secured by the guarantee of other powers is out of date."[32]

NOTES

1. See STK, 2 October 1971.
2. STK, 11 August 1972.
3. Speech of 6 September: FAM, vol. 6, no. 3, September 1973, p. 17.
4. STK, 16 January 1971 (Razak's address); The Times, London, 23 January 1971 (the communique).
5. The Times, London, 11 August 1973: FAM, vol. 6, no. 3, September 1973, p. 6.

6. STK, 27 November 1971.

7. Algiers speech, FAM, vol. 6, no. 3, September 1973, p. 21.

8. STS, 18 March 1973.

9. Kompas, Djakarta, 20 March 1973, as quoted in STS, 21 March 1973.

10. See the report by S. M. Ali and V. K. Chin in New Nation, Singapore, 26 November 1971.

11. The full text is set out in Appendix A.

12. Merdeka and The Nation, quoted in STK, 30 November 1971.

13. See James Morgan in FEER, 4 December 1971.

14. FEER, 11 December 1971.

15. Sunday Times, Kuala Lumpur, 28 November 1971.

16. Ibid.

17. STK, 13 January 1972.

18. Ibid.

19. FEER, 12 February 1972.

20. See Bob Hawkins in FEER, 4 March 1972. The fact that Foreign Minister S. Rajaratnam of Singapore later suggested the "regularization" of political meetings of the five Foreign Ministers along the lines of the Kuala Lumpur conference shores up the conclusion that if ASEAN were not a political body at least the line distinguishing between its institutionalized economic and cultural work and the political consultations of its Foreign Ministers becomes so thin as to be hardly worth insisting upon. See also James Morgan in FEER, 26 April 1972.

21. New Nation, Singapore, 20 April 1972.

22. Current Notes on International Affairs, Canberra, October 1972, pp. 501-2.

23. Ibid.; and FAM, vol. 5, no. 3, September 1972, p. 46.

24. MD, 2 December 1972, p. 4; SWB-FE/4554, 19 March 1974.

25. New York Times, 23 February 1971.

26. MD, 2 December 1972, p. 8.

27. BP and STK, 16 February 1973; MD, 23 February, 1973, p. 5.

28. STK, 23 February 1973. See also Felix Abishegenaden in BP, 12 March 1973.

29. MD, 20 May 1973, p. 1; ARB, May 1973, p. 1761; FAM, vol. 6, no. 2, June 1973, p. 30.

30. STK, 23 June 1973; Japan Times, 24 June 1973.

31. Japan Times, 10 May 1974.

32. Interview with Pang Cheng Lian, New Nation, Singapore, 3 June 1974.

3

ALTERNATIVE
APPROACHES

What alternatives to neutralization are in fact available to Southeast Asia? One of the virtues of Tun Razak's iniative in pressing his own scheme so hard is that others in the region had to re-examine and rationalize their own positions on the basic issue of minimizing big-power interference. Thus the ASEAN Committee of Senior Officials decided at its first meeting that "other alternative means" than neutralization had to be considered for implementing the goal of a zone of peace, freedom, and neutrality as set out in the Kuala Lumpur Declaration. What about neutralism on the Cambodian-Burmese model, neutrality a la Sweden, or the nonalignment of Nehru, Nasser, and Nkrumah? At the other extreme lies alignment (that is, bilateral or multilateral defense alliances carrying a commitment to the political support of the military protectors), and in between are the more conventional mechanisms of nonaggression pacts and collective security arrangements. The "critique" presented at the Kuala Lumpur Conference in 1971 adds yet another possible response in the form of "quasi-parliamentary diplomacy at the regional and global levels."

PRECEDENTS: SWEDEN AND SWITZERLAND

The first task is to consider the principal precedents in international law for the neutralization idea, and to see which are most favored in Southeast Asia. The concept of neutrality in modern international law and diplomatic usage goes back to the Swiss experience in the fifteenth and sixteenth centuries. Neutrality first developed as a policy within Switzerland, since the Helvetic Confederation was built up by new cantons being admitted on condition that they remained neutral in any quarrels between the existing members. The cantons then "sat still" in the wars of the European Reformation in spite of their differing Catholic and Protestant loyalties within the confederation. Swiss neutrality was thus more than the expression of an act of will by the Swiss people; it was an organic product of the two principles of federalism and freedom by which the Swiss nation has grown and survived.

In six hundred years it was broken only by Napoleon and by the Allies who defeated him in the wars of the French Revolution. The Allies restored Swiss neutrality in 1815 under their guarantee, described by a leading Swiss authority on the subject as an imposition that the Swiss at that time could not "escape" and which had the "foreseen" result of attempts at interference in the internal affairs of Switzerland over a period of some thirty years.[1] The fact that none of these attempts succeeded was due largely to the peacetime disharmony of the Allied victors and the Swiss skill in playing them against one another.

Then in the later nineteenth and twentieth centuries the Swiss found that neutrality was the only way in which they could contain their own internal divisions—between French, German, and Italian culture and between opposing religious faiths and political ideologies. A war for Switzerland was doomed to turn into civil war, with some of the population supporting different sides. Switzerland's neutral role was helped by its geographic advantage of controlling the Alpine passes: Belligerent neighbors were satisfied that these access routes would be denied to their enemies as well as to themselves, and as long as Swiss arms provided a credible means of preventing an enemy from using them, the neutrality was respected.

Sweden's practice of neutrality is more recent, dating only since the end of the nineteenth century. In 1914, when it was first seriously tested, it did not prevent international speculation that Sweden might throw in her lot with the Germans. The triumph came in the Second World War when, despite the failure of Denmark and Norway to stay out, Sweden succeeded in preserving its essential neutrality (although not its complete freedom of action) throughout.

For Austria neutrality came in 1955 as a prerequisite of national reunification after ten years of partition by the four Allied occupying powers. The Soviet Union was willing to withdraw from Austria only if the Austrians accepted neutrality (a position to which they were led by, among other things, the persuasion of Pandit Nehru); prior to the State Treaty that restored Austrian sovereignty a memorandum was signed with the Soviet Union in which the Austrian government accepted an obligation "to practice in perpetuity a neutrality of the type maintained by Switzerland."

Europe also offers the examples of Belgium (1839-1919), Luxembourg (1867-1919), the Vatican (1929 to date), the city states of Cracow (1815-46) and Danzig (1919-39), Malta (1802), Albania (1913), Trieste (1945-54), and others. The Congo was neutralized from 1885 to 1907,

Honduras from 1907 to 1923, Samoa from 1886 to 1899. And Iceland declared its own permanent neutrality in 1918.[2]

In Asia, Burma, Cambodia, and Laos are regarded as professing some degree of neutrality in their international relations. "Burma's foreign policy," according to Maung Maung, "is one of positive neutrality." Burma has always been concerned lest the common forums for Asian, Afro-Asian, or nonaligned nations come to be regarded by the rest of the world as just another bloc like the others. No treaties or guarantees define Burma's position, but its consistent preference for staying out of international movements or organizations has gained it a reputation for neutrality.

"Independent and neutral Cambodia," Prince Norodom Sihanouk explained to the Bandung Conference in 1955, "now finds herself on the separating line of two civilizations, of two races, of two political worlds . . . as such she has the dangerous privilege of putting to the test the application of the principles of Pancha Shila" (the five principles of peaceful coexistence).[3] Later, after Cambodia had enacted a Neutrality Law renouncing alliances, he wrote for an American periodical, "We are neutral in the same way Switzerland and Sweden are neutral—not neutralist like Egypt or Indonesia . . . our votes in the United Nations . . . are often not 'aligned' with those of the bloc of 'neutralist' nations."[4] At the Geneva Conference in 1954, Cambodia and Laos were neutralized, although, at Khmer insistence, they retained the right to maintain effective national armed forces and to retain foreign military missions. But the provisions of the Geneva Accords, including that of 1962 on Laos, were infringed in one way or another by most of the key signatories, and neither country can be regarded as a happy example of neutralization.[5]

MULTIPLE NEUTRALIZATION

There is one important respect in which the Malaysian proposal for neutralization differs from all these European and Asian examples. There is no precedent for multiple neutralization—that is, neutralization for a group of nations as distinct from a single nation. Professor Stargardt in a lecture given in Singapore in 1971 drew attention to this fact:

Regional neutralization has its own implied limitations. Blocs of neutrals are as much a contradiction in terms as a party of independents in parliament. Each can only defeat its own aims, and we have seen that leaders of neutral states in the region have been conscious of this. Whether it is possible at this stage to avoid this problem by the formation of some kind of neutral confederation is, at best, an open question. Development has probably not yet gone this far, either in economic or in political terms. It would at least involve a common foreign policy, although leaving wide scope for intraregional differences whose solution would have to exclude military means. It would, further, require some kind of military coordination, exclusive of the influence of the great powers. None of these problems are insurmountable but they could become so if they are not faced. Above all, success would depend on the practiced recognition of the equality of all nationalities, ethnic, religious and social groups living within such a confederation. Once it becomes practiced, this may grow under its own momentum if the volatile forces seeking short-term advantage from divisive policies can be held in check.[6]

It is because of these contradictions that a guaranteed neutralization of Southeast Asia would require a fixed, agreed, and effective machinery for the peaceful settlement of disputes within the region. Neutrality towards the outside powers is not enough: The Southeast Asian states should also be neutral among themselves.* If the Philippines and Indonesia were to come to blows over the treatment of Muslims in Mindanao, their Malaysian and Thai partners would have to keep the peace, and this obligation could not be tucked away under the carpet as an inconvenient chore that the world could overlook. Almost any official fighting in the region would affect shipping, and the interest of the maritime powers would lie in the effective policing of the sea lanes, whether by an intraregional system or something else.

What else then, if not neutralization? Ghazali bin Shafie has pointed out that the security arrangements the countries of the region have employed so far have not had the desired results of removing the problems of subversion and infiltration of insurgents. "The alternative security arrangements in terms of a balance of power with offshore American air-power, or a purely Asian balance of power or an Asian collective security pact are unlikely to prove effective or credible, even if in fact one or other variation could be constituted."[7]

---

*However, the use of the word "particularly" in the ASEAN officials' definition of neutrality (see Chapter 2 above) implies that they envisage some degree of intervention by Southeast Asian states among themselves.

ALIGNMENT OR SELF-RELIANCE?

It would be possible in theory for the region's governments to agree that their best path was to align themselves behind a powerful protector. This was precisely what the Thai, South Vietnamese, and Philippine governments did during most of the postwar period, hitching their wagon to the star of Uncle Sam. North Vietnam equally opted for Sino-Soviet patronage, and even the outbreak of the Peking-Moscow slinging match has not altered its basic international orientation, only forced it to sit carefully on that particular fence so as to offend neither side excessively. (Indeed the Swiss jurist whose views have been quoted above has tried to make a case for saying that the "neutrality" of Hanoi with regard to China and Russia is legitimately a part of the region's experimentation with the whole idea of neutrality. [8])

But now the big power that has played the strongest role in Southeast Asia, the United States, is reducing its presence and lowering its commitment. It is no longer possible, after Vietnam, for Southeast Asians to dream that American troops will come to save them from aggression. It would in any case be too humiliating to the region's sense of nationalism for overt alignments of the SEATO type to be reconstituted. And the need for such alignments is surely irretrievably past. Some of the regional leaders, notably President Suharto and his military colleagues in Djakarta, believe that China might still try to take advantage of any regional disorder to promote her own proteges, and they worry lest the indigenous will and means to resist prove too weak. Razak predicates his belief in neutralization on a quite different premise, that a Chinese attack could conceivably take place only in the context of a general world war. It is common ground to both Suharto and Razak that insurgency is essentially an internal problem which can and must be combatted internally, though there can be fine differences of emphasis over the role of foreign encouragement and aid. In the upshot an alignment with any one of the big powers is extremely unlikely.

The smaller Southeast Asian countries want to keep their international defense arrangements intact (the American bases in Thailand and the Philippines, the British and New Zealand units in Malaysia and Singapore, SEATO) until there is something equally credible to replace them. In Razak's words, "the neutralization proposed is a long-term objective towards which we are working; the Five-Power arrangements are for the purpose of meeting our present defense needs."[9] But there is no desire to crawl back behind the comforting protection of the American tent. Not only is the credibility of U.S. protection badly bruised after Vietnam and the Guam Doctrine, but the Asian nationalism of the 1970s is too strong for the humiliation of overt protectorate status.

Indonesia, the only ASEAN nation lacking institutionalized external defense assistance, is especially vocal on the need for the region to become self-reliant in every way—politically, economically, and militarily—and this call is now echoed by the others in ASEAN. One might ask whether the Indonesian attitude to the United States and to SEATO is not comparable with the French attitude to the United States and NATO—that is, chilly in public speech but warm in underlying action. It is probably true to say that the Indonesians would prefer the American presence in Asia to phase out gradually rather than create a sudden invitation for a corresponding Soviet or Chinese intrusion. But there is no lobby in Indonesia or elsewhere in Southeast Asia for a politically committing defense link with the United States, and the United States is at present the only conceivable big-power patron for the region.

COLLECTIVE SECURITY

What, then, about intraregional collective security? This is the essence of the Russian proposal for an Asian collective security system, though advocated on a pan-Asian and not merely a Southeast Asian scale. But the Brezhnev Doctrine, as President Suharto has called this scheme, is rendered suspect by its authorship. Since the Soviet presence and influence in the region is waxing rather than waning, any Soviet-backed proposal tends to be seen as a means of maximizing that greater presence. The fact that any such development would be regarded by China as provocative adds another damper to its attractiveness. And the fact that the Brezhnev proposal would include Japan, India, Pakistan, Bangladesh, and even China in one single collective security network would mean that the big Asian powers would be given an authority in Southeast Asia that the South east Asians are anxious to deny them. "To bring in the big countries in Asia into such a scheme," said Razak to Malaysian correspondents after discussing the matter in the Kremlin in 1972, "will be to bring in problems which we small nations may find difficult to resolve."[10] In blunter language, Suharto told C. L. Sulzberger of the New York Times in 1973, "We want ASEAN to strengthen regional independence and avoid having this area become a regional cockpit. Therefore we automatically reject the Brezhnev Doctrine."[11] A subregional Southeast Asian system of collective security might still be agreed upon as a possibility, and there are signs that ASEAN might gradually be moving in that direction—a development that is taken up in more detail in Chapter 17. But clearly a defensive alliance among the Southeast Asian countries themselves would not of itself achieve regional freedom from the interference of the big external powers.

NONAGRESSION PACTS

A network of nonagression pacts might be another answer. It would be possible to construct a system of interlocking bilateral agreements whereby China, the United States, and the USSR each undertook not to attack any of the Southeast Asian states. However, the experience of Hitler is still recent enough to raise doubts about the value of such promises. A similar result might be brought about by pledges within the United Nations, and the Committee of ASEAN Officials has apparently found itself in substantial agreement on suggesting a U.N. Declaration of Southeast Asia as a Nuclear-free Zone or Zone of Peace and Neutrality, following the initiative of Srimavo Bandaranaike in asking for similar treatment with respect to the Indian Ocean. At the United Nations the moral onus would be on the big powers to support such a declaration. Indonesia is particularly concerned to obtain from Peking, Washington, and Moscow a public commitment not to send nuclear submarines, that is to say submarines equipped with nuclear missiles, into Southeast Asian waters. This could also be regarded as an example of "quasi-parliamentary diplomacy, " with the U.N. General Assembly playing the role of world parliament.

Another example would be the attempt by Indonesia in 1970 to secure an Asian solution to the Cambodian crisis.[12] When the Lon Nol regime in Phnompenh came under attack from Communist forces the Indonesian government was highly sympathetic, and army leaders were apparently keen to support Lon Nol in various material ways. Adam Malik, the Foreign Minister, was, however, opposed to any intervention of Indonesian arms, troops, or military advisers, and he convened a Conference of Foreign Ministers of Asian and Pacific countries in Djakarta. Twenty governments were invited, but ten of these did not accept: Afghanistan, Burma, Ceylon, China, India, North Korea, Nepal, Pakistan, North Vietnam, and Mongolia. The ten that did participate were more or less pro-Western—Australia, Japan, South Korea, Laos, Malaysia, New Zealand, Philippines, Singapore, Thailand, and South Vietnam. These Foreign Ministers passed on 17 May a predictably worthy but vague resolution,[13] and set up a task force comprising representatives of Indonesia, Japan, and Malaysia to lobby the United Nations and the Geneva signatories to take steps to stop hostilities in Cambodia. The task force duly visited New Delhi, Warsaw, Ottawa, London, Moscow, and New York during June 1970, but little notice was taken of it.

Malik's Conference was not successful, and big power escalation of the war in Cambodia could not be avoided or undone merely by an assembly of Asian verbal protest. The conference nevertheless stands as an example of Indonesia's concern for Southeast Asian security against Communist attack, and its lack of success played a role in stimulating Malaysia to take up its neutralization proposal at the highest level a few months later. In Djakarta the conference has come to be regarded in retrospect as an important diplomatic initiative, perhaps the most significant by Indonesia since the Bandung Conference of 1955.[14] Whatever the anticipated difficulties or possible failure, Asians should at least, in the Indonesian view, attempt to solve a problem of this kind, particularly when so many of the non-Asian powers involved are unprepared to do much about it. An international conference draws attention to Asian concern. One result of the Djakarta Conference was the later appointment of Indonesia to the International Control or Supervisory Commission in Indochina under the Paris Accords of 1973.

NOTES

1. A. W. Stargardt, Problems of Neutrality in South East Asia: The Relevance of the European Experience. (Singapore: Institute of South East Asian Studies, 1972), p. 2.

2. See Black et al., Neutralization and World Politics (Princeton: Princeton University Press, 1968), pp. 31-35.

3. Asian-African Conference, Bandung, Indonesia 1955 (Djakarta, 1955), quoted in Stargardt, op. cit., p. 12.

4. Foreign Affairs, vol. 36, no. 4, July 1958, pp. 582 ff.

5. See Arthur J. Dommen, Conflict in Laos: The Politics of Neutralization. (New York: Praeger, 1964); and George Modelski, International Conference on the Settlement of the Laotian Question 1961-62. (Canberra: Australian National University, 1962).

6. Stargardt, op. cit., pp. 24-25.

7. FEER, 27 August 1972. Cf. William P. Bundy in Foreign Affairs, vol. 49, no. 2, January 1971, p. 193: "The plain truth is that no security arrangement or combination of security arrangements can be designed in Southeast Asia that remotely covers conceivable forms of aggression."

8. Stargardt, op. cit., p. 22.

9. STK, 27 July 1971.

10. STK, 6 October 1972.

11. New York Times, 18 March 1973.

12. Lau Teik Soon, Indonesia and Regional Security: The Djakarta Conference on Cambodia (Singapore: Institute of Southeast Asian Studies, 1972).

13. FAM, vol. 3, no. 1, June 1970, pp. 50-53.

14. Michael Leifer, "Indonesia's Future Role," in The World Today, London, vol. 26, December 1970, p. 516. See also Adam Malik, "Djakarta Conference and Asia's Political Future," in Pacific Community, vol. 2, no. 1, October 1970, p. 67.

PART

II

SOUTHEAST ASIAN ATTITUDES

The attitude of the Republic of Indonesia toward any proposal of policy for the future diplomacy of Southeast Asia is obviously critical. Although Indonesia can boast a gross domestic product of only U.S. $14,000 million, only a quarter of the combined figure for the region, the country is so vast in its potential and so self-confident of its eventual political destiny that its views on all regional questions are conceded to be of the greatest importance. Although Indonesia is not in a position to force the other countries to agree with her, it is still not possible for them to insist on something for the region with which Indonesia disagrees—and since Indonesia's latent economic power has over the past few years become so obvious and so attractive to the outside world, the opposition of Indonesia is extremely damaging for any regional proposal. It is for this reason that of all the attitudes of the smaller states of Southeast Asia toward the neutralization proposal one is led to discuss first the attitude of Indonesia.

Indonesia is in area the fourteenth largest and in population the fifth largest nation in the entire world and is by any criterion the largest nation in Southeast Asia. The energy and determination of so many of her inhabitants, to which the Dutch and Japanese imperial forces—as well as American, Chinese, and Soviet diplomats— can testify, adds another ingredient to the Indonesian equation: In addition to being the largest state in the region she is also one of the most determined and ambitious.

There was an amusing exchange at the end of the seminal conference in Singapore in the middle of 1971, called "New Directions in the International Relations of Southeast Asia," in which the Indonesian Foreign Minister, Adam Malik, referred to the book War and Peace in Southeast Asia written by one of the other participants in the conference, Peter Lyon. Discussing neutralization in his book, Lyon had observed that the withdrawal of the great powers from Southeast Asia must mean one of two things: "Either it means the arrival of a new hegemony, and in Southeast Asia today this can be only China in the face of the United States; or it means an area of contrasting, perhaps warring local powers (with Indonesia and Vietnam doubtless trying to rule the local roosts) and with the permanent possibility of great power intervention." Malik's comment, which provoked the laughter of scholars and writers attending the conference, was: "Well, thank you so much indeed, Mr. Lyon, for awarding Indonesia with a major power status. Indonesia, together with other ASEAN member countries, is trying hard to prevent your prediction becoming a reality."[1]

The view offered by Peter Lyon about the future potential of Indonesia and Vietnam is in fact widely shared among observers of Southeast Asia. These are the only two countries within the region that show any signs of developing in the future into powers possessing both the will and the capacity to be of significant influence not only throughout the Southeast Asian region as a whole but even beyond. The capability of the Vietnamese to involve their neighbors and the great powers in their internal, subregional, and ideological affairs needs no rehearsal here. The Indonesian potential is less widely appreciated, but it is not so many years ago that they astonished the world, under President Sukarno, by persuading the great powers to force Holland into surrendering the sovereignty of West Irian, by daring to take on (virtually alone) the armed might of Great Britain in the war of confrontation over the inclusion of Sabah and Sarawak into the new Federation of Malaysia in 1963, and finally by defying the Americans and forging an alliance with China that struck a chill in both Washington and Moscow, let alone in some of the smaller Asian capitals.

Indonesia is, however, different in very important respects from her four partners in ASEAN and from most of the other states in Southeast Asia as a whole. Like Vietnam, but unlike any of the others, Indonesia had to fight for her independence against the armed forces of a European power. The Indonesians thus bring to international and diplomatic problems a taste of blood which expresses itself in self-confidence, sometimes in toughness and bluster, but always in spirit. Their subsequent experiences after independence was finally wrung from a reluctant Netherlands were, however, far from happy. The challenge of materializing the ideas of nationhood and modernization across these huge, disparate, and separated islands was greater than that faced by almost any other country in the Third World with the possible exception of India. Yet Indonesia inherited from its colonial power nothing like the relatively efficient bureaucracy and education system that the British left behind in India, and nothing like the beginnings of economic advancement and scientific and industrial development that had been built up in India by the end of the Second World War. Indonesia was and remains one of the poorest countries in the world in terms of income per head, and is certainly the Cinderella among the ASEAN states in terms of standard of living.

With a weak civil service, an impossibly strung-out terrain, very little funds, and political and regional divisiveness, Indonesia did not promise well in the first few years of the new republic. The proliferation of political parties and the impossibility of getting a strong continuing government by coalition looked to prove fatal to the Indonesian experiment. But it was saved by the remarkable Sukarno, who, although reckoned by most Westerners and many Asians as a comic opera character, a buffoon and a philanderer, was also a statesman of remarkable vision and drive who, more than any other man, made Indonesia mean something to the vast majority of its citizens. Sukarno, the demigod, the orator, the man of charisma and sparkle, was able to inspire ordinary folk with the idea of modern nationalism, and under his regime, culminating in the virtual dictatorship he managed to secure as a result of balancing the right-wing military and Islamic leaders on the one hand against the left-wing Communist Party on the other hand, succeeded in putting Indonesia on the diplomatic map. He lacked any real interest in economics, and during this whole period the Indonesian economy stagnated tragically. He finally overreached himself in the mid 1950s and toppled from power when an abortive coup d'etat engineered by an obscure colonel—apparently with the intention of murdering the leading right-wing generals so that Sukarno and the PKI (the Indonesian Communist Party) could consolidate their dictatorship—was foiled through inefficiency and bad luck, catapulting General Suharto, who until then had been a mild and obscure senior member of the armed forces leadership, into the succession to Sukarno.

FOREIGN POLICY AFTER SUKARNO

Since 1965-66 Suharto has consolidated his position as the leader of the army and of the nation, has legitimized his government through elections and through the creation of a new political party encompassing the nonreligious establishment forces throughout the country (the civil servants, the professional men, the trade unions, the peasant and cooperative groupings), and by patiently laying the groundwork for Indonesia's economic development, utilizing the best indigenous "technocrats" available.

In the beginning the Suharto regime inevitably gained a reputation for being pro-Western, though in reality this was more a case of Indonesia's turning against the powers that had supported the PKI, namely the Soviet Union and China. In reaction against the bombast of Sukarno, the government of Suharto maintained at the beginning a low posture in international affairs. Only in 1970, five years after its installation, did his government begin to play an active role on the international scene, by which time the country was regarded as being morally, if not explicitly, in the Western camp. This was partly the result of the fact that the right-wing generals relied on the Americans for military supplies and training, partly of the implications of the new economic policy they undertook.

There were many American advisers and American-trained Indonesian economists who helped to shape the new policy from about 1966 onwards, a policy of opening Indonesia up to the international capitalist economy, restoring a role to indigenous private enterprise, and attracting foreign aid and investment. The promulgation in 1967 of the Foreign Investment Law under which whole sections of the economy came under the control of American, Japanese, European, and Overseas Chinese investors, and the establishment of the Inter-Governmental Group on Indonesia (a body comprising the principal countries giving foreign aid to Indonesia) were seen by many outside observers, especially in the Communist camp, as placing the Indonesian economy in the Western orbit.

Technically Indonesia did not exclude Communist countries, and the Foreign Investment Law, for example, made provision for the inflow of capital from the Soviet bloc as well as from the West. But the fact remained that at the moment when Indonesia's economy seemed on the verge of collapse in 1965-66, the countries that most readily offered help and capital were those in the West.[2] This does not mean that Indonesia broke off her economic ties with the socialist countries. During the same period that the Indonesian economy was getting this tremendous boost from Western investment, Bulgaria, East Germany, and Czechoslovakia also gave assistance in building factories, a cement mill, and a radio station in Indonesia.

In 1970 the Suharto regime began its tentative re-entry into international diplomacy,[3] largely because of the Cambodian crisis, which alarmed the military leadership considerably. The entry of Vietnamese Communist forces into Cambodia in that year seemed in Djakarta to confirm the view that Vietnam was a belligerent power determined to force the other countries of the region into communism against their will. There were even generals who believed that Indonesia ought to send troops into Cambodia, although the opposition that this idea encountered from almost all civilian circles prevented it from being realized.[4] The Indonesian government did, however, convene the Djakarta Conference on Cambodia, which allowed Indonesia to play host to a wide range of countries, mainly pro-Western, interested in a peaceful solution to the Cambodian problem. President Suharto began a series of visits to West European countries and to the United States. He attended the Lusaka Conference on Non-Aligned Nations in 1970, and it was there that he first heard the Malaysian proposal for the neutralization of Southeast Asia expounded.

In the following year the Indonesian Foreign Minister, Adam Malik, was elected President of the United Nations General Assembly, and the seal was thereby set on Indonesia's return to the family of nations and to leadership in world diplomacy. Relations with Holland changed perceptibly during these years, and the rapprochement between the former colony and the former metropolitan power came to a climax when Suharto visited Holland in 1970 and Queen Juliana visited Indonesia in 1971. In 1972 President Suharto extended his visits to Australia, New Zealand, and the Philippines, and significance was attached to the military hardware (16 Sabre jet planes) that the Australian government donated to Indonesia as a result of that visit, opening what seemed to be an emerging defense relationship between these two countries.

One reason for the hesitancy of Suharto in entering into international affairs was the considerable differences of viewpoint within political circles in Djakarta. Among the generals themselves there was some disagreement, although it would be fair to describe the military leaders as being relatively hawkish, apprehensive of the international communist "threat," and unready to embark on a normalization of relations with China and the Soviet Union, whereas the civilian leaders are pragmatic, more inclined to the basic nonalignment philosophy of the earlier Sukarno period, and more sophisticated in their perceptions of the changing power structure of Asia and the Pacific. Malik, the Foreign Minister, represents the latter strand in the foreign policy fabric, but he has often had to temper his real inclinations because of the pressure of military opinion.

Indonesia was nevertheless a founding member of ASEAN in 1967 and has set great store by the development of intraregional relations. In spite of the war of confrontation between 1963 and 1965, it is with Malaysia that relations have become closest and warmest —partly because of similarities of language, temperament, cultural background, and religion, partly because of the similarity of economic ideas and a common trust in private enterprise involving a legitimate business role for the Overseas Chinese in Southeast Asia. Mutual visits between Indonesia and Malaysia have become frequent; the two countries undertake joint military action in the border area between Sarawak and Kalimantan, where Communist insurgents are still fighting the Malaysian army; they have adopted a common spelling system, have taken a common stand over the deinternationalization of the Straits of Malacca, and have begun a number of economic collaboration projects, including assistance to Malaysia in setting up a state oil corporation modeled on the highly successful Pertamina of Indonesia.[5]

It is against this background that the neutralization proposal has been received and discussed in Indonesia. The reaction was not at first positive, indeed it was highly skeptical, but when the Indonesians realized how serious Tun Razak and his colleagues were about their proposal, they entered into the debate with the fullest sense of its importance.

In December 1970, after the Lusaka Non-Aligned Conference, Tun Razak of Malaysia visited Djakarta and explained his ideas to the Indonesian President. Suharto, according to the joint communique issued afterwards, "showed his appreciation of the issue of the neutralization of the Southeast Asian region. He also re-emphasized the Indonesian stand that to guarantee peace and stability in the region of Southeast Asia the countries in the region must possess adequate national defense strength to the extent of being able to face threats from any quarter. The two heads of government re-emphasized that basically, progress, peace and security in the region were the responsibility of the Southeast Asian countries themselves."[6]

MALIK VOICES RESERVATIONS

Probably the fullest single statement of the compromise position that has evolved in the Indonesian power structure was given by Malik at a meeting of the Press Foundation of Asia held in Bali in September 1971, after the Malaysian proposal had been given a considerable airing but before the Kuala Lumpur Declaration. This speech is worth citing at some length where it focuses on the neutralization idea, because in it Malik conveys the complications and the apprehensions that underlie the Indonesian attitude:

In my view three alternatives are open to us. We could align ourselves with any one or a combination of powers whom we would trust to help secure our safety and well-being; we could obtain the concurrence of the major powers to declare Southeast Asia a neutralized zone, free from big power interference; we could develop among ourselves an area of indigenous sociopolitical and economic strength.

The first alternative looks like the easiest way out but is at the same time the least productive. It would in essence amount to an acceptance and adjustment to the powers that be. It will not be in the interest of Southeast Asia to see any single power within the new constellation assume a position of paramountcy, as this would only lead to continued tensions or even confrontations between the major powers. Since alignments, by definition, work towards a position of dominance of one element over the others, we would, by aligning ourselves, in fact perpetuate the very same situation in which Asia has found itself since colonial days: an arena of strife and turmoil where conflicts of outside interests are actually being fought out.

The second option may appear to be a more attractive modus vivendi than the first. It has been put forth several times in the past by some European leaders and suggestions of a similar nature were made again in recent months by some Asian leaders themselves. Thinking on this concept has so far been understandably vague and any reservations one may have are often linked to one's own interpretation of the type of neutralization contemplated.

If the neutralization envisaged is of the type of Switzerland or Austria, then it would be difficult to see even a remote similarity of conditions and strategic interests between such a vast and diverse area as Southeast Asia and a country like Switzerland or Austria. Hence, it seems to me still a rather distant possibility to ever get the four major powers, given their divergent interests and designs towards the area, voluntarily to agree to its neutralization. Moreover, neutralization that is the product of "one-way" benevolence on the part of the big powers, at this stage, would perhaps prove as brittle and unstable as the interrelationship between the major powers themselves.

The third choice, in my personal view, would be the most desirable as it would be the most effective in securing long-term stability and harmony in this part of the world.

I strongly believe that it is only through developing among ourselves an area of internal cohesion and stability, based on indigenous sociopolitical and economic strength, that we can ever hope to assist in the early stabilization of a new equilibrium in the region that would not be the exclusive "diktat" of the major powers. However dominant the influence of these big powers may be, I think there is and there should be scope for an indigenous Southeast Asian component in the new, emerging

53

power balance of the region. In fact, I am convinced that unless the big powers acknowledge and the Southeast Asian nations themselves assume a greater and more direct responsibility in the maintenance of security in the area, no lasting stability can ever be achieved.

It is only through such a Southeast Asian presence in the power equation that we can ever hope to persuade the major powers to take into acocunt our wishes and aspirations and the directions and forms in which we want to develop. At this transitional stage, in which the international constellation of forces is moving towards new balances of accommodation, we are afforded an opportunity to contribute our concepts into the mainstream of the thinking and searching that is going on. It is a unique opportunity and we should not waste it. Once a new equilibrium is crystallized, we may not be able to do so anymore.

To this end, therefore, the nations of Southeast Asia should consciously work towards the day when security in their own region will be the primary responsibility of the Southeast Asian nations themselves. Not through big power alignments, not through the buildup of contending military pacts or military arsenals, but through strengthening the state of our respective national endurance, through effective regional cooperation, and through cooperation with other states sharing this basic view on world affairs.

It is here that the importance of such an organization as ASEAN comes to the fore, as basically reflecting the determination of its member countries to take charge of their own future and to reject the assumption that the fate of their region is to continue to be determined by outside powers. It is here that the role of the nonaligned group of nations assumes particular significance, as one refusing that the fate of the world be decided by the confrontation between two polarized power blocs. And although some may consider the influence of nonalignment to be marginal, the important contribution of this group of nations has been to enhance mobility in international relations and thus reduce the possibility of frontal clashes between the contending blocs.

Of course, to be able to wield a proportionate and effective influence within the future balance of forces in the region, Southeast Asia needs first to attain a commensurate strength, based on a certain degree of internal prosperity and stability. It is precisely here where the concurrence and support of the major powers could be of crucial importance. For there seem to be hopeful signs of a growing realization on the part of some of the big powers, that to assist in the stability and economic prosperity of Southeast Asia may in the end prove to be a much better and less costly investment towards lasting security than would the present cycle of direct military interventions and confrontations.

The vision that is alive in Indonesia is of a Southeast Asia working together in freedom, equality and peace towards greater stability and prosperity; a Southeast Asia, supported in its economic development by the developed nations of both West and East; and guaranteed against nuclear attack or blackmail by the nuclear powers. [7]

In Kuala Lumpur, on the eve of the Declaration, Malik elaborated a little further on the neutralization idea: "If it means to free the region from outside interference," he said, "in principle we shall have no objection." He would prefer to wait to hear other countries' views before making up his mind, but he called for Malaysia to focus specifically on the problems that faced the countries of the region. What, for example, should be done, he asked, if a nuclear-armed vessel belonging to one of the big powers wanted to pass through the Strait of Malacca?[8]

It should be noted that of all the Indonesian leaders, it was Malik who responded most quickly to the change in the position of China and to the change in American policy toward China during this period. Whereas the Indonesian generals were suspicious and alarmed at the Kissinger diplomacy from 1971 onwards and the Nixon visit to Peking, Malik welcomed these developments, although with some reservations. "China and the United States," he said after the Shanghai communique between President Nixon and Prime Minister Chou En-lai, "will continue to have special interests in Southeast Asia. Despite their recent declaration [that is, of their respective noninvolvement in Southeast Asia] we cannot expect them to forget these altogether, but we can hope that their activities in this area will be limited. We hope China will reduce her support for national liberation movements. We can hope that the United States, after her involvement in Indochina, will not want to involve herself again in like manner."[9]

PRESIDENT SUHARTO'S VIEWS

It was, however, for President Suharto himself to give the authoritative comment on neutralization. He told an Asian editor in April 1971 that the Malaysian proposal would get "our fullest attention, " adding, "However, I wish to stress again that most decisive is the national resilience of each nation in Southeast Asia itself. "[10] On the eve of his visit to France at the end of 1972 Suharto told Le Monde:

> The project for the neutralization of Southeast Asia has as
> its goal the liberation of our region from the dangers which
> threaten it. These dangers can take any form: physical,
> Communist, ideological infiltrations or subversion, or
> threats in the economic, political or cultural fields. South-
> east Asia must free itself in order not to become a region
> for confrontation between certain big powers. Even when
> a solution will have been found to the Vietnam conflict,
> there will always be differences between the United States,
> the Soviet Union and China, which pursue their efforts to
> try and consolidate their influence in this part of the
> world. As long as the big powers try to use our region
> as a tilting-ground, as long as they seek to establish
> spheres of influence here, we will have neither tran-
> quility nor peace. The only way for Indonesia to face
> such a situation is to reinforce national resistance on
> all planes—political, ideological, economic, cultural
> and military. For the neutralization of Southeast Asia
> to succeed, each country must act in this way. We are
> now collaborating on that.[11]

And on a later occasion, the President declared:

> What we want is the birth of a new Southeast Asia that
> can stand on its own feet and not let its future be de-
> cided by outside powers. Such a Southeast Asia,
> where there is no conflict, no suspicious feeling, and
> no foreign intervention, would be able to make a posi-
> tive contribution to world peace. [12]

The concept of national resilience or building up self-reliance is Indonesia's unique contribution to the Southeast Asian debate. It stems from the faith of Indonesian leadership in the capacity of the region to solve its own problems if left alone, and it is reinforced by the instinctive dislike on the part of the largest country within the region for the idea of foreign commitments in the region. The feeling behind all this reaches back into Indonesia's modern history, and it was well set out by Malik after the Djakarta conference on Cambodia in 1970, when the idea of neutralization was still very new. In an article in Pacific Community, he wrote:

Military alliances or foreign military presence does not enhance a nation's capacity to cope with the problem of insurgency. The price for such commitments is too high, whereas the negative ramifications for the nation are too great. I am confident that this challenge can best be met by strengthening the national resilience, by way of continuing top-priority commitment to economic development next to maintaining political stability and high morale and combat-readiness of the armed forces; by infusing a sense of participation and responsibility into the various currents of political and social groups in the country and by nurturing a mutual respect among the racial and ethnic groups and religious minorities. Above all, the political systems in all these countries should, in the first place, make possible the pursuit of planned economic development, without which all other problems will remain insoluble.

Since many of the Asian countries are facing quite similar domestic problems of insurgency and subversion, some kind of working arrangement should be possible among those countries in their efforts to meet the common threat. A kind of understanding among the countries concerned reflecting the general pattern of political, economic and social reform which they are carrying out will be necessary to forge such a working arrangement. To this end a continuing dialogue on matters pertaining to the general interest of the region is a prerequisite for establishing meaningful communication. For each country in the region, a concentration on programs of economic development should be the primary preoccupation, while at the same time striving for independence from burdensome military alliances.

In a sense the Asian countries, in their quest for peace and progress in the face of existing superpower rivalries and looming internal subversion, have to conduct their international relations on the principle of nonalignment. This then is the pattern of diplomacy that emerged from the Djakarta conference. [13]

DISLIKE FOR MILITARY PACTS

There is a strong dislike among the Indonesian leaders for military pacts of any kind. There was an immediate reaction, for example, when Lee Kuan Yew, the Prime Minister of Singapore, on a visit to Bangkok urged the United States to maintain a military presence in Thailand at the beginning of 1973. "If Indonesia was asked to provide military bases for foreign countries, " said Malik in commenting on the Lee Kuan Yew call, "we would certainly say: 'Go to hell.' It should also be asked why Lee Kuan Yew asked for military presence in Thailand, not in his own country."[14] The Indonesian Foreign Minister went on to say that foreign bases in the ASEAN countries were temporary, and when pressed to say what temporary meant he answered, "Temporary may mean five years, or even ten years, but for us the sooner the better."[15] Malik later defined temporary as meaning the time during which the presence of the foreign forces or bases concerned was felt to be necessary by the host country, but he warned that their presence would only increase the host country's dependence on foreign powers, delay the time necessary to achieve self-reliance, and invite other powers to move in and influence the balance of power.[16]

He commented again, this time in Singapore, "If one nation, or a number of nations of ASEAN, think that they still need foreign troops, it is up to them. It is within their sovereignty . . . but from Indonesia's point of view, we have never accepted, invited or agreed to foreign military bases . . . if we want to implement the ideal of neutralization, then the area to be neutralized should not contain foreign military bases of one power or another. The alternative is, all powers may equally have their bases in the country. Perhaps the second alternative is even more difficult to implement."[17] When there were rumors, hardly reliable but nevertheless worrying, about the possibility of Singapore inviting a Soviet replacement for the Australian military presence in Singapore, an anonymous Indonesian defense ministry official was quoted as saying that the existence of a big-power naval base in Singapore would obstruct the creation of a neutral Southeast Asia.

The burden of the Indonesian objection to neutralization is its perpetuation of a sense of dependency by the region on the great powers. Indonesians have a great deal of sympathy with the viewpoint expressed most strongly by Singapore, that since no one big power is likely to dominate the region again, it is better to have them offsetting each other through some kind of equal presence in the region. The Indonesians are certainly not happy at the prospect of a sudden alteration in the balance of big power interests in Southeast Asia that would inevitably accrue to the benefit of China and the Soviet Union and to the detriment of the American presence. They do not often say so, partly out of a natural pride and partly out of the knowledge that they themselves are likely to be the last to be affected by such a change in the balance of power. But the point was well expressed by a former diplomat, Nugroho, who wrote in 1972:

> If the isolationist trend and the war-weariness in the
> United States grow further, the United States may aban-
> don South Vietnam to the mercy of the DRV. In that
> case it will be a matter of time before the whole of
> Vietnam becomes Communist. Laos and Cambodia are
> likely to follow in due time, because if the United States
> pulls out of Vietnam she is not likely to stick her neck
> out for Laos and Cambodia. Such a development will
> pose a further threat to Thailand and Malaysia, both
> already suffering from endemic communist insurgency
> and subversion. In such a state of affairs, the rest of
> Southeast Asia may turn more towards the United
> States and her Western allies for protection. [18]

The Indonesians are not quite as nervous as some of the smaller states of Southeast Asia about the future intentions of great powers (particularly China) in the region, nor are they exposed to the memories of expansionism and aggression by powers within the region of the kind that Malaysia and Singapore had to endure during the Sukarno war of confrontation.

The initial Indonesian instinct, therefore, was to dilute the proposal for neutralization under big-power guarantee by arguing that guarantees should be sought from a much bigger group of powers, including Western Europe and Japan. But at heart the Indonesians are not keen on the idea itself and would prefer that the countries of Southeast Asia move slowly but steadily toward a common front based on internal strength and a growing economic development in the region, a growing sense of meeting the needs of social development as well as economic growth, which would enable them to become simply less apprehensive about (and less vulnerable to) the intentions or potential disruption of the great powers.

NOTES

1. ND, pp. 201-2.
2. O. G. Roeder in FEER, 7 May 1970, p. 15; Lau Teik Soon, Indonesia and Regional Security: The Djakarta Conference on Cambodia (Singapore: Institute of Southeast Asian Studies, 1972), pp. 6-7.

3. See Robert C. Horn, "Indonesia's Response to Changing Big Power Alignments," in Pacific Affairs, vol. 46, no. 4, Winter 1973-74, p. 515.

4. O. Sutomo Roesnadi, "Indonesia's Foreign Policy," in Trends in Indonesia (Singapore: Institute of Southeast Asian Studies, 1972), p. 63.

5. See, however, John Hoffman in New Nation, Singapore, 7 May 1971, for an account of Indonesian-Malaysian tensions.

6. FAM, vol. 3, no. 2, December 1970, p. 85.

7. FEER, 25 September 1971, pp. 32-33.

8. STS, 23 November 1971.

9. STK, 11 March 1972.

10. Interview with S. M. Ali, New Nation, Singapore, 13 April 1971.

11. Patrice de Beer, Le Monde, 19 November 1972.

12. STK, 5 April 1973.

13. "Djakarta Conference and Asia's Political Future," Pacific Community, vol. 11, no. 1, October 1970, p. 74.

14. BP, 18 January 1973.

15. STK, 18 January 1973.

16. STS, 10 February 1973; ARB, March 1973, p. 1630.

17. STK, 20 January 1973.

18. Nugroho, "Southeast Asian Perceptions of the Future of the Region," in ND, p. 18. See also Peter Polomka, Indonesia's Future and South-East Asia (London: International Institute for Strategic Studies, 1974), pp. 25-26 and 35.

Malaysia did not achieve its political independence from British rule until 1957, by which time Indonesia and the Philippines had already consolidated their independence from prewar colonialism, while Thailand had never succumbed to it. It is somewhat remarkable, therefore, that it turned out to be Malaysia that took the initiative in proposing neutralization as a regional goal.

The explanation is perhaps to be found in the experiences of the Malaysian leaders during their first decade and a half of national independence. The first period in Malaysian foreign policy is described by Stephen Chee as "leaning to one side."[1] In some respects Malaysia did not start out as an avowedly pro-Western state. The new government declared, for example, that its intention was to be "on the most friendly terms with all countries in the world," and Malaysia did not join the Southeast Asian Treaty Organization. However, the perils of independence led Malaysia initially to secure protection from the former colonial power, which in this case had peacefully handed independence to her on a platter. Malaysia signed a mutual defense treaty with Great Britain similar in some respects to that which the Philippines enjoyed with the United States. Peking was quick to recognize the newly independent state, but the Chinese offer to establish diplomatic relations was ignored in Kuala Lumpur, where the preoccupation was still with the Chinese-led Communist insurgency. The Malaysian Communist Party (MCP) had fought the government in Malaysia since 1948, and the so-called Emergency was not officially ended until 1960. The government could hardly afford to make overtures to the Communist countries when it was still in the process of breaking the back of such a formidable local insurgency.

The outlook the Malaysian leaders had of the world outside at this time was that of a bipolar system in which the so-called Free World faced monolithic Communism. Some events during the late 1950s

61

and early 1960s reinforced their view of China as an aggressive state, notably the war against Tibetan rebels in 1959, the border conflict between China and India in 1962, the escalation of the Vietnam War, and the spreading influence of the Communist Party of Indonesia. Tunku Abdul Rahman, the first Prime Minister of Malaysia, was particularly shocked by the subjugation of the Tibetans, and he took something of an international lead in supporting the Tibetan case in the United Nations.

Underlying all of these problems was the fact that Malaysia differs from the other Southeast Asian countries (with the rather special exception of Singapore) in embracing a Chinese minority that is not merely a minority but constitutes some 40 percent of the total population. The most common view political leaders from the Malayan community had of their Chinese colleagues was as a group of people difficult to control, vulnerable to hostile ideology, not necessarily loyal to the state in which they resided, and yearning for their land of origin and its culture. It seemed sensible to argue that a policy of isolating the local Chinese in Malaysia from the mainland of China would promote the integration process in the new state. It was for t his reason that diplomatic relations were not established with Taiwan and consular relations were only set up there in 1964. Malaysian leaders wanted no truck with any kind of China, neither Communist nor Nationalist.

ANTICOMMUNIST FOREIGN POLICY

Reinforcing all these attitudes was the idiosyncratic figure of the Tunku himself, a man whose basic sympathies and instincts were anti-Communist and pro-Western. At the beginning of its existence, Malaysia had a very weak foreign service, and Malaysian foreign policy in the early years was almost a one-man show.[2] The first official visit made by the new Prime Minister to a foreign country was in 1958 to South Vietnam, where the Tunku protested his solidarity with President Diem, adding: 'It is a mistake for Southeast Asian countries to concern themselves unduly with world and Afro-Asian politics when politics in Southeast Asia itself is in the melting pot.'[3] In 1960 the Malaysian government even sent surplus war equipment to Saigon, and in 1961 the Association of Southeast Asia was formed largely on the initiative of the Tunku himself with those two SEATO allies, Thailand and the Philippines, as the other partners.

It was difficult to avoid the impression that Malaysia was a country increasingly becoming identified with the policy of combatting international communism and containing China. And this in turn was underlined by the high degree of economic dependence on Britain in particular and on the Western nations in general for markets, for sources of imports, for aid, and for capital investment. Development planning in the early years of Malaysia was premised on a large-scale inflow of external funds; more than that, it was based on the assumption that spending on defense could remain small in spite of the demands of the insurgency. The Anglo-Malayan Defense Agreement (AMDA) was a way of getting military security on the cheap, in order to maximize the development of the civilian economy.

For all these reasons, during the first phase of Malaysia's foreign policy the ruling elite leaned towards a policy of commitment to the Western alliance. This provided the external security needed for the process of nation-building and socioeconomic advance. Thus, in the pursuit of diplomacy towards the Commonwealth and leaning towards the West, the Tunku omitted to cultivate friends among the enlarging circle of Third World countries.

This first began to matter seriously in 1963, when the new Federation of Malaysia was formed, whereby peninsular Malaya, which had been independent from 1957, was joined with Singapore and with the two Borneo states of Sabah and Sarawak to form the new Federation of Malaysia. The Federation became an international issue from the very day it was formed, in the sense that it was opposed by Indonesia, led to the breaking of diplomatic ties with the Philippines, intensified the antagonism of China, and exposed Malaysia to hostile diplomacy led by the Soviet bloc at the United Nations. During the two years in which the Federation was "confronted" by Sukarno, the Malaysian leaders were forced to acquire new perspectives about world politics. The initial effect of the military engagement with Indonesia was to move Malaysia closer to the West and make her even more reliant on British military support. But this could only be a temporary and short-term prop to Malaysian independence.

Meanwhile it was clear even in Kuala Lumpur that the division of the international communist camp had gone so far that it could no longer be regarded as tentative or insignificant. Polycentrism in the eastern camp had become a reality. It was therefore possible for the first time to think of the Soviet Union in different terms from China. It remained the sentiment among the Malaysian leaders that the evil genius behind confrontation was the PKI, and that behind the mask of the PKI lurked the leaders of the People's Republic of China. There were open references by ministers to China's "grand design" and to the dedication of Peking to "militant revolution through subversion and infiltration."[4] During this period the Vietnam War had again escalated, and the cultural revolution was beginning to make Chinese foreign policy more belligerent. In the course of all this Malaysia became more committed to the support of American intervention in Vietnam and shifted to oppose the admission of China to the

United Nations. In 1966 Malaysia joined ASPAC, thus demonstrating solidarity with the overtly anti-Communist states of the Asian-Pacific region.

At the same time, the confrontation experience drove the Malaysians to seek new friends among the Afro-Asian countries in order to expose the pretensions of Sukarno, whose credentials in the Afro-Asian nonaligned movement were impeccable. Tunku Abdul Rahman and other Malaysian Ministers began for the first time to fly frequently to places like Algiers and Cairo in order to plead the Malaysian case. They lobbied for admission to the Conference of Non-Aligned States, and they inaugurated a policy of actively making friends with almost any country that was not unfriendly to Malaysia. This culminated in the rapprochement with post-Sukarno Indonesia and with the Philippines and the revival of regional cooperation in the shape of ASEAN in 1967. There were even overtures to the Soviet Union that resulted in the signing of a trade agreement and the subsequent establishment of diplomatic relations. During this period Malaysia's foreign policy could perhaps be described as "still committed" although moving towards a more independent position. Ironically, although Malaysia depended upon British military support, first in containing the communist insurgency and then in defeating the confrontation attack from Indonesia in 1963-65, Malaysians became apprehensive after 1965 about the possibility of Britain's supporting the Singapore side after the separation crisis.

It had always been felt that the British were more committed to Singapore than to Malaysia, and when the British had to take a position on the numerous disputes that came to the surface after Singapore's secession from the Federation of Malaysia in 1965, suspicions were aroused in Malaysian minds. Then came the British government's decision, for economic reasons, to withdraw its military presence in Southeast Asia. The links with Britain began to be eroded, with the untying of the Malaysian dollar from its peg to the pound sterling, and the alteration of some of the Commonwealth trade preferences. Malaysia for the first time began to accept American aid, and the outcome of the confrontation experience was to push Malaysia into a greater awareness of the wider world of America and Afro-Asia. Perhaps the best statement for this middle period of Malaysian foreign policy was made by Ismail in parliament in 1966:

> We are not committed to any power bloc, and we crystallize our attitude on any issue strictly on its merit in the light of our national interest. In that sense we are not aligned. We never claim ourselves to be neutral. In the realm of ideas, and in the choice between right and wrong, we can never remain neutral.[5]

SHIFT TO NONALIGNMENT

But from 1968 onwards there is a new phase in which the road towards nonalignment and neutrality is much more positively taken. A greater clarity in foreign policy is discernible in Kuala Lumpur, a more vocal articulation of the goals of Malaysian foreign policy, and a greater expenditure of energy in actual diplomacy. "What is new, basically," said Stephen Chee, "is the adoption of a political entre-preneurship role in Malaysian foreign policy."[6] This, of course, is the neutralization proposal.

The realization that the Americans were not going to win the war in Vietnam, the withdrawal of the British military commitment, the Nixon Doctrine, and the re-entry of China after the end of the Cultural Revolution all led to an appreciation in Kuala Lumpur of the vital importance of China policy. As long as the Americans and the British had provided both tactical and strategic defenses against any hostile powers, there had been no need to alter the Malaysian attitude towards China. But once this position began to crumble, it became necessary to consider more rationally the question of how to deal directly with the Chinese-Southeast Asian relationship. In 1970 Malaysia was admitted to the Lusaka Conference of Non-Aligned States, and the new Prime Minister, Tun Abdul Razak, set out there his ideas about the neutralization of Southeast Asia. During this more recent period particular attention was paid to developing stronger ties with Indonesia, under the conviction that regional cooperation was absolutely essential in the era of world diplomacy and that Indonesia must play a full part in this. Malaysia established diplomatic relations with all the Indochinese states and with most of the East European states, while Tun Razak paid official visits to Poland and the Soviet Union in 1972.

CHINA AS THE KEY

Since 1971 Malaysia has actively sought a rapprochement with China, voting in the United Nations that year for the Albanian resolution calling for the seating of China. It was then recognized beyond question by the Malavsian leadership that China existed and had to be persuaded to live with Southeast Asia. It was more difficult, how-ever, to hit upon the right formula or basis upon which diplomatic relations could be established between Malaysia and China. A great deal of talking was done in the period between 1971 and 1974, using the diplomacy of sport, medicine, and commerce in the absence of any more formal channels. Malaysia needed to be assured that China would not continue to support the Malayan Communist Party, at least not in any significant way. Malaysia needed to be assured by China that the Voice of Malayan Revolution radio broadcasts would come to an end, at least insofar as they came from Chinese soil. Finally the Malaysians needed to be assured about the status of the 220,000 Chinese living in Malaysia who do not have Malaysian citizenship and are technically stateless. The Malaysian government was reluctant to reward them with citizenship, yet if they were to be taken under Peking's wing the moment a Chinese embassy was established in Kuala Lumpur it would greatly unsettle the internal racial balance and atmosphere within Malaysia.[7] On her side, China was not willing to commit herself to a hands-off policy towards these stateless Chinese, partly out of considerations of ethnic responsibility and partly because she feared that if she renounced them, Taiwan would make capital out of it in the competition for the loyalty and support of the Overseas Chinese in Southeast Asia as a whole.

Meanwhile the economy of Malaysia has sufficiently developed and diversified to enable the country to consider a more detached and independent attitude not only toward the United Kingdom but also towards the United States. There is now a great deal of Japanese investment in Malaysia, and the New Economic Policy elaborated in the Second Malaysia Plan of 1971-75 offers an umbrella beneath which a considerable amount of Russian, East European, and even Chinese support has been able to come into the Malaysian scene. In spite of what one writer calls the "constant patronizing advice by Indonesian military leaders that Malaysia should learn from the 1965 PKI coup and be cautious in making friends with Communist China,"[8] the Malaysians pushed firmly and patiently ahead with their opening to Peking. Heavy increases in defense expenditure assisted the process by which Malaysia became able to dispense with Western military assistance and foreign bases. In spite of the Five-Power Defense Pact, which replaced AMDA, Malaysia has publicized her lack of interest in the extension of these Commonwealth defense arrangements, indicating that Australian withdrawal was acceptable—and that indeed by 1976 it might have become necessitated by the expansion of Malaysia's own armed forces and their need for facilities.

The Malaysian position on neutralization is one, clearly, of unremitting approval; indeed, as the author of a glamorously attractive regional plan that has brought her name to world attention in a serious and flattering light, Malaysia is never likely to jettison her ideas on this subject. When things go badly for neutralization, it can be explained that it was only intended as a long-term goal and as providing a context or a framework within which regional tactics and strategy in the new era could be plotted. When things go well for neutralization, it can be taken as a vindication of the Malaysian plan. Either way Malaysian public opinion is satisfied and the momentum of regional leadership in foreign policy can be maintained.

But the motives for Malaysia's attachment to neutralization should now be clear. It stems primarily from Malaysia's perception that apart from its own internal and subregional problems, the biggest single "external" problem of Southeast Asia is the uncertainty surrounding China's future intentions. Neutralization was a device offering China an honorable bridge to the normalization of relations with the region on mutually satisfactory terms. The twin elements in the attraction of neutralization for Malaysia were as a carrot-and-stick for China and as a beacon by which Malaysia could claim regional leadership and international respect. But whether the same energy would be invested by Malaysia in the neutralization drive after the breakthrough with China in May 1974 remained to be seen. Neither Razak nor Chou En-lai referred to "neutralization" as such during their public exchanges in Peking. Had neutralization already served its purpose for Malaysia?

NOTES

1. Stephen Chee, "Malaysia's Changing Foreign Policy," in Trends in Malaysia II, (Singapore: Institute of Southeast Asian Studies, 1974), p. 37.
2. See Marvin C. Ott, "Foreign Policy Formulation in Malaysia," Asian Survey, vol. 12, no. 3, March 1972, p. 225.
3. The Times, London, 9 February 1958.
4. Quoted in Chee, op. cit., p. 44.
5. Quoted in Peter Boyce, Malaysia and Singapore in International Diplomacy (Sydney: Sydney University Press, 1968), p. 4.
6. Chee, op. cit., p. 47.
7. See Harvey Stockwin in FEER, 15 October 1973, p. 14.
8. Chee, op. cit., p. 56.

6

THE PHILIPPINE
POSITION

Not long after the Malaysian government had launched its proposal for the neutralization of Southeast Asia, Tomas Benitez, a member of the Constitutional Convention, which was then deliberating on necessary constitutional changes, introduced a resolution that would have the effect of declaring the Philippines in a new charter to be a neutral country. A provision allowing for the neutralization of the Philippines was in fact contained in the Independence Act of 1935, and President Quezon twice pleaded with Roosevelt—in 1939 and again after Pearl Harbor in 1941—to implement this, but in vain.[1] The Foreign Secretary, Carlos P. Romulo, replying to Benitez, commented that he himself had argued that neutralization was the answer for the Philippines as far back as 1945 at the United Nations charter meeting in San Francisco. He went on to express the view that "the ultimate security of this region lies in an understanding among the four powers that will not allow any single power to build a hegemony over this region. . . . It is my hope that a sort of neutralization pact can be agreed upon by these powers, or a nonaggression pact." He was referring here to the United States, the Soviet Union, China, and Japan.[2]

This was the time when the Philippines was beginning to make its opening to the left in international relations. After a long period of the nation's being labeled as a "client state" of the United States since its independence in 1946, the administration of President Marcos began a series of initiatives designed to open up a relationship in various ways with China, the Soviet Union, and other Communist states. In his state-of-the-nation address to the Philippines Congress at the beginning of 1971, Marcos called for a reorientation of foreign policy to gain new friends while strengthening relations with the old ones. Diplomatic and trade relations with Communist countries would be established. Despite some opposition in Congress, there was some exchange of trade and cultural delegations with Communist countries, and a three-man delegation led by Congressman Diaz Antonio toured the Soviet Union and Eastern Europe in the spring of 1971. The Chinese Prime Minister, Mr. Chou En-lai, intimated to Filipino visitors that China would welcome diplomatic relations.

THE DISPUTE OVER SABAH

Nevertheless the Philippines had reservations about the neutralization proposal when it came to the Kuala Lumpur meeting of November 1971. President Marcos had already told correspondents in Manila that the Philippines had to choose between two options—a trust in the United States and SEATO on the one hand or neutralization on the other—and he described the latter scheme as "a novel concept to the point where it is an experiment."[3] Before the session of Foreign Ministers of ASEAN in Kuala Lumpur, Foreign Secretary Romulo told Tun Razak that the Philippines wanted to know if the neutralization plan would "prejudice territorial boundaries and certain commitments" made by the Philippines, a reference to the dispute over the sovereignty of Sabah and to the U.S. defense treaty.[4] Not only that, he had to take into account at Kuala Lumpur the ambition of his President to play host, in order to enhance his domestic support, to an Asian summit of heads of government that might conceivably bring about a settlement in Vietnam. The specific problem of the Asian summit was sidestepped by the ASEAN Ministers through the device of legal terminology, so that everybody was satisfied. But after the Kuala Lumpur Declaration, Romulo described it as "a long-range program which will take some time to put into full effect" and which would not immediately affect either existing agreements or the settlement of problems between member states of ASEAN.[5] In other words the Sabah claim was still technically open and in dispute, and the Philippines had not committed itself to abandoning its American alliance.

THE U.S. ALLIANCE

President Marcos subsequently made friendly references to the neutralization proposal,[6] and he sometimes expressed views that came very close to those of Tun Razak—for example, when he told a Thai editor early in 1973 that "the principal threat and danger to the stability of our governments is internal subversion. There will not be, for the next ten years, I believe, external aggression."[7] Yet the Philippines' schizophrenia over its relationship with the United States continued to make it difficult to regard the Philippines as a willing

69

supporter of neutralization. On the one hand Romulo repeated on many occasions that, for political and psychological reasons, the bases would have to be phased out. "The elimination of these bases from the Philippines," he said in a television interview in 1973, "will give us a more flexible stand in our international relations with other countries." He added that the U.S. bases eroded the integrity of Philippine sovereignty.[8] The agreement with the United States, which was negotiated together with a military assistance program in 1947, was originally designed to continue for 99 years, but the termination date was later brought forward to 1991, and there is speculation now that it may be brought forward again.[9]

But President Marcos has reminded Filipinos that the financial loss in foreign exchange from closing the bases would be in the order of U.S. $130 million a year, and that about 26,000 Filipinos employed in these bases would lose their jobs. A rather similar tug-of-war went on over the vexed question of preferential trade, although this finally expired in July 1974, under the Laurel-Langley agreement. During the later part of 1973 the Philippines and the United States were renegotiating their commercial and military agreements.

This left the Philippine leaders in a position of accepting the intellectual arguments of neutralization but pleading time in which to clarify their own ideas and desires regarding their relationship to the United States while at the same time they insisted on continuing to press Malaysia on the awkward dispute over the sovereignty of Sabah.

NOTES

1. See Peter Lyon, War and Peace in South-East Asia, p. 175.
2. STK, 11 June 1971.
3. New Nation, Singapore, 19 November 1971.
4. Ibid., 25 November 1971.
5. Sunday Times, Singapore, 28 November 1971.
6. For example, STK, 15 September 1972.
7. BP, 26 March 1973.
8. ARB, June 1973, p. 1842.
9. See Trends in the Philippines, (Singapore: Institute of Southeast Asian Studies, 1972), pp. 32-33.

Thailand has traditionally prosecuted a foreign policy of accommodation with the dominating power in the region in order to protect her territorial integrity and national sovereignty and to reduce to a minimum the possibility of outside interference in her own domestic affairs. This was the case when the Thai kingdom had to deal with the colonial powers of Europe in the nineteenth century and with Japan during the Second World War, and it has continued into the postwar period in the form of the Thai alliance with the United States. Indeed Thailand became more heavily aligned with the Americans than almost any other state in Southeast Asia, identifying with the old policy of containment of China and playing willing host to an American military presence which at its height saw almost 50,000 U.S. troops and airforce men stationed at various U.S. bases in Thailand. Bangkok became the headquarters of SEATO, Dulles's instrument for resisting Communist aggression in Southeast Asia, and the Thais fostered a close relationship with Taiwan, which became the third largest foreign investor in Thailand after Japan and the United States. [1]

This policy was not much complained of within Thailand, although there were occasional stirrings of nationalism. This was largely because of the firm grip successive military dictatorships have exercised over the country, beginning in the early postwar period with Marshal Sarit and continuing until 1973 with the condominium of Marshals Thanom and Praphass. The military view of Thai objectives in foreign policy was not unanimous, but those who did think about the problem were by a considerable majority in favor of the U.S. link and against a dialogue with either the Soviet Union or China, let alone North Vietnam.

There were some generals and colonels who believed that a deal with China might remove at a stroke the problem of insurgency within Thailand, but most civilian advice was to the contrary, to the effect that only domestic reforms and internal actions by the Thai government could secure the certain failure of the various insurgent groups in their attempted revolutions, which were not fully dependent on foreign support. There was no dispute that Chinese, Russian, North Vietnamese, and Pathet Lao help had been given to the Thai insurgents: Chinese and Soviet arms and propaganda materials were found on Thai soil, and it was known that leaders of the insurgency movements had been trained in Communist states. There was also the continuing radio propaganda, believed to come from Chinese soil. But there has always been in Bangkok a view, albeit often a minority one, that the five or seven thousand insurgents who are seriously troubling the security of Northeast Thailand could not be sustained in their partial control of limited areas of Thai territory only by Chinese, Vietnamese, or Laotian support: They must have something to offer the local populace that the Thai government has not been able to rival. The Thai government's activities in the remoter parts of its outer provinces are notoriously minimal, and the services it provides are in some areas nonexistent.

DETENTE WITH CHINA

For these reasons the Thai opening to China took place later than the efforts of some of the other Southeast Asian states, and Thailand had the embarrassment of providing the ground from which many of the U.S. bombing raids during the later stages of the Vietnam war were launched. But gradually a less inflexible line toward China has evolved, and a Defense Minister and a Deputy Foreign Minister have visited Peking on unofficial missions connected with sport and trade. The Defense Minister, an influential air force leader, was optimistic on his return about the Chinese being willing to cease their support for insurgency in Thailand, although it was later suggested that his report of what Prime Minister Chou had actually said had been misinterpreted and that the undertaking by the Chinese Prime Minister was not in fact so specific. [2] Nevertheless, from the time that China entered the United Nations in 1971, the attitude of the Thai government toward Communist states, particularly China but also the Soviet Union, has become more ambiguous and less rigidly hostile. This greater flexibility in foreign policy was inherited by the new civilian government of Prime Minister Sanya which took office at the end of 1973.

When the Malaysian proposal for neutralization was first aired, Thai reaction was fairly hostile. Field Marshal Thanom, then the Prime Minister, visited Kuala Lumpur in the middle of

1971, before the Chinese entry into the United Nations, and made it clear that he could not accept the neutralization of Southeast Asia because of the Chinese backing that was given to the insurgency in Thailand, although he recognized in a joint communiqué that the proposal was well-intentioned. [3] But within weeks the China question came up for the last time in the General Assembly, and the Thai delegation to the United Nations voted for the entry of the People's Republic, recognizing the direction in which the stream of international opinion was going. It was this development, combined with the imminence of President Nixon's visit to Peking (bitterly criticized in Bangkok), that led the Foreign Ministers of the five ASEAN nations to agree to meet in Kuala Lumpur in November 1971 to discuss the new situation.

At Kuala Lumpur, Thanat Khoman, the veteran Thai Foreign Minister, arrived shorn of his office by a military coup d'état which had clamped down on the partial restoration of parliamentarianism the Thanom regime had experimented with during the preceding months. One of the reasons given for halting the limited return to democracy was the instability caused by the American change of policy toward China and the Chinese entry to the United Nations, which it was feared would encourage the Chinese residents of Thailand to go all out in support of the Communist insurgents. Thanat did not in fact last for very long as a representative of the new government, but he did go to the Kuala Lumpur meeting, accompanied by military advisers, as a special envoy of the Thanom regime. He declared in Kuala Lumpur that Thailand saw no reason for the time being to give up its obligations under existing agreements with the United States and other foreign countries, at least not until the time when the prospects of peace, freedom, and neutrality were completely assured. He afterwards explained that when he signed the Kuala Lumpur Declaration on the neutrality of Southeast Asia on behalf of the Thai government the definition of "neutrality" he had in mind was that of "seeking freedom from interference by outsiders in our internal affairs, and pledging in return that we would not meddle in other people's affairs." He stressed that he did not consider that he was supporting a view of neutralization or neutrality that would embrace nonalignment, noninvolvement, or not leaning on one side or the other. [4]

NEUTRALIZATION UNRELIABLE

An editorial in the Bangkok Post following the Kuala Lumpur Declaration was representative of the government's view. The Declaration was, the newspaper said, "a beautiful document but it

73

has no teeth." It referred to the neutrality of Belgium, which did not prevent that country from conquest in the 1940s. "The type of neutrality we hope for," it went on, "is that of the Swiss," and the virtues of self-defense were praised. The editorial concluded,

> We in Thailand cannot sever our ties with SEATO, inviting predatory powers to move in and fill the vacuum for their own imperialist interests. Until and unless international Communists stop their support of guerillas and insurgents inside Thailand and other countries in the region, we will have to continue to rely on a deterrent like SEATO. SEATO will only become redundant when all outside powers directly respect the neutrality and freedom of the countries in Southeast Asia. It would be dangerous to let our guard down, especially now. If we let it down now, the Communists will have no respect whatsoever for our neutrality. [5]

The Malaysian press did not take quite such a gloomy view of the Thai attitude—a newspaper close to the Malaysian ruling party reported that some words of Thanat shortly after the coup d'etat in Bangkok justified the reading that Marshal Thanom felt neutralization could be made to work if China were to agree to it. [6]

During the course of 1972 the most powerful voices in Thailand did not speak sympathetically for neutralization or neutrality. General Praphass declared: "Thailand cannot be neutral, being so near the war in Indochina and being subject to covert aggression—unlike Malaysia, Singapore and Indonesia." [7] Praphass said that it was possible for the latter three countries to go toward neutrality because they were "far from the war scene," whereas Thailand had been "infiltrated and intruded by the Communist insurgents." He added decisively, "We don't agree with this particular neutralization. I don't see that neutralization could help stop war and solve other problems." [8] In Kuala Lumpur, Prime Minister Razak told his Parliament that he had asked for a clarification of statements attributed to General Praphass to the effect that neutralization was "not suitable to Thailand," and that he had been assured in reply that the actual words of the Deputy Chairman of the ruling National Executive Council of Thailand had been: "This is only the beginning, and therefore we should not talk about it." [9]

But during the course of 1973, as the climate for a more flexible policy toward the Communist powers improved in Bangkok, less rigid stances were taken. Mr. Chartchai, the active Deputy Foreign Minister in both the Thanom and Sanya administrations, reaffirmed

Thai support for the Kuala Lumpur Declaration, explaining that American troops were in Thailand only for the purpose of guaranteeing the Vietnam ceasefire, and that the process of their gradual withdrawal had already begun. [10]

It should, however, be borne in mind that this more sympathetic view of the neutrality declaration was accompanied by some irritation on the part of Thai opinion to the effect that the country was being pushed by its friends for their own purposes. "Some of the ASEAN members," the Thai-language newspaper Thai Rath said early in 1973, "want to push Thailand into becoming a buffer state against Communist countries while they are trading with Communists"—a hit against Singapore especially, and also Malaysia. [11]

The new civilian government that took power at the end of 1973 did not make any startling innovations in foreign policy, no doubt because of its tenuous legitimacy as a caretaker regime. Pending the creation of a more securely based government, the position in the early part of 1974 remained open. It might only be added that one of the views that would have to be taken into account by any more or less popular government in Bangkok would be that expressed by the opposition from time to time under the military dictatorships, to the effect that Chinese hostility to Thailand was not inherent but a product of the Thai alliance with the United States. This point was most graphically made when Thanat, in one of his more flexible phases early in 1969, publicly proposed that a dialogue with China be instituted, suggesting that a suitable emissary to Peking for this purpose might be the highly respected and independent-minded editor, M. R. Kukrit Pramoj. But the latter dismissed the idea with a characteristically curt note in his newspaper, Siam Rath, in which the key sentence was "If the purpose of talking with China is to ask China questions on why they want to destroy Thailand, then it is a waste of time, since we know the answer, that is that Thailand is on the American side." [12]

THANAT'S VIEWS

Thanat is no longer in power, but his view of foreign affairs is still respected in Bangkok, and he is more free to express his true feelings since the military dictatorship has been dissolved. For this reason, a widely-published article he wrote at the beginning of 1973 is worth noting. In this article [13] Thanat argued that neutrality, "if practiced truly," was the only policy that could enable the small developing nations of Southeast Asia to steer a path through "the present polycentric world" created by the emergence of new power centers in China and Japan and by the renunciation, in the Guam Doctrine, of U.S. worldwide responsibilities.

But "neutrality will work only if the neutral countries can secure the respect of other countries for their neutrality. International treaties are not necessarily the best guarantee, for international agreements and declarations are honored only so long as it suits countries to honor them." Citing the contrast between Belgium, which had not been able to back up its neutrality with any significant strength of its own, [14] on the one hand, and Sweden and Switzerland on the other, Thanat argued that armed neutrality was the best formula. "Neutral nations are required by their neutrality to prohibit the establishment of foreign military bases on their soil. But shunning military alliances does not mean that the neutral nations should allow themselves to be caught militarily unprepared completely."

And independence meant not only military but economic muscle. "Economic strength may be an even more effective guarantee for the preservation of neutrality than military strength. Independence in the political and military fields cannot truly exist for a country which is in a state of dependence on foreign aid and whose economy is more or less dominated by foreign interests." This view of the most distinguished and experienced Thai expert on diplomacy corresponds very markedly with the Indonesian concept of neutralization, and it suggests that the support by any Thai government for neutralization would have to be regarded as support in principle and in the long term rather than support for a program that is considered to be a practicable possibility in the near future.

NOTES

1. See generally Astri Suhrke, "Smaller-Nation Diplomacy: Thailand's Current Dilemmas," in Asian Survey, vol. 11, no. 5, May 1971, p. 429; and Michael Morrow, "Thailand: Bombers and Bases—America's New Frontier," in Journal of Contemporary Asia, vol. 2, no. 4, 1972, p. 382.

2. See Japan Times, 18 February 1974; and Stewart Dalby, "Slow Changes in Foreign Policy," "Survey on Thailand in The Financial Times, 19 April 1974.

3. FAM, vol. 2, no. 2, June 1971, p. 85.

4. Japan Times, 22 April 1973.

5. BP, 30 November 1971.

6. Utusan Melayu, Kuala Lumpur, 24 November 1971.

7. BP, 8 August 1972.

8. ARB, September 1972, p. 1163.

9. STK, 19 December 1972; FAM, vol. 5, no. 4, December 1972, pp. 115-16.

10. STK, 2 February 1973.

11. Quoted in Japan Times, 5 March 1973.

12. Siam Rath, 19 March 1969, as quoted in Suhrke, op. cit., p. 437.

13. "Neutrality—With Strength, " Japan Times, 22 April 1973.

14. Cf. Dr. Thanat's earlier remark in STK, 16 June 1971: "How can we think that Asian nations can be more successful than countries in Europe?"

8

THE SINGAPORE
POSITION

Singapore is in an unusual situation compared with the other countries of Southeast Asia, mainly because she is so small and therefore so vulnerable to outside forces of all kinds and from all quarters, particularly from nearby quarters. The nightmare that haunts even the Singapore leaders of today, ten years after their republic's independence as a separate state, is that one day they may wake up to find that they have been asked to go to Collyer Quay to hand over the city to an Indonesian admiral, or to the Johore causeway to hand over the keys to a Malaysian general. This is to put Singapore's apprehensions at their most extreme. It is enough for the purposes of clarifying Singapore's attitude to the neutralization proposal to quote a passage from the first President of Singapore, Inche Yusof bin Ishak, in an address to parliament soon after Singapore's independence. "So many of our neighbors," he said, "and we ourselves would not have had a separate existence if purely Asian forces were to settle the shape of decolonized Asia."[1] He was referring to the 1963-65 confrontation by Indonesia, which without the opposition of British arms could well have succeeded in reducing Singapore to an adjunct of Indonesia.

RELATIONS WITH INDONESIA AND MALAYSIA

To counter the threat of absorption by Singapore's two neighbors, Malaysia and Indonesia, the new republic attempts to maximize its economic utility to those two countries and to reduce its dependence on them to the greatest possible extent by becoming self-reliant in defense and manufacturing, to quote two recent examples. Singaporeans like to talk of themselves as constructing a "global city," in the words of Sinnathamby Rajaratnam, the Foreign

Minister. "We draw sustenance," he once said, "not only from the region but also from the international economic system to which we as a Global City belong and which will be the final arbiter of whether we prosper or decline."[2] Singapore has thus encouraged as great a diversification of foreign investment into its economy as possible, hoping to give all powers throughout the world a stake in the continued independent status of its tiny and fragile state.

Another vivid image came from the Prime Minister, Lee Kuan Yew: "I take comfort from the fact that even in the dark ages there were places like Venice which shone out and lit the way back into the Renaissance. And perhaps this is the role we may be asked to play. But I would like to believe that we can be the sparking plug for a great deal of cooperative endeavor . . . and economic and social well-being—for a better quality of life in Southeast Asia."[3] The idea that Singapore is a "brain center" for the region, conserving and supplying technology and professional and scientific services of various kinds to neighboring countries, is one that gives satisfaction to Singaporeans, if it is slightly scornful of the feelings of its neighbors, who are made to see themselves, in this metaphor, as the "muscle" to Singapore's "brain." As Chan Heng Chee has observed, ideology as a factor in Singapore's foreign policy is clearly subordinated to the far more pressing interests of economic growth and military security.[4]

The corollary of this from the point of view of the relation to the big powers is that Singapore fervently believes in interesting everybody from all over the world in Singapore and in Southeast Asia in order to give everybody enough to want to protect but without giving anybody enough to be tempted to dominate. Singapore would be the last state in the region to put its faith in an ideological label like neutralization without gaining any substantial benefit.

In fact, Singapore's fears are now somewhat diminishing as a result of the improved relationship the Lee Kuan Yew government has been able to achieve in the past two or three years both with Malaysia and Indonesia. The Prime Minister's visit to Djakarta in the middle of 1973 was a key event in this development, and the fact that he laid a wreath at the graves of the two Indonesian marines who were executed in Singapore in 1968 for their crimes committed in Singapore during the war of confrontation in 1963-65 went a long way to heal the wounds this unhappy legal tangle had caused.[5] For the many Indonesians who now feel that they have begun to make some economic progress and can achieve something by themselves without reliance on neighbors like Singapore, the attitude toward Singapore is more relaxed, more friendly. It is no longer seriously argued that Indonesia should as a matter of high priority seek to replace on Indonesian soil the facilities she at the moment borrows or uses from Singapore, such as ports and sophisticated banking and other services.

The argument is rather that Indonesia should proceed along its own path weighing its own national interest as well as it can, regardless of whether this is good or bad for Singapore, and that a successful, prosperous, and friendly government in Singapore is better than one driven to seek the patronage of China or other foreign powers. The Singapore government naturally does as much as possible to convince Indonesia and Malaysia that Singapore is not a Chinese state but rather a multiracial and polycultural state in which English is better understood and more widely used than, for example, Chinese and whose business interests are firmly linked with those of the West. [6] Adam Malik, Indonesia's Foreign Minister, paid tribute to this policy when he said in 1973: "Singapore is not a racial community, although that may be the first impression when we first see it. Singapore should be allowed time to develop into a single and unified nation."[7]

The relationship with Malaysia is much more tense, partly because of the physical proximity of the two countries, which face each other across a short causeway, and partly because of their common experience under British rule. Since the separation of 1965, there has been a gradual but continuous process of adjustment as the divergent national interests of each of the two countries became more apparent. The joint airline, Malaysia-Singapore Airlines (MSA), was split into separate national airlines in 1971 despite its record of profitable operations for a quarter of a century. The currencies were finally separated more recently, in 1973, and the interchangeability of the Singapore dollar and the Malaysian ringgit or dollar came to an end. It used to be said at the beginning of the 1970s that there were only three things left in common between the two countries, namely MSA, the stock exchange, and the Straits Times. By now even these joint enterprises have split up as a result of the gradually divergent needs and policies of a basically rural and agricultural nation on the one hand and an almost totally urban and industrial city-state on the other.

Another area in which there is tension is defense, where under the British yoke there had been a collaboration between Malaysia and Singapore. Today the training facilities for jungle warfare in Malaysia are not made available to Singapore troops, nor has the Singapore air force been given access to the desolate islet of Bukit China, where the Malaysians conduct aerial bombardment exercises. The fact that Singapore used Israeli advisers in building up its defense forces after the separation of 1965 caused some offense in political quarters in Kuala Lumpur. But these tensions should not be exaggerated. In the last year or two there has been a marked improvement in the official relationship between the two governments, culminating in mutual visits by the two Prime Ministers.

SKEPTICAL ABOUT NEUTRALIZATION

Given these two basic facts about Singapore's foreign policy, namely her need to keep the more distant big powers in play in order to minimize the risk of pressure by her immediate neighbors and her highly pragmatic and business-oriented approach to diplomacy, it was inevitable that the Singapore reaction to Tun Razak's proposal for the neutralization of Southeast Asia would be skeptical. Lee Kuan Yew put it very bluntly during his visit to Djakarta in 1973, saying that it was a fact of life both for the present and for the near future that big power guarantees would not be forthcoming. Neither the Americans nor the Russians had given any commitment in this respect, nor could China make any meaningful commitment in view of her lack of naval power. In Lee's view, there would still be considerable jockeying between the big powers to see how each could get more than the others out of the Southeast Asian power balance. [8] The same message of reservation on highly practical grounds was echoed by many officials and commentators in Singapore. Jackie Sam, a leading columnist of the day, observed at the time of the Kuala Lumpur Declaration that neutralization would require many of the Swiss attitudes of determination, discipline, sacrifice, and cooperation, as well as a fundamental unattractiveness on the region's part as a prize for any big power. [9] Clearly these conditions were not being met and were not likely to be met in the near future. The Foreign Minister, Sinnathamby Rajaratnam, dwelt on the unhappy example of Laos, which proved that a guarantee can be quite useless if a big power changes its policy unilaterally to suit its own interests. [10]

In another comment, Rajaratnam noted that while the Southeast Asian nations could not be certain of persuading the great powers to accept the neutralization of the region, they did have it in their power to make conditions in Southeast Asia such that neutralization would become the only proposition open to the big powers. This could be done by strengthening the structure of the region itself "so that we do not provide opportunity to big powers to intervene in our affairs. They intervene only when we offer temptations for intervention by having internal conflict among ourselves or having a domestic situation of great instability."[11] In this respect the Singapore reaction to the Malaysian proposal echoed the Indonesian one by saying that the first priority was for Southeast Asia to put its own house in order, and only then could the big powers be invited to make a formal recognition of the desire by the region to be declared neutral.

Tommy Koh, the Dean of Law at Singapore University and a former ambassador to the United Nations, explained in an article soon after the Kuala Lumpur Declaration that very few of the nations of Southeast Asia genuinely feared for their independence (this list would include Cambodia and Laos, and possibly Singapore, but none of the others). The majority of the nations of Southeast Asia preferred to rely on policies of alignment, of alliance with powers outside the region, on military preparedness, or on the potential maneuvers of diplomacy. There was no apparent convergence of interest toward Southeast Asia on the part of the big powers outside, and Koh believed that the only circumstances in which neutralization would become attractive were if the Vietnamese war were to spill over into Thailand or Malaysia, or if the rivalry between the big powers over the Indian Ocean were to become much fiercer. And in any case, the Singapore ex-diplomat concluded, Indonesia would not be a willing backer of neutralization. "No country," he said, "with aspirations to big or middle power status could accept neutralization."[12]

A more recent representative comment was that given in an editorial by New Nation, the Singapore newspaper, after Adam Malik's Gandhi Memorial Lecture in Kuala Lumpur at the end of 1973. The Indonesian Foreign Minister had argued that there were five preconditions for the realization of a neutral Southeast Asia: (1) The countries in the area must be ready to cooperate, (2) they must minimize conflicts and differences, (3) they must refrain from taking sides in big power politics, (4) they must not invite external powers into the region to solve internal disputes, (5) there must be "national resilience and regional cohesion." The Singapore newspaper observed that the last two of these conditions remained targets rather than realities, and that until they were realized "neutralization must remain largely a topic of discussion and debate."[13]

But it must still be said that the Singapore leaders have given the neutralization proposal its due credit. The Prime Minister once remarked to an American correspondent, "If the Chinese, Russians and Americans agree that neutralization is in their joint interests, there could be a neutral Southeast Asia. Then that, I think, is the best answer."[14] It will be forgiven that some readers of his remarks on that occasion recalled that three years earlier he had said, "I am nonaligned in the sense that I do not want to be involved in power blocs. . . . Where my security and survival [are] threatened, I cannot be neutral."[15] But this perhaps would be unfair. The Singapore view on neutralization was simply expressed by Rajaratnam just after the Kuala Lumpur Declaration when he said, "We are all agreed on the concept itself. To be quite frank, we all have different approaches to this goal."[16]

It is to be noted finally that Singapore was well aware of the Chinese factor behind the Malaysian proposal. The New Nation observed in an editorial just before the Kuala Lumpur Declaration:

> Malaysia's strategy seems to be to offer as a bait to China regional neutralization—which, its officials have now admitted, implies the eventual abrogation of the Commonwealth five-power defense agreement and will also presumably mean an end to SEATO and the American bases in both Thailand and the Philippines. "If you live up to the U.N. charter," the ASEAN line to Peking could be, "and stop this overt interference in our affairs, then we will gradually disengage from our Western military entanglements. But we must do it in step, and we want to see something from your side, some evidence of change in your patronage of our local Communist minorities, before we take the risk of sending our Western friends home." If this is a correct interpretation of Tun Razak's proposal, then it seems on the face of it to be a good strategy. It would put the ball in Peking's court. The trouble is that while China's ping-pong players are only too eager to come out and do battle, Peking's diplomats look like taking their time over Southeast Asia. ASEAN may have to live with the tensions of a non-neutralized region for many years. [17]

Both in its appraisal of the Razak initiative, and in its comment as to its practicability, this editorial reflected a common view in Singapore.

AMERICAN PRESENCE PREFERRED

When it came down to it, Singapore was almost always in favor of retention of American military support. This came out very well in Lee Kuan Yew's press conference after his official visit to the Philippines at the beginning of 1974. He indicated in Manila his concern that the Watergate affair and American domestic problems were weakening the capacity of the United States to react to developments in Southeast Asia. It was necessary, he said, to strike a balance between the growing Soviet capacity, Japan's interest in free passage through Southeast Asian waters and open trade with the region, the legitimate interests of China, and the continuing global interest of the United States in ensuring that "no major or super power exerts an overwhelming pressure on any single important part of the world, and that includes Southeast Asia."[18] The same message was very strongly delivered by Lee when he visited Thailand in 1973, in the course of a striking call for the maintenance of an American military presence in Thailand. Thailand is regarded by Lee in particular (and, with less fervor, by others in Singapore) as the crucial "domino" in the region. If the Thais are able to cope with the threat of communism, both internal and external, then the other countries in the Malay archipelago could feel reasonably assured of their future. But if Thailand were to cease to act as a buffer against further Communist expansion from China and Indochina, then the future prospects of both Malaysia and Singapore would be considered somewhat dim. [19]

Just as Singapore's attitude to neutralization is a healthily skeptical one, so is its attitude toward ASEAN itself. As Goh Keng Swee, Deputy Prime Minister, once observed when speaking about the difficulties of forming a common market in Southeast Asia, "It is not that we are against regional schemes of cooperation, trade liberalization, common market, or whatever; on the contrary, we stand to benefit substantially if these things could successfully be implemented. Our reservations rest on the will and ability of other parties concerned to plan and, more important, to implement these plans."[20]

In the end, Singapore's difficulty with the neutralization concept stems from its all too close familiarity with the gap between Southeast Asian protestations and Southeast Asian actions. There is no shortage of good will or of exhortation to do the right thing; what is in short supply is the energy and determination to carry out the requirements of these plans and ideals, and Singaporeans are fundamentally skeptical about the likelihood of the other Southeast Asian governments being able to pursue the infrastructure of neutralization with sufficient vigor and zest. This enables the Singaporeans to take the position that neutralization is an excellent idea, and what a good thing it would be if it could only be realized, and that one should hope for the best but plan for the worst.

NOTES

1. The Times, London, 9 December 1965.
2. The Mirror, Singapore, vol. 8, no. 7, 14 February 1972.
3. STS, 22 December 1968.
4. "Singapore's Foreign Policy 1965-68," in Journal of Southeast Asian Studies, vol. 10, no. 1, March 1969, p. 177.

5. See ARB, June 1973, pp. 1830-31.

6. See Seah Chee Meow, "Singapore's Foreign Policy in Southeast Asia: Options for National Survival," in Pacific Community, vol. 4, no. 4, July 1973, p. 535; and Dick Wilson, The Future Role of Singapore (London: Royal Institute of International Affairs, 1972).

7. STS, 18 January 1973.

8. STK, 28 May 1973.

9. New Nation, Singapore, 18 November 1971.

10. Ibid., 24 November 1971.

11. Ibid., 15 April 1972.

12. STS, 19 January 1972.

13. New Nation, Singapore, 24 October 1973.

14. Sunday Times, Kuala Lumpur, 21 March 1971.

15. STS, 16 November 1967.

16. FEER, 4 December 1971.

17. New Nation, Singapore, 12 November 1971.

18. BP, 18 January 1974.

19. Lee told Theh Chongkhadikij, Editor-in-Chief of the Bangkok Post, that President Nixon should keep some bases in Thailand: "This will be useful to all other countries in Southeast Asia in preventing the relentless erosion through insurgency which corrodes away one country after another, but which requires sanctuaries from which the insurgents sally forth. If Thailand is able to maintain her independence on the basis of the Nixon Doctrine, then the survival of the other countries in Southeast Asia will not be in jeopardy." BP, 13 January 1973.

20. Asian Pacific Record, Singapore, vol. 1, no. 8, November 1970, p. 8.

9

THE BURMESE
POSITION

The father of modern Burmese nationalism, General Aung San, was one of the earliest advocates of regional collaboration in Asia. He spoke of multilateral cooperation with neighboring nations as enriching and beneficial, and he stressed that a small country like Burma would be better off placing its trust in a regional organization than in the strength of its own puny forces. [1]

But Aung San was cut off in his prime, and under its two great postwar leaders, U Nu and Ne Win, Burma has pursued single-mindedly the most scrupulously neutral path of any goverment in Asia. As a Malaysian observer put it, Burma "adheres strictly to its policy of neutrality, even to the point of offending neighbors in order to maintain the stance." [2] The reasons for this choice of policy can be found largely in the situation the Burmese nationalist leaders inherited when they won independence from Great Britain. They had experienced military defeat by the Japanese, and they had chafed all the more uncomfortably under the British yoke because in the period preceding British imperialism the Burmese had been highly active and expansionist toward their neighbors. Freedom of action in international affairs has therefore become a symbolic and emotional issue for the Burmese of today.

The Burmese government has faced insurgency from rebels attempting to establish secessionist states in numerous minority areas, by communists of various persuasions and supported at various times by external Communist powers, and by opposition groups driven to insurrection in order to recover political power; Burma has furthermore experienced the incursion of both Nationalist and Communist Chinese troops across her borders. Having insisted from the very beginning on asserting independence from Great Britain by refusing to join the Commonwealth, as India and Pakistan did, Burma proceeded to make it very clear that she would join no camp. Although her relations with India have been perhaps closer than with any other neighbor, her determination to reduce the economic status of the Indians who had emigrated to Burma and to terminate their favored position in the Burmese economy, resulting in a large-scale exodus back to India, has invited Indian resentment.

Toward China, Burma has maintained a steadily correct and at times cordial relationship which has survived the periods of Chinese antagonism, such as those that occurred during the Cultural Revolution in 1967. [3] As between the United States and the Soviet Union, Burma has maintained a doggedly correct neutral stance and is one of the few neutral countries to have carried its neutrality to the extent of giving up foreign aid. Toward the other smaller states of Southeast Asia, Burma has maintained a curiously distant and aloof posture, refusing to be drawn into any regional groupings and refusing to cooperate with any regional initiatives.

BURMA'S BRAND OF NEUTRALITY

Burmese neutrality is often said to be unlike any other in the world, in the sense that Burma has no close friends and does not seem to want them. The position of Burma is so unusual that it has managed to maintain a diplomatic presence in all three of the major divided countries—Vietnam, Korea, and Germany. The Burmese leadership prides itself on the fact that Burma does not belong to any club, not even the club of so-called nonaligned states, but makes up its own mind on each specific issue in world affairs.

One important component of this policy involves a respect for the strategic interests of China, which means not permitting Burmese territory to be used in any way that could be thought of as a threat to China. It is probably for this reason that in 1968 the Burmese government refused to join other Asian nations in approving the five-year work plan and the setting up of a permanent bureau to build an Asian highway connecting Europe with Southeast Asia. The United Nations officials at the United Nations Economic Commission for Asia and the Far East (ECAFE) in Bangkok attributed Burma's noncooperation in this scheme to the fact that the Burmese government "was wary of offending China, which has dubbed the highway an imperialist plan to encircle China."[4]

The Working People's Daily has stated on a number of occasions that Burma would never join any Asian regional bloc. Regionalism has been rejected in Rangoon because it is believed that it inevitably stems from outside forces, notably the United States in the case of Southeast Asia, rather than from states indigenous to the region itself. It was this habit of thinking, for which some justification can be found, that caused the Burmese to be suspicious of Tun Razak's proposal for neutralization.

Even in its fight against the Communist Party of Burma insurgents in various parts of the hinterland, General Ne Win made it clear that Burma would not abandon its neutrality, as India did in 1962, by seeking military assistance in any massive way either from the United States or the Soviet Union. "We are fighting with our own might," he once said. "We do not depend on others. As said before we must be on our own. We will then fight with what we have. In short we will never give up our neutral policy despite all these happenings and even if others want war."[5]

In spite of the threat from Communist insurgents and Chinese hostility, Burma terminated the American military aid program that had been quietly proceeding for several years with very little publicity. Substantial quantities of arms and equipment were in fact supplied by the Americans, particularly in the period following the breach with China in 1967, but in 1970 these arrangements were brought to an end by the Burmese side, and General Ne Win even turned down an American offer of surplus military equipment at cut-rate prices. It was decided, apparently, that more U.S. aid of this kind was not desirable, presumably in order not to provoke Peking any further. The final visible presence of the U.S. military aid program departed from Burma in the middle of 1971.[6] But the Burmese were courageous enough to assert their displeasure with China's support of the Burmese Communist insurgents as well as to criticize America for interference in Southeast Asia.

A Burmese scholar has pointed out that one reason for Burma's disinterest in the Malaysian proposal for the neutralization of Southeast Asia could be the fact that Burmese neutrality is based largely on its uniqueness. Her task of maintaining neutrality and retaining international acceptance of that neutrality was made easier because Burma was "the lone working neutral in this part of the world. Her neutrality, by contrast more easily identifiable, is made credible, acceptable, and workable."[7] In a collective neutralization of Southeast Asia, it is inevitable that some states would be more neutral than others. Being considerably less important in the international power stakes than other countries in Southeast Asia because of her limited resources, manpower, and strategic situation, Burma was able to take advantage of the unimportance of being the lone neutral. And indeed the Burmese openly wonder to what extent some of the other small nations in the region really desire to be left alone.

NEGATIVE REACTION TO MALAYSIAN PLAN

Nevertheless the Burmese tradition of neutrality excited hopes in Malaysia that the Ne Win administration would support the Razak proposal. It was generally agreed, in Adam Malik's words, that "within his own heart, Burma's General Ne Win accepts the idea" of neutralization.[8] But when Tun Razak visited Rangoon in order to solicit support for his proposal he had to return home somewhat disappointed. Burma, he explained to his countrymen on his return, "has always been neutral. However it will take part in a regional plan only if all the other countries are genuinely neutral."[9]

Some interest was created in 1973 when Ne Win visited Indonesia and ventured a little more positively into the regional diplomatic scene than he had been known to before. Referring to the tendency toward detente in other parts of the world, the Burmese Prime Minister declared at a state banquet given in his honor by President Suharto that it was also necessary to strive for peace and stability "in our own region." He went on to say that "when circumstances are favorable it will be necessary for nations of the region to get together and confer on ways and means of how to achieve this objective of creating peace and tranquility in the area."[10]

This uncharacteristic contribution from the Burmese leader attracted an immediate response in the Southeast Asian press. The Straits Times in Kuala Lumpur observed that his speech aligned Burma for the first time with the Philippines and Thailand, which had also been advocating a conference of Southeast Asian nations following the Paris agreement that terminated the Vietnam War in its international aspects.[11] A commentary on Radio Djakarta explained that Burma had shied away from international activities in the past in order to concentrate on domestic issues. "Perhaps growing stability in Burmese political and economic development," it went on, "has provided an opportunity for Burma to think about its relations with other countries in Southeast Asia."[12]

But Ne Win went on to Kuala Lumpur after visiting Indonesia and made it clear there that his government had not changed its policies and would pursue its own ideas of international detente at its own pace. While Burma supported the underlying principles of ASEAN and of the neutralization proposal, President Ne Win was not prepared to make any commitments so long as the Indochina situation remained a fluid one and until perceptible progress was made toward neutralization.[13]

The position has not apparently changed since then, although there are frequent indications that Burmese political life may be undergoing some change in the direction of liberalization and that a more forthcoming attitude toward regional neighbors might soon become apparent. It still seems that Burma would almost inevitably be the last state to sign up for regional neutralization and would only be satisfied if every other state had already committed itself to the same process. [14]

NOTES

1. See quotations in Maung Kyaw Thet, "Some Burmese Views on the Neutralization of Southeast Asia, " in ND, pp. 150-51.
2. FEER, 25 June 1973.
3. See Robert A. Holmes, "Burma's Foreign Policy Towards China Since 1962, " Pacific Affairs, vol. 45, no. 2, Summer 1972, p. 240.
4. Asian Recorder, vol. 14, no. 6, 5 February 1968, p. 8155.
5. Rangoon Radio, as cited in Robert A. Holmes, "China-Burma Relations Since the Rift, " in Asian Survey, vol. 12, no. 8, August 1972, p. 692.
6. See Holmes, op. cit., pp. 692-93.
7. Maung Kyaw Thet, op. cit., p. 146.
8. STK, 11 March 1972.
9. Sunday Times, Kuala Lumpur, 20 February 1972.
10. Speech of 11 June 1973; see ARB, July 1973, p. 1909.
11. STK, 13 June 1973.
12. 11 June 1973; see ARB, July 1973, p. 1909.
13. FEER, 25 June 1973; see also ARB, March 1973, p. 1622.
14. Ne Win told Razak in April 1974 that Burma would be prepared to join ASEAN once its members had demonstrated their complete neutrality. Japan Times, 9 April 1974.

10

Indochina was the area of Southeast Asia for whose angry problems the concept of neutralization was first floated by Western statesmen as a solution. Yet precisely because of the ravaging wars that have plagued the four states of Indochina almost continuously for the past three decades, this strategic mainland section of Southeast Asia still resists neutralization. It is common ground among most of the advocates of Southeast Asian neutralization that the plan is not truly realizable until the fighting has stopped in Indochina.

CAMBODIA: A PIONEER OF NEUTRALITY

This is less true of Cambodia and Laos, the two smaller countries of Indochina, than of Vietnam. Indeed Cambodia, under its great contemporary leader Prince Norodom Sihanouk, became one of the most outstanding practitioners of neutrality to be found anywhere in the world. Cambodia has always been hemmed in, on one side by Thailand and on the other by Vietnam, and without the support of French imperialism, for its own reasons, and without the particularly energetic leadership that the royal family was able to give at a decisive moment of its history, Cambodia might well have disappeared from the list of twentieth century nation-states, carved up between its two bigger neighbors. Yet it has survived, and that survival in the post-French era owes a great deal to Chinese support—which in turn was possible, given the firmly non-Communist domestic policies of Sihanouk, by a particularly scrupulous and imaginative policy of neutrality in foreign relations.

Sihanouk during his brilliant career managed to irritate almost everyone and yet to retain the ultimate respect and recognition of the major powers—the United States, the USSR, and China—as

91

well as of Thailand and Vietnam. By the time the Malaysian neutralization proposal was made, Sihanouk was no longer at the helm of Cambodian affairs, and indeed, it had been the Cambodian crisis resulting in the exile of Sihanouk to Peking and the installation of the Lon Nol regime in Phnompenh in 1970 that led the Indonesians to hold their path-breaking Djakarta conference on Cambodia, [1] and it was that experience in Southeast Asian diplomacy which encouraged Tun Razak of Malaysia subsequently to elaborate his own neutralization proposal.

The President of the Council of Ministers in the new government, Sirik Matak, told Le Monde soon after the Malaysian initiative that the neutralization of Indochina "is certainly the ultimate goal." He added, "It conforms to our aspirations, but the road to it has a long way to run. We must first put an end to aggression and then ask the big powers to give their guarantee."[2] A few weeks later the Council of Ministers, under Chief of State Cheng Heng, decided that they would support the declaration of neutrality or neutralization made at Kuala Lumpur by the five ASEAN states in November 1971.[3] The Cambodian observer who was invited to attend the sixth Foreign Ministers' Meeting of ASEAN, held in Thailand in April 1973, was fairly forthcoming on the question. Cambodia, said Korn Orn, Secretary of State for Community Development, was "determined to remain faithful to her policy of independence, peace, and neutrality." But he went on to explain that his government had been "obliged to ask" for American air support in order to "enforce respect for the national sovereignty and territorial integrity of the Khmer Republic (Cambodia)."[4]

LAOS SUPPORTS PROPOSAL

If Cambodia is only too anxious to be neutralized under some kind of formula such as Tun Razak's, so is Laos. The situation of these two mini-states of the Southeast Asian mainland is similar. Laos, like Cambodia, is a nation squeezed between Thailand and Vietnam, two more populated, more powerful, and more dynamic nations. To the north, Laos faces a Chinese frontier, which means that, even more than Cambodia, it is obliged to consider Chinese sensibilities in any foreign policy decision. Unlike Cambodia, Laos has no seafront and is entirely surrounded by these overpowering neighbors, dependent on Cambodia, its southern neighbor, for its outlets to world maritime trade. Like Cambodia, and in even stronger degree, Laos owes its survival to French imperialism. Finally, Laos affords the only example in Asia of an attempt to declare some form of international neutralization, in the Geneva

Accord of 1962. In 1974 there was yet another attempt to form a coalition government, which it was hoped would "bring a final neutralist solution."[5]

The formula by which this weakest state in Southeast Asia has succeeded in preserving its independence, albeit only in a technical sense at times, has been the device of a coalition government in which right-wing and left-wing forces are technically collaborating. In practice, of course, the country's territory is divided between communist or Pathet Lao control on the one hand and Vientiane or pro-Western control on the other. Prince Souvanna Phouma endeavors to act as a neutral bridge between the two factions and is currently succeeding better than at some periods in the past. Whenever he has spoken on the question of neutralization he has been in favor of it. When he visited Malaysia shortly after the Kuala Lumpur Declaration, he told his hosts, "We don't have to join ASEAN to support this neutrality plan because we are already neutral." The great powers, he went on philosophically, would not seriously guarantee one Southeast Asian country alone. "But if we are together . . . maybe we can get it."[6]

The endorsement of the Kuala Lumpur Declaration was confirmed in the joint communique issued by Prince Souvanna Phouma and Tun Razak at the end of the former's visit.[7] The Straits Times editorial on the following day noted that the Laotian prince had not concealed his disappointment over the failure of the 1962 international neutralization of Laos. "But Prince Souvanna Phouma agreed to give neutrality another try."[8] The Laotian Ambassador to Thailand, Keo Viphakone, told the Sixth Meeting of ASEAN Foreign Ministers at Pattaya in April 1973 that his government was "resolved to follow the path of peace and neutrality, to apply the five principles of peaceful coexistence in foreign relations."[9]

NORTH VIETNAM IS HOSTILE

There is little doubt where the instincts of Cambodia and Laos lie when it comes to neutralization. The problem is that they do not decide the destinies of Indochina, which are held in the much larger and stronger hands of Vietnam. Since the early postwar years this tragic nation has been effectively divided into two separate states, whose separateness has now gained worldwide recognition: the Democratic Republic of Vietnam, based in Hanoi, which is communist and which controls the northern part of Vietnam, and the Republic of Vietnam, based in Saigon, which is anticommunist and which controls large parts of southern Vietnam. If at any time the two halves of this war-torn country become reunited, then Vietnam would play a crucial role in the affairs not merely of Indochina and of the continental part of Southeast Asia but of the entire region. The Chinese, the French, and the Americans have in succession had occasion to test the tenacity and willpower of this nation. But for the time being the two halves are separated by apparently unbridgeable ideological differences, strengthened by a long-standing historical diversity of culture and ethnic origins within Vietnam. It is therefore necessary to consider separately the attitude of first North Vietnam and then South Vietnam toward the neutralization proposal. [10]

One of the earliest comments from Hanoi on the general idea of neutralization came in 1964, when U. S. President Lyndon Johnson made a proposal of peace based on the neutralization of both parts of Vietnam. Radio Hanoi declared at that time, "How dare Johnson raise the problem of neutralization of both North and South Vietnam while he knows full well that our people would never accept the neutralization of North Vietnam."[11] This position of rejecting neutralization and insisting on standing together with other Communist nations, has been consistently repeated in the decade since then. When the Kuala Lumpur Declaration was published, the comment of the North Vietnamese government was that as long as the status quo was maintained, to neutralize Southeast Asia would be to legitimize the American presence in the region. [12]

There are a number of factors to explain this unrepentantly hostile attitude. For one thing, North Vietnam is a country at war. It needs military assistance and alliances in its endeavors, and it is therefore hardly consistent for it to adopt a neutral policy. It is difficult enough, one might add, for the Vietminh to walk the tightrope between Moscow and Peking let alone attempt to balance between the Eastern camp and the Western camp. Furthermore, if neutralization were to be accepted after the end of the war each country's armed forces would have to be reduced, and the former belligerents would have to give up military aid and submit to international supervision. In the case of North Vietnam this would deprive Hanoi of perhaps the most likely means whereby it could achieve its long-sought objective of unifying the whole of Vietnam by force. Finally, the Kuala Lumpur Declaration version of neutralization would inevitably mean closer regional cooperation in Southeast Asia. It would mean the institutionalizing of collaboration in common organizations, which might lead to regional integration. In such an event, Hanoi would inevitably have to fear the possibility of being outvoted in what would be a predominantly anticommunist and pro-Western grouping. The North Vietnamese leaders might also well be apprehensive at the prospect of opening their closed society to outside influence, which might lead to a faster liberalization than they would like, thus threatening their internal stability.

Nevertheless, when it became apparent that the Kuala Lumpur Declaration was the prelude to a general aura of detente in the region and in the world at large, with President Nixon visiting Peking and Moscow and with China entering the United Nations, the Hanoi line began to soften. A broadcast from Hanoi in December 1971 explained that although ASEAN was an instrument of American imperialism, interventionism, and aggression, the Kuala Lumpur Declaration nevertheless reflected to some extent "the change in the power balance in Southeast Asia and the world in favor of the forces of revolution and progress and to the disadvantage of imperialism and the forces of reaction."[13] When the Paris peace talks began a year later, Nguyen Thanh Le, the spokesman of the North Vietnamese delegation, told the press that "what we want is to establish a zone of true neutrality in these countries. To achieve this the United States must withdraw its troops and liquidate its bases in the area." It was on the basis of this remark that the Malaysians have said ever since that North Vietnam had endorsed its neutralization proposal.

There is, however, much ground to be covered before it can be said in any meaningful way that the North Vietnamese will support the Malaysian plan. For one thing, Hanoi has continued to attack the pro-Western regimes in Southeast Asia in the most impolite and provocative terms. Adam Malik, the Indonesian Foreign Minister and one of the architects of ASEAN, has been described in a North Vietnamese newspaper as "one of the most brazen mouthpieces of the United States," because he had claimed that the Americans were not trying to destroy the dikes in North Vietnam by bombing, [14] and Hanoi rejected the ASEAN bid for a truce in the Vietnam War as "absurd" because it "made no distinction between 'aggressor' and 'victims.'"[15] As long as these attitudes persist, it must seem inevitable that North Vietnam would be the last and most reluctant candidate for a Southeast Asia neutralization program.

SOUTH VIETNAM IS ALSO HOSTILE

The position is not much better in the South, where an equally extreme pro-Western regime presents almost the counterpart of the Hanoi reaction. At the beginning of 1970, President Nguyen Van Thieu stated quite categorically that "the Republic of Vietnam cannot be a neutral nation."[16] A short time afterwards his Foreign Minister, Tran Van Lam, observed that if there was to be a cease-fire in Vietnam, the government in the south "should preserve for itself the right to modernize its armed forces . . . and to participate in regional military alliances if necessary."[17] There are good reasons for such a negative attitude. Neutralization in the South Vietnamese book is associated with the idea of coalition government, or collaboration with the hated Communists of the north, a policy the Saigon administration has vehemently opposed. Furthermore, it is contradictory for Thieu, as it is for the North Vietnamese, to advocate neutrality while his country is at war and relying so heavily on the help of his allies in fighting the Communists. To advocate or accept neutrality in these circumstances would be virtually to disarm oneself. President Thieu and his colleagues in Saigon distrust the Communists and do not think that the conditions for neutralization exist in Vietnam.

Once the Malaysians had come out with their neutralization proposal, and possibly because of the Malaysians' reputation for anticommunism and for stout resistance to Communist insurgency in their own country, the Saigon attitude was softened. In an early speech following the Razak proposal, President Thieu again rejected the idea of a coalition with the Vietnamese Communists, but asserted that South Vietnam "wished to be friends with all nations, regardless of their political regimes, on condition that they respect our territorial integrity, our sovereignty, and our national interests."[18] On the eve of the Kuala Lumpur meeting of ASEAN ministers, South Vietnamese Foreign Minister Tran had stated that neutralization could only be acceptable "if there is a concrete guarantee of the United Nations, and if the right of self-defense is clearly permitted against aggression in any form."[19] And President Thieu, in his first public comment on the Kuala Lumpur Declaration by ASEAN at the end of 1971, rejected it. He made it clear that he saw it as merely a thinly disguised method by which the Communists could assume a role in the government of South Vietnam.[20]

This was before the Nixon visit to China, and the next public statement by Thieu to the Western press was given while Nixon was actually in Peking. Thieu's position was slightly more conciliatory. He did not think that the five nations in ASEAN could represent all Southeast Asia, and for that reason he welcomed a conference of all the Southeast Asian nations, including North Vietnam, to discuss a possible common stand on the evolving international situation. To put it another way, Thieu did not wish to rubber-stamp what had been signed at Kuala Lumpur, but he was ready to rediscuss it in order to put his conditions for neutralization. Clearly, if South Vietnam was to be neutralized, North Vietnam should also be neutralized. But he went on to say that South Vietnam would like to see the development "of a buffer zone with international guarantees against invasion," comprising the ten Southeast Asian states. He also insisted that if any country was going to be neutralized to serve peace in Southeast Asia, it should be the big powers and not the small nations, because it was they who had the intention and the means to aggress. "No great power, " he said, "should mount an aggression in Southeast Asia, no great power should use the territory of any country in the region to stage an aggression against any other country, and among Southeast Asian nations no one should violate or permit others to use its territory to violate the territorial integrity of a third nation."

Finally, South Vietnam would not have to change its policy in order to adhere to a neutralization plan because South Vietnam had no aggressive designs, did not belong to any military alliance, and did not allow anybody to use its soil to mount aggression against other countries. But it was impossible to trust the Communists because "to ask the aggressive Communist imperialists to refrain from aggression and to ask them to guarantee the right of small nations to live is a very difficult thing to do." It was in this interview that President Thieu rejected the phraseology of neutralization. "I do not think, " he told the New York Times, "neutralization is the correct word to describe our goal. The three superpowers should be neutralized while the weak states in Southeast Asia should be turned into a buffer zone which is not violated by anyone. . . . We do not want any foreign bases here or any alliances in this area." Neutralization was too vague a term, and was liable to be misinterpreted by the Communist side, and it would be better to use the phrase "common stand."[21]

The idea of a Southeast Asian conference was repeated in President Thieu's message to the National Assembly in October 1972; he stated that the only desire of noncommunist Asia was "to neutralize the activities of the big powers in this area." Despite the differences in their political regimes, all the countries of Southeast Asia had the common goal of opposing external intervention. Perhaps "the time has come to convene a conference of all the countries of Southeast Asia including North Vietnam."[22] By the standards of South Vietnamese politics, this must be taken as a remarkable change of front. Yet the mutual antipathy between South Vietnam and ASEAN has prevented any real dialogue. A South Vietnamese Foreign Ministry spokesman, Thai Ha Chung, said in April 1973 that his government would like to join ASEAN, since it believed "in the benefit of regional cooperation for peaceful development." But Mr. Chung went on to complain that "ASEAN has never shown an interest in the contribution, however modest, that we may bring to the organization."[23] Both South and North Vietnam were invited, along with Cambodia and Laos, to send observers to the Sixth Ministerial Meeting of ASEAN at Pattaya in Thailand in that month. Neither in fact participated, and Chung said that in the view of the South Vietnamese government no practical purpose would be served by sending an observer to attend the opening and closing ceremonies of the meeting without taking part in the substantive discussions in between.

To sum up, South Vietnam is no longer categorically opposed to real neutralization, but it is very considerably skeptical about its materialization and feels out of sympathy with the neutral instincts of the ASEAN governments. It is thus a common thread in both Saigon and Hanoi that neutralization will not be allowed to become a weapon in the fight for the future of South Vietnam, although it might conceivably become a device to govern the international relationships of both North and South Vietnam once the war is over.

NOTES

1. See Lau Teik Soon, Indonesia and Regional Security: The Djakarta Conference on Cambodia (Singapore: Institute of Southeast Asian Studies, 1972).
2. Le Monde, 3 December 1971.
3. Le Monde, 12 February 1972.
4. ARB, May 1973, p. 1761.
5. FEER editorial, 8 April 1974, p. 13. See generally Arthur J. Dommen, Conflict in Laos: The Politics of Neutralization (New York: Praeger, 1964); and Hugh Toye, Laos: Buffer State or Battleground (London: Oxford University Press, 1968).
6. STK, 17 December 1971.
7. STK, 18 December 1971; FAM, vol. 4, no. 4, December 1971, p. 90.
8. Ibid.
9. ARB, May 1973, p. 1761.
10. See Nguyen Manh Hung, "The Two Vietnams and the Proposal for a Neutralized South East Asia," in ND, p. 137.
11. Radio Hanoi, 12 February 1964, quoted in Hung, op. cit., p. 143.
12. See Hung, op. cit., p. 143.
13. VNA, broadcast of 1 December 1971; Japan Times, 2 December 1971.
14. Quan Doi Nhan Dan (an army newspaper), Hanoi, 1 August 1972, as reported in a Reuter despatch from Hong Kong, BP, 2 August 1972.
15. North Vietnam News Agency, 10 August 1973 (see ARB, September 1973, p. 1163).
16. Chinh Luan, Saigon, 28 January 1970, quoted in Hung, op. cit., p. 140.

17. Speech at National Defence College, 3 March 1970, quoted in Hung, op. cit., p. 140.

18. Speech at National Military Academy, 18 December 1970, quoted in Hung, op. cit., p. 140.

19. Tien Bo, Saigon, 19 November 1971.

20. 1 December 1971, Vietnam News Release No. 71/45, 7 December 1971; New York Times, 5 December 1971.

21. Interview with C. L. Sulzberger, New York Times and Daily Telegraph, 25 February 1972.

22. Sunday Times, Kuala Lumpur, 29 October 1972.

23. STK, 17 April 1973.

PART

III

**EXTERNAL
ATTITUDES**

It was a matter of disappointment for Tun Razak of Malaysia
that the Americans have never given their unreserved approval to
the neutralization scheme but have instead been negative about it
from the very beginning. In the words of Lee Kuan Yew, the Singaporean Prime Minister, "the United States has not been forthcoming
about the proposal for a number of reasons. It does not believe it
is timely to support this proposal, particularly as the Indochina conflict is far from resolved."[1] When Tun Razak visited Washington
just before the meeting in Kuala Lumpur that led to the Kuala Lumpur
Declaration at the end of 1971, he had informal talks with President
Nixon, but they produced no words of sympathy or understanding that
the Malaysians could quote in support of their neutralization proposal.[2]

Indeed, when it came to the point, the Foreign Ministers of
the five ASEAN states found when they met in Kuala Lumpur that
American diplomats were making a strong pitch to the various delegations along the lines that any excessively neutralistic statement
by them in Kuala Lumpur could only do harm to the future prospects
of retaining an American presence in Asia. It would, the American
diplomats argued, strengthen the neoisolationist lobby in the United
States and make it more difficult for the administration in Washington to continue to convince Congress of the need to maintain forces
and give material support to the noncommunist countries in Southeast Asia.[3]

UNITED STATES NOT ENTHUSIASTIC

In the annual report by Secretary of State William P. Rogers
on U.S. foreign policy published in March 1972, there was only

103

one reference giving any kind of attitude on the neutralization proposal, and that was under the general heading of the Nixon Doctrine.
It was there explained that the growing applicability of the Nixon
Doctrine to Asia was becoming evident from a number of developments during 1971, of which one was the Kuala Lumpur Declaration
enunciating "as a long-term goal recognition of their area as a zone
of peace, freedom, and neutrality." But Mr. Rogers continued in
his report, "However, the effectiveness of any plan ultimately to
reach this objective will depend on the secure independence of Southeast Asian nations and on the attitudes of their neighbors."[4] This
was hardly an enthusiastic comment, and one is reminded of the view
held in the mid-1960s in Washington: "We believe," as William P.
Bundy then put it, "that it is an incredible gesture of faith to suppose
that North Vietnam and Communist China would leave alone a Southeast Asia from which the Western presence was effectively withdrawn."[5] There has been no lack of writers pointing out that innumerable difficulties would stand in the way of any formal guarantee by
the United States of the neutralization of the countries of Southeast
Asia.[6]

On the other hand there has been a gradual awareness among
Americans since the end of 1971 that it is possible to adopt the view
that, as a long-term goal, the neutralization plan is both acceptable
and useful. It is common ground among American leaders today that
it is now not only possible but desirable for the United States to prepare to pull out its combat military forces from the Southeast Asian
mainland, to rely in the future on a combination of economic and
military aid, a more imaginative diplomacy, and mobile forces (particularly air and naval) operating from offshore bases in the western
Pacific. This three-tiered program for the protection of U.S. interests in Southeast Asia (nowadays defined with rather more discrimination than in the days of Dulles and Rusk) is not inconsistent with
neutralization. George McT. Kahin, to quote one American scholar
on Southeast Asian affairs, has argued that neutralization would
assist U.S. objectives in the area. In cutting its military ties with
Thailand, he told the Singapore Conference on New Directions in the
International Relations of Southeast Asia in 1972,

The United States should concurrently make a major effort to arrange for its neutralization. A neutralization
of continental Southeast Asia—Thailand included—would
conform with Peking's basic security interests and considerably decrease China's fear of encirclement. With
the neutralization of the states adjacent to her southeast
border she would not have the worry that a hostile
power—whether the United States or Soviet Russia—

104

might threaten her from a base within one of them. Being so heavily preoccupied with her Soviet and Mongolian borders, China would undoubtedly find it advantageous to be freed from concern over her 2,000-mile frontier with the states of Southeast Asia. There is a sufficient convergence of interests between the United States and China to warrant their making a serious attempt to effect a neutralization of continental Southeast Asia once the Indochina war has ended; and it might be possible to relate such an effort to a peace settlement there. [7]

The hope of relating a Vietnam peace settlement to Southeast Asian neutralization has not been realized. But the arguments put by Kahin are repeated in American foreign policy debates by a number of respectable experts, and the climate has become less negative toward neutralization than it was before. There are also, naturally, Southeast Asians who argue that neutralization would serve U.S. interests. Thus Goh Cheng Teik of the University of Malaysia told the same Singapore Conference in 1972 that many Thais and Filipinos were opposed to the dissolution of the American-led alliance system in Southeast Asia and the Pacific. But he went on to explain:

Nevertheless, there is one way in which the United States can reconcile her new perception of China's stance with the requirements of Thai and Filipino security, namely the neutralization of Southeast Asia as proposed by the Malaysian government. The United States does not need to isolate herself from a neutralized Southeast Asia. On the contrary, she will be asked to stay, to play a great power role in concert with Russia and China in order to ensure that the neutralized status of all the Southeast Asian states is not violated—either by intraregional and/or extraregional forces. [8]

BIG POWER CONSIDERATIONS UPPERMOST

When one searches the public record of those members of the American government responsible for policy toward Southeast Asia, there is indeed a noticeable readiness to accept some kind of hands-off policy in which the United States, the Soviet Union, and China would collaborate. The emphasis in the statements of these officials, however, is on the interest of the great powers rather than the interest of the Southeast Asians themselves. Ambassador William H. Sullivan, who had been a major policy maker in the State Department in Washington before his appointment to the Philippines, declared in a major speech in September 1973 that it was "essential" for the United States to retain its military presence in the area so as to reassure its friends that they were not being abandoned. The American goal was to "maintain the equilibrium of great powers"; he went on to explain: "That equilibrium will be a great canopy so that other countries of Asia will not have to look over their shoulder at the menace of attack from the mainland." In maintaining this equilibrium, all the great powers would have to have influence and presence in Southeast Asia. But since some countries in the region were still incapable of fully defending themselves, the United States accepted the need for a "continued, limited military presence . . . and continued economic presence." Sullivan conceded that the Philippines, Indonesia, Malaysia, Singapore, and Thailand were all in stronger and more stable circumstances than they had been since the end of the Second World War, but if any protecting was still needed the United States would be ready to underwrite it.[9] Sullivan added in response to questions after a later speech that neutralization of Southeast Asia at this time would be "not only premature but perhaps idealistic," and that it would be "more constructive" for the states in the region to build up their own internal strength while allowing the great powers continued access to the region in order to balance each other. "Neutralization in a passive sense does not look to me an ideal prescription for Southeast Asia."[10]

Four months later the Deputy Secretary of State, Kenneth Rush, further elaborated the theme that the United States was building new relationships with China, the Soviet Union, and Japan in order to oppose attempts by anyone to dominate Asia and the Pacific. A major aspect of the new relationships between the big powers was their "agreement to oppose attempts by anyone to impose hegemony in the Asian-Pacific region."[11]

It is fairly clear from all this that the Americans are not unsympathetic toward the reasoning behind the Malaysian neutralization proposal. They would, however, undoubtedly prefer not to have the plan made so specific; they dislike the United States being placed equally with the Soviet Union and China as big powers whose actions in the region are harmful to the region, and they perhaps suffer from some unconscious resentment at the first major independent diplomatic initiative to be made in the modern period by a group of Asian countries usually regarded as friendly toward the United States.

American interests in Southeast Asia are as important as the American presence that supports them. As a leading maritime nation and exponent of free trade, the United States has a strong interest in the maintenance of the international seaways through Southeast Asia, a fact that has already brought the United States into dispute with Indonesia and Malaysia over the question of the deinternational- ization of the Straits of Malacca. American investment in Southeast Asia is still larger than any other nation's, although Japan is rapidly catching up. The United States counts as anticommunist allies no fewer than eight of the ten governments whose participation in the neutralization scheme is envisaged by the Malaysians—Cambodia, Indonesia, Laos, Malaysia, the Philippines, Singapore, South Viet- nam, and Thailand—and it would be idle to attempt to argue that any other big power has a stronger political position in the region.

But in the end one comes back to the superpower considerations that dominate debates in Washington. The U.S. interest is either to deny or to make difficult any further entry into Southeast Asia on the part of the Soviet Union and China. In the old days this was thought of as a single objective, to be applied against both the Soviet Union and China equally. But now that the Sino-Soviet dispute has changed this premise, there is a subtle alteration in the attitude toward China. It has already been noted in this book how easy it is for Southeast Asians to worry about the possibility of their region being assigned to a Chinese sphere of influence as a result of a summit meeting be- tween the U.S. President and Chairman Mao. The United States has accustomed itself to the rules of detente with the Soviet Union, and it is now experimenting along the same lines with China. It does look as if the Americans have it in mind to allow the Chinese to take up some of the slack in Southeast Asia as a means of preventing the Russians from gaining anything from the partial U.S. disengagement. It would be too crude to say that Washington would like to play China against the USSR in Southeast Asia. But it would be realistic to as- sume that the Americans will not be unhappy over the process of normalization of relations between China and Southeast Asia, and it would be only sensible to recognize that the Americans respect South- east Asian concern over China's future intentions and understand some of the motivations behind the neutralization proposal.

CANADIAN CAUTIOUSNESS

What has been said about the United States could very generally apply also to Canada. There was a curious misunderstanding in the earlier months of the Razak premiership when the Malaysian leader asked for Pierre Trudeau's help in putting his arguments to the lead- ership in Peking. Razak's intention was to try to take advantage of the apparently successful and rather warm relationship this fellow- Commonwealth Premier had succeeded in forging with Peking. But

Trudeau rebuffed the approach on the grounds that Canada could not plead Malaysia's case in Peking, to which Razak immediately riposted that he had only asked the Canadian leader to explain in Peking Southeast Asia's desire for peace. [12] This was something of a storm in a teacup, but even when Razak was able to talk to Trudeau in Ottawa in October 1971, just before the Kuala Lumpur Declaration, the furthest that the Canadian Prime Minister would go in the joint communique was to express his "interest and understanding" in the neutralization plan: no word of support. [13]

NOTES

1. STK, 28 May 1972.

2. STK, 7 October 1971.

3. See the report by James Morgan in FEER, 4 December 1971.

4. U.S. Department of State, United States Foreign Policy 1971 (Washington, D.C.: Government Printing Office, 1972), p. 52.

5. In A. Buchan, ed., China and the Peace of Asia (London: Chatto and Windus, 1965), p. 30.

6. See, for example, Pracha Guna-Kasem, "The Future Role of the United States in South East Asia," in ND, pp. 96-97.

7. "The Role of the United States in South East Asia," in ND, p. 80.

8. Goh Cheng Teik, "The United States and Southeast Asia: Past, Present and Future," in ND, p. 102.

9. BP, 14 September 1973.

10. BP, 26 September 1973.

11. Japan Times, 23 January 1974.

12. STK, 26 and 27 January 1971.

13. STK, 9 October 1971; Sunday Times, Kuala Lumpur, 10 October 1971; FAM, vol. 4, no. 4, December 1971, p. 27. For Canada's record of caution in dealing with the region's problems, see Lorne J. Kavic's "Canada and the Security of Southeast Asia," in Zacher and Milne, eds., Conflict and Stability in Southeast Asia (New York: Anchor Press, 1974), p. 383.

The Soviet Union has for a long time had political, economic, and military interests in Southeast Asia. The maritime sealanes of the region connect the Black Sea with Vladivostock and the Siberian Far East ports, constituting the only sea passage between the USSR's eastern and western coasts that is open year-round. This Russian stake in the status of Southeast Asian waters as international maritime highways came into the limelight in early 1972, when the Soviet Union was the first big power to make a public protest against the joint declaration by Malaysia, Indonesia, and Singapore at the end of 1971 deinternationalizing the Straits of Malacca and Singapore. The Soviet ambassador in Tokyo paid a call on the Japanese Deputy Foreign Minister to ascertain his government's position on the Straits question, and was reported as saying that the Soviet Union regarded them as international waterways. Subsequently a Soviet emissary visited Djakarta and Kuala Lumpur and repeated the Soviet position that it could not accept deinternationalization of the Straits.[1] It was thus possible for the Chinese to gain advantage from this confrontation by denouncing the Soviet Union for "casting a covetous eye on the Strait of Malacca."[2]

Added to the importance of the sealanes is the trade the Soviet Union conducts with Southeast Asia, especially in such raw materials as rubber. The Russians had an important military stake in Indonesia during the earlier days of the Sukarno regime in the 1950s and early 1960s, before the Indonesian President launched into his alliance with China. And of course the Russians had had a stake in North Vietnam from very early on after World War II; Soviet arms and economic aid were instrumental in supporting the Vietminh government, first against the French and then against the Americans in their struggle to win control of the whole of Vietnam. The Soviet Union thus regards itself as a rival of the United States and China for influence in the region.

Soviet ambitions in Southeast Asia were, however, badly set back at the end of 1965 when the unsuccessful coup d'etat against the right-wing Generals in the Indonesian Army brought about the eventual end of the Sukarno regime and its replacement by the military government of President Suharto. Communist influence in Indonesia was severely reduced, and although the brunt of the anticommunist feelings of the new government was borne by China, which Suharto and his colleagues felt had backed the attempted coup against them, there was a residual hostility toward the Soviet Union as well.

But after the beginning of 1969 a new page was turned in Soviet relations with the region. A detente was undertaken with governments in the region that had previously been very strongly pro-Western and resistant to Soviet overtures. This new phase in Soviet diplomacy was doubtless precipitated by the British decision in 1968 to withdraw its military presence from east of Suez and by the advance signals of the forthcoming Nixon Doctrine under which the Americans too would gradually disengage militarily from the region. The new Soviet policy was also a reflection of the continuing impasse with China, highlighted by the clashes on the Ussuri River on the Sino-Soviet border at the beginning of 1969.

The new detente was manifested by the visit to Moscow of Lee Kuan Yew, Prime Minister of Singapore, in 1970. In the same year Moscow negotiated a trade agreement with Thailand. In 1971 Russian technicians were sent to Indonesia again for the first time in five years, and in the spring of 1972 there was a much-publicized visit to Moscow by the First Lady of the Philippines, Imelda Marcos, who had a long audience with Prime Minister Kosygin.

THE SOVIET COLLECTIVE SECURITY PLAN

One of the principal initiatives undertaken by the Russians in their new quest for influence in Southeast Asia was their collective security proposal for Asia, first adumbrated by V. V. Matveyev in an article in Izvestia in May 1969 and then elaborated the following month by Leonid Brezhnev, First Secretary of the Soviet Communist Party, on the occasion of the Moscow international meeting of the Communist and Workers' Parties. [3] Neither of these discussions was very specific in nature, and from the beginning the Soviets reserved as many options as possible in interpreting their somewhat vague proposal. In the spring of 1972 the Soviet Ambassador to Thailand, A. A. Rozanov, urged this "system of collective security" on the Asian nations assembled for the annual meeting of ECAFE, giving the proposal an economic and commercial dimension as well as a political one. [4] But the proposal was doomed from the start by its transparent anti-Chinese motivation. Peking was quick to attack it, denouncing it as an "anti-China military alliance . . . picked up from the garbage heap of the warmonger Dulles. "[5] It was clear that the Soviet Union hoped to corral Japan, India, Pakistan, Afghanistan, and Bangladesh into its proposed system, which would have the effect of isolating China. But, as Dennis Bloodworth of the Observer commented, "The small nations are becoming increasingly suspicious of big brothers who fly monster kites, even if the strings attached to them are longer. "[6]

A typical though restrained official assessment of the Soviet position in the region by the end of 1973 was given by Ghazali bin Shafie of Malaysia in a speech in Singapore:

> The Soviet Union . . . appears to be moving in the
> Pacific region with a design and a purpose. This may
> be because she has never really played a role in the
> Pacific or because there is a clear and undivided focus
> of attention and interest brought about by the Sino-Soviet
> dispute. Because of the Sino-Soviet dispute, however,
> Soviet interest and activities are invariably analyzed
> within that perspective. It would seem that any Soviet
> initiative that is designed or even only as to appear to
> further the Soviet cause in the dispute is not likely to
> gain the supoort of countries in the region. This fac-
> tor is unfortunate because the Soviet Union has much
> to contribute to the development of the region. [7]

So strong are some suspicions of the Soviet Union in this region that Prime Minister Lee Kuan Yew once went so far as to make a public suggestion for a joint naval task force comprising ships from the American, Japanese, Australian, and West European fleets to counter the Soviet presence in Southeast Asian waters. [8]

SOUTHEAST ASIA IS COOL

At all events the proposal for a collective security system has failed to gain support in Southeast Asia. General Suharto has stated forthrightly, "We want ASEAN to strengthen regional independence and avoid having this area become a regional cockpit. Therefore we automatically reject the Brezhnev Doctrine. "[9] Adam Malik, the Indonesian Foreign Minister, added that the Soviet collective security scheme was "biased to one side, " and that any genuine collective scheme should include China, the United States, and the Western European powers, not merely the Asian states and the USSR. [10]

111

In April 1973, A. E. Nesterenko attempted at the annual meeting of ECAFE in Tokyo to undo some of the damage that Soviet vagueness had caused. "In our view, " he told delegates from almost all the Asian countries, "the Peoples Republic of China would be a fully-fledged member of such a system of collective security."[11] But this was not repeated sufficiently frequently or strongly by the Soviet leaders to erase the impression that their real interest was in isolating China from the other Asian powers. Mr. Brezhnev's visit to India in 1973 carried the Soviet proposals a little further, but can hardly be said to have enlarged the circle of acceptance of them. In an address to the Indian Parliament, Brezhnev linked the collective security proposal with the recent initiative from within the region for neutalizing Southeast Asia and for declaring the Indian Ocean a nuclear-free zone or zone of peace. But India preferred to support the principles of peaceful coexistence in a general way without formally engaging in a project that might bar the road to reconciliation with China.[12]

The renewed emphasis given to the collective security proposal after the Paris Peace Conference, at which it became clear that the Americans were going to withdraw their troops from Vietnam, brought home the anti-Chinese sentiment. The Hungarian newspaper Nepszava published in January 1973 an unusually comprehensive article, "Asian Security and Chinese Foreign Policy, " in which it was stated that while the ending of the Vietnam war opened good prospects for collective security and improvement of relations with the United States, "the attitude of China, in the Asian region as well as in international politics as a whole, gives cause for alarm."[13] Similarly Brezhnev, speaking in Alma-Ata in August 1973, underlined the anti-Chinese aims of the Soviet proposal, and a leading commentator in Pravda accused the Chinese of "hegemonistic aspirations . . . evidenced above all by their activities in Southeast and South Asia, including the old idea to create, under Peking's patronage, a kind of military and political group of states in Southeast Asia."[14]

RAZAK IN MOSCOW

The Soviet reaction to the Malaysian neutralization proposal had originally been far from enthusiastic. But gradually there was a slightly more positive reception given to it. Early in 1971, V. L. Kudryavtsev, leading an Afro-Asian Peoples' Solidarity Organization mission to Kuala Lumpur, told Malaysian reporters that the Soviet Union welcomed all policies of neutrality and nonalignment if they were "directed toward all countries."[15] In January 1972 an

Izvestia article declared that the position claimed by the five ASEAN states in their Kuala Lumpur Declaration "lacked consequence, " observing that neutralization was particularly difficult to square with Philippine and Thai adherence to Western military blocs.[16] But on the eve of Tun Razak's visit to Moscow toward the end of 1972, the Soviet press unveiled a more responsive view of neutralization. In July, V. Pavlovsky described the Kuala Lumpur Declaration as "in accord with" the Soviet proposal.[17] Pravda in September called it "an idea that cannot be underestimated, " praising Malaysia for following "an independent and realistic" foreign policy course, in which the proposal for the neutralization of Southeast Asia had evoked "an extensive response the world over."[18] It was possible for an Asian correspondent in Moscow to speculate that the Soviet Union was interested in the Malaysian proposal because "assuming that it would have to be guaranteed and accepted by all the big powers, it would give the Soviets a legitimate presence in the area."[19]

Razak spent two and a half hours with Kosygin, and he learned that the Russians would prefer the larger collective security agreement, which would embrace Japan, Pakistan, and India as well as the smaller states. The furthest the Soviet Prime Minister would go was to say, "We understand the interest of Malaysia in normalization of the situation in Southeast Asia, which also is manifested in the plan for the neutralization of Southeast Asia. We respect many of the views contained in this plan." But the Soviets put forward, as eagerly as the Malaysians had stressed neutralization, their own idea of collective security in Asia, in which they were ready to cooperate with all states, including Malaysia. In the final joint communique at the end of the Razak visit there was a polite agreement to disagree. The Soviet Union stated its views on ensuring security in Asia on a collective basis, while "the Malaysian side, in its turn, informed the Soviet side of the essence of the proposal for the neutralization of Southeast Asia."[20] Razak said afterwards that when the Russians told him that neutralization was similar to collective security, he told them that "he appreciated this, but added that Malaysia preferred a neutrality plan which would be applicable to a smaller region such as Southeast Asia." And a little later he explained to Malaysian reporters that "to bring in the big countries in Asia into such a scheme will be to bring in problems which we small nations may find difficult to resolve."[21]

If the Russians had hoped that their collective security idea could be regarded as in some way supplementary to Razak's plan for neutralization, they were disappointed. They were in fact more interested in selling their concept of collective security in Asia than in listening to Razak's idea about neutralization. Nevertheless the neutralization policy was at least preferable in Soviet eyes to the policy of overt reliance on Western security alliances that had preceded it. Neutrality could be viewed as the first step toward the eventual acceptance of Soviet-style collective security, given the failure of the Brezhnev Doctrine to be eagerly accepted in the region when first adumbrated.

NOTES

1. See Michael Leifer and Dolliver Nelson, "Conflict of Interest in the Straits of Malacca," in International Affairs, London, vol. 49, no. 2, April 1973, pp. 194-95; Geoffrey Jukes, The Indian Ocean in Soviet Naval Policy, Adelphi Paper No. 87 (London: International Institute for Strategic Studies, 1972); and M. Pathmanathan, "The Straits of Malacca: A Basis for Conflict or Co-operation?," in ND, p. 186.

2. Peking Review, 17 March 1972.

3. Izvestia, 29 May 1969; and Pravda, 8 June 1969. See generally Alexander O. Ghebhardt, "The Soviet System of Collective Security in Asia," Asian Survey, vol. 13, no. 12, December 1973, p. 1075; and V. Pavlovsky, "Collective Security: The Way to Peace in Asia," International Affairs, Moscow, July 1972, p. 23.

4. FEER, 8 April 1972.

5. Peking Review, 4 July 1969. See generally Melvin Gurtov, "Sino-Soviet Relations and Southeast Asia," in Pacific Affairs, vol. 43, no. 4, Winter 1970-71, p. 491.

6. Observer Foreign News Service, 10 October 1972.

7. MD, 31 October 1973, p. 10.

8. STK, 28 May 1973.

9. Interview with C. L. Sulzberger, New York Times, 18 March 1973. See also Peter Howard, "A System of Collective Security," Mizan, vol. 11, no. 4, July-August 1969, p. 199.

10. The Mirror, Singapore, 10 September 1973, p. 2.

11. Japan Times, 14 April 1973. See also the Novosti correspondent's letter to the Indian Express, 24 May 1974, quoting Brezhnev's view that China would become an equal partner.

12. See ARB, December 1973, pp. 2279-80.

13. 21 January 1973, cited in Ghebhardt, op. cit., p. 1089.

14. Moscow Radio, 15 August 1973; and I. Aleksandrov in Pravda, 26 August 1973. See also Ian Clark, "Collective Security in Asia: Towards a Framework for Soviet Diplomacy," Round Table, London, no. 252, October 1973, p. 473.

15. STK, 5 March 1971.

16. Izvestia, 2 January 1972.

17. Pavlovsky, op. cit., p. 27.

18. See STK, 4 and 18 September 1972.

19. Dev Murarka, Observer Foreign News Service, 4 September 1972.

20. Soviet News, 3 and 10 October 1972; STK, 6 October 1972; FAM, vol. 5, no. 3, September 1972, p. 35.

21. STK, 4 and 6 October 1972.

13

THE CHINESE
POSITION

The chief target of the neutralization proposal, so far as the Malaysians are concerned, is, understandably, China. Of all the big powers, China worries Southeast Asia most because its potential interest, reinforced by the links of history and migration, is so much greater than its current derisory presence in the area. It is obvious that, whatever happens over the forthcoming decade or two, it will result in a more significant Chinese relationship with Southeast Asia and a greater increase in China's interest than that of any other big power. China is not only the giant behind Southeast Asia's shoulder, she is a sleeping giant with memories of earlier involvements and with appetites not yet clearly defined.

The apprehensions nursed about China by Southeast Asia may be summarized under three heads: China's past actions, China's present irritations, and the future potential of Chinese intervention. President Suharto of Indonesia has put the first factor very bluntly: "it has been proved that China lent its support" to the attempted left-wing coup in Djakarta in 1965. His government, Suharto told a Western correspondent at the end of 1972, considered China's attitude "an interference in the internal affairs of Indonesia."[1] Similar comments could be cited from other leaders in the region, and a former Singapore High Commissioner to Malaysia, Chiang Hai Ding, has observed that "while China seems to have matured as a power vis a vis the great powers, it nevertheless continues to serve as a source of inspiration for revolutionary communist forces in our region."[2]

PEKING'S SUPPORT FOR REVOLUTIONARIES

The extent and importance of any Chinese participation in the planning of the so-called Gestapu affair in Indonesia in 1965 remains controversial. Nevertheless, the Chinese have consistently supported the Communist-led liberation movement of South Asia and find themselves, therefore, giving material aid to people who are in a state of violent resistance and insurgency against the established governments of most of the Southeast Asian states. The extreme provocations have recently been reduced but not eliminated. One of the most irritating of them is the "radio war." The neutralization proposals have been sharply attacked by two of the clandestine radio stations that support, in Malay and Burmese, the Communist insurgents in those countries, namely the Voice of Malayan Revolution (VMR) and the Voice of the People of Burma (VPB). These two radio stations began regular services in 1969 and 1971 respectively, and there is a Voice of the People of Thailand (VPT), which has been broadcasting on behalf of the Communist insurgents there since 1962. Even when a Chinese table-tennis team visited Thailand and Malaysia in 1973, as part of the thaw, the VMR and VPT, while welcoming the "envoys of peace" from China, used the occasion to attack the two host governments and took the position that public opinion had forced the visit upon them.

The Southeast Asian governments are fairly certain in their own minds that these radio broadcasts come from stations in Chinese territory, presumably in the deep south of Yunnan province where it juts into Laos and Burma toward Thailand. The Chinese deny this. They do admit to giving help to the insurgents in Southeast Asia, but this help is regarded as coming from the Chinese Communist Party and not from the Chinese government, and the distinction between the two is labored to Southeast Asian visitors in Peking. It enables them to help their insurgent friends while disclaiming any official responsibility. Another irritant is the continued asylum the Chinese give to the leaders of the various Communist Parties of Southeast Asia. The first vice-chairman of the Communist Party of Burma, U Ba Thein Tin, and the leading Central Committee member of the Communist Party of Indonesia, Jusuf Adjitorop, are among the two outstanding exiles resident in China. The latter is the leader of what remains of the pro-Chinese group within the Communist Party of Indonesia. A senior leader of the Communist Party of Malaya has on occasion made an appearance in Peking.

These exiles are not often publicly seen, and major statements by Adjitorop or Ba Thein Tin are highly infrequent. They are there, however, along with leaders of the Communist Party of Thailand, to be reactivated if a further turn of policy in Peking should so require. A pro-Chinese Communist Party did not emerge in the Philippines until 1968 and was not publicly acknowledged by Peking until 1970. Since the Chinese were at that time about to embark on a series of exchanges with the Philippine government and with established commercial and intellectual circles in Manila, there has not emerged any similar Filipino figure in Peking.

The Southeast Asian leaders are not nowadays frightened of inevitable Chinese aggression. The most accepted view is that China is most unlikely to undertake a forceable expansion into Southeast Asia along Hitlerian lines, even when she acquires the military capacity to do so. But there are two factors that might tempt the Chinese to become involved in Southeast Asia in the future that are somewhat worrying. One relates to Sino-Soviet competition, and the other to the presence in Southeast Asia of some 15 million Overseas Chinese.

SINO-SOVIET COMPETITION FOR REBEL PATRONAGE

China's problem in reconciling its government's need for normal diplomatic relations with the governments of Southeast Asia on the one hand, and its ideological commitment to support its fraternal revolutionaries overseas on the other hand, was also faced by the Soviet Union at an earlier stage. The Russian response was often to abandon its ideological commitments in the interests of Soviet strength, and there are many examples of this in the Middle East. But China would find it difficult to dissociate entirely from the left-wing insurgency in Southeast Asia, if only because it would drive these parties into the hands of the Soviet Union. So long as the Sino-Soviet dispute continues, it is likely that Peking will want to continue supporting these movements. Like the radio stations, the local Communists in Southeast Asia provide a useful means of bringing pressure to bear on the governments in the area. There is no reason why Peking should not continue to try to get the best of both worlds by gradually improving official relations with the governments while at the same time continuing to extend moral support to those in arms against them.

The official explanation given to visitors to Peking from Southeast Asia is that China is bound to support liberation movements although it will not interfere in internal affairs and does not regard revolution as exportable. Ideas, of course, know no frontiers, and it is in this way that the clandestine broadcasts are justified, although the Chinese have implied that the radio is under the control or in the territory of Communist Laos or Vietnam. This line of policy has been played down since the end of the Cultural Revolution: whereas Lin Piao, Mao Tse-tung's former deputy, pledged support specifically to Southeast Asian "armed struggles" in his report to the Ninth Congress of the Communist Party in 1969, Chou En-lai's less extreme report to the Tenth Congress in August 1973 referred only in general terms to the "just struggles of the Third World." After Tun Razak had been to Peking in 1974 to sign the historic agreement on diplomatic relations, he claimed that "Chairman Mao Tse-tung and Premier Chou and other leaders of China have categorically assured us that they regard the remnant terrorists in our country as our internal problem that is for us to deal with as we think best."[3]

The most worrying aspect of this is the evidence that the Chinese regard the Russians as provocatively expanding their presence in Southeast Asia in a way that could conceivably justify Chinese retaliation or emulation. An article by Hsiang Tung in the People's Daily published in Peking in March 1974 under the title "The Soviet Revisionist Social-Imperialists' Expansion in Southeast Asia" issued a long list of grievances on this score.[4] "In their contention for hegemony in Asia with the other super-power in recent years," Hsiang observed, "the Soviet revisionist social-imperialists have been stepping up their expansion in the Southeast Asian countries in an attempt to control and lord it over Southeast Asia and place it under their sphere of influence so as to realize their fond dream of building a great Russian empire." This People's Daily writer accused the USSR of sending warships into the Indian Ocean to form a Soviet "permanent fleet" there. Hsiang cited the dozen or so ports of which the Soviets had acquired the use in the Indian Ocean and the recent upsurge of exchanges between the Soviet Union and Southeast Asia:

> In the name of "trade" they dispatched "merchant ships," "trawlers," and warships to show their flag in various Southeast Asian ports. Under the pretext of "overhauls," and "replenishment" of fuel and provisions, they tried to grab t he right to use various Southeast Asian ports and turn them later into military bases as a foothold for further expansion in Southeast Asia. To acquire the right to use the port of Singapore, the Soviet revisionists have sent a "shipping experts delegation" and a "shipping delegation" to Singapore. In addition they dispatched spies to conduct subversion and disruption there. All this had aroused the vigilance of the Singapore authorities. In Malaysia, the Soviet revisionist ambassador took advantage of his diplomatic privileges to make frequent tours of Malaysia's remote areas in his scheme to acquire the rights to use Malaysian ports. In Thailand Soviet revisionist diplomats conducted activities along the coastal lines of the Isthmus of Kra in Southwestern Thailand, thus arousing discontent from the Thai government. The Soviet revisionists have also stretched their claws to

Indonesia and the Portuguese-occupied part of Timor
Island. Disregarding Indonesia's sovereignty over her
territorial waters, the Soviet revisionists sent their
"trawlers" to run amuck in Indonesian territorial
waters. Furthermore, it was disclosed that they are
making painstaking efforts to build a naval base in the
Portuguese-occupied part of Timor Island and for this
purpose have held frequent consultations with the Por-
tuguese authorities. What warrants particular attention is that in recent years, the Soviet revisionists
have loudly trumpeted "internationalization" of the
Malacca Strait.

The calculation behind these moves, in the view of the People's
Daily writer, was to secure for the Soviet Pacific fleet, based in
Vladivostock, free passage through the Malacca Straits into the Indian Ocean to join force with the Mediterranean and Black Sea fleet
in an attempt to establish hegemony in these vast waters. Meanwhile the Soviets also attempted to press their "Asian collective security system" on the Southeast Asian governments, offering friendship treaties similar to that signed between the Soviet Union and
India.
The article by Hsiang concluded:

It could be seen from the Soviet revisionists' undertak-
ings in Southeast Asia that the threats to the peace and
security of Asia today come from the contention in Asia
between the two superpowers. Only by eliminating the
superpowers' intervention can the peace and security
of Asia be secured. By carrying out expansion in
Southeast Asia, the Soviet revisionists have shown themselves up as social-imperialists. Whatever be their
plots and tricks, the Soviet revisionists cannot deceive
the daily-awakening people of the Southeast Asian countries. Southeast Asia belongs to the people of Southeast Asia, not to either of the superpowers.

It is perhaps understandable that the kind of language used here
which is not untypical and is calculated to alarm those in authority
in Southeast Asia, who perceive in the language the possibility of
Chinese intervention in the area to obstruct the Soviet Union.

THE OVERSEAS CHINESE FACTOR

The second factor is no less important. The position of the
Overseas Chinese in Southeast Asia has been difficult and controversial

all along, and it can be argued that the policy of the Chinese Communist government in the past 25 years has been on the whole more internationalist and statesmanlike than that of its predecessors. Chinese policy toward this group of communities has veered from unthinking support to cold rejection. In the years immediately following the Bandung Conference of 1955, Prime Minister Chou En-lai devoted considerable energy to a policy of encouraging the Chinese in Southeast Asia to become citizens of the states in which they resided, thus abandoning the traditional claim of allegiance to the Peking government. The Dual Nationality Treaty concluded with Indonesia in 1959 was an example of this position, in which the Chinese in Indonesia were asked to decide between Indonesian or Chinese citizenship, and the Chinese government accepted responsibility for the repatriation of those who declared for Chinese citizenship. This treaty failed in the end because it was not sufficiently flexible to deal with the problem of the middle group of Chinese who neither wished to take up Chinese citizenship and return to China nor to take up Indonesian citizenship, and who thus remained stateless.

But when China has been going through revolutionary periods, such as the Cultural Revolution, the government has sung a different tune, encouraging the Overseas Chinese to rebel against their host governments and to introduce Maoist revolutionary communism. It was the flagrant interventions of this kind during the Cultural Revolution period, particularly in Burma, which had been so friendly to China before, that dismayed and alarmed the Southeast Asian governments.

Since then, Chou En-lai's statements have gone back to the earlier policies. He told the Australian Prime Minister, Gough Whitlam, at the end of 1973 that he was glad that many Chinese had adopted Australian nationality. In 1974, during Tun Razak's pathbreaking visit to Peking, Chou and his colleagues spelled out their policy in more detail. On 31 May the two Prime Ministers issued a joint communique:

> [The Chinese government] takes note of the fact that
> Malaysia is a multiracial country with peoples of
> Malay, Chinese, and other ethnic origins. Both the
> Government of the People's Republic of China and the
> Government of Malaysia declare that they do not
> recognize dual nationality. Proceeding from this
> principle, the Chinese Government considers anyone
> of Chinese origin who has taken up of his own will or
> acquired Malaysian nationality as automatically for-
> feiting Chinese nationality. As for residents who re -
> tain Chinese nationality of their own will, the Chinese

Government acting in accordance with its consistent policy, will enjoin them to abide by the law of the Government of Malaysia, respect the customs and habits of the people there and live in unity with them, and their proper rights and interests will be protected by the Government of China and respected by the Government of Malaysia. [5]

Vice-Premier Li Hsien-nien, standing in for Premier Chou at a banquet that night, referred to this same question in his speech:

Owing to historical reasons, there are considerable numbers of people of Chinese origin living in Malaysia and other Southeast Asian countries. The Chinese Government's policy on this matter is consistent and clear. We encourage them to take up of their own will the nationality of the country of their residence. Anyone of Chinese origin who takes up of his own will, or acquires, the nationality of the country of his residence, automatically forfeits Chinese nationality. We would like to see them make a contribution to the country of their residence and work for the enhancement of friendship between the peoples of China and of the country of their residence. As for those residents abroad who retain Chinese nationality of their own will, we enjoin them to abide by the law of the country of their residence and live in amity with the people there. Their proper rights and interest will be protected by the Government of China. [6]

Tun Razak told his enthusiastic countrymen after his return to Kuala Lumpur that the Chinese government had agreed to "far-reaching and historic commitments" with regard to the Overseas Chinese. It believed their destiny was with the countries and peoples among whom they had lived for so long, and that they should "integrate themselves in the countries of their residence and they should form an integral part of the local society and not consider themselves separate from it."[7] The official Indonesian radio commentary warned that "observers believe that Chinese support of communists in Malaysia will be quietly continued, while the abolition of the dual nationality of Chinese residents will be on paper only."[8]

The Chinese Foreign Minister, Chi Peng-fei, told his Indonesian counterpart, Malik, in Paris at the beginning of 1973 that the Commission for Overseas Chinese Affairs had been abolished—

news greatly welcomed in Southeast Asia because it was this body, during the period when it was controlled by Cultural Revolution extremists, that had excited Overseas Chinese in Southeast Asia to take part in subversion. It is feared by the skeptics of Chinese pronouncements that at times of stress chauvinism might reappear in China and lead the Chinese government of the day to send gunboats or indulge in other Palmerstonian diplomacy designed to protect the interests of the Overseas Chinese when they come into conflict with the aims and aspirations of their hosts.

Here again, the question is complicated by a quite separate factor, namely the continued competition for legitimacy between Peking and Taiwan. As long as Taiwan offers an alternative Chinese government, Peking is reluctant to drop its support for the Overseas Chinese. If it let down its overseas "kith and kin, " it could be sure that Taiwan would make good propaganda out of the fact and would broadcast it very loudly throughout Southeast Asia that the Chinese government in Peking no longer cared for its compatriots abroad. Just as the Chinese Communists are obliged to support the Southeast Asian Communist Parties because of their fear of giving an entry to Russia, so they feel obliged to support in some degree Overseas Chinese communities in order not to give an entry to Taiwan.

MALAYSIA'S BAIT TO CHINA

It was thus that by the beginning of 1974 China lacked diplomatic relations with Malaysia, Singapore, Thailand, or the Philippines, and that Chinese relations with Indonesia had remained suspended since 1967. This was a quite artificial state of affairs and one that was worrying to both sides. There is no doubt that it was one of the considerations behind the neutralization proposal, as a speech by Tun Razak, the Malaysian Prime Minister, at the beginning of 1971 (delivered, it should be noted, before China had succeeded in entering the United Nations) makes clear:

It is a fact that China for the most part has been excluded from the mainstream of international affairs for more than two decades. I do not think it is profitable, at this point of time, to go into the whys and wherefores of this.

What is of more immediate relevance is that as a result, a natural result some might say, China does not accept the international order as it exists today and seeks to upset it because, in her view, she has been deliberately excluded.

123

The countries of Southeast Asia are her immediate neighbors and are the first to live with the consequences of her policies. As an example, I might add, insofar as Malaysia is concerned, there is a constant barrage of radio broadcasts from China called "Suara Revolusi Malaya, " or Malayan Voice of Revolution, which contains not merely virulent propaganda attacks on my government but also detailed instructions on the lines of action that subversive elements should take.

The countries of Southeast Asia are, after all, independent countries who form a part of the existing order and who cannot accept its overthrow. The question, therefore, is this: Is there room for adjustment and accommodation so that there can emerge in time an international order—I refer specifically to an order in Southeast Asia—which is acceptable to all and which is compatible with the legitimate national interest of all countries concerned? Surely there must be.

Malaysia for its part accepts the fact that China has a right to play her part in international forums, and to have an interest in the affairs of Asia. Our support for China's membership to the United Nations and in particular, our proposal for the neutralization of Southeast Asia, are clear manifestations of this belief.

But we cannot accept or tolerate any form of interference in our internal affairs, which we shall resist to the best of our ability. In the interest of our own survival we have a right to call on the assistance of anyone wishing to assist us. This surely cannot be denied.

For our part therefore, we wait to see China's response, whether she for her part recognizes and respects our independence and integrity and our legitimate interests in Southeast Asia.

We are aware that persuading China to accept the credibility of the proposal for the neutralization of this area, or indeed even perhaps to view the concept of neutralization favorably, will not be an easy task.

Obviously verbal eloquence alone is not enough. We in this region will have to demonstrate by positive words and deeds that neutralization is the only answer in the otherwise grim and certain prospect of conflicts that confront Southeast Asia.

Malaysia is convinced that the countries in this region can by a discernible consistency of policy and action reassure China that peace, stability, and neutrality are what Southeast Asian nations are truly striving for.

But China too has to reassure us of her intentions and her policies.

Of course, the accumulation of years of bitterness, frustrations and fear cannot be overcome overnight. We will require much patience. We will need to move step by step, feeling our way carefully in a matter which, so far as the countries of Southeast Asia are concerned, involves our very survival.[9]

SOUTHEAST ASIAN DETENTE WITH PEKING

Since the entry of China into the United Nations at the end of 1971, there has in fact been a considerable thaw in the relationships between China and the Southeast Asian countries. Malaysia has taken the lead in negotiating, mainly in New York but also through mutual visits by commercial and sports missions, culminating in the Razak visit of 1974, a recognition formula. One of the biggest difficulties was the question of the 220,000 stateless Chinese living in Malaysia, whom the Chinese government was reluctant to accept as having no obligations toward itself. There were similar exchanges, though on a somewhat lower key, with Singapore. The Singapore government was apprehensive about the temptations that would be placed in the way of any representative of the Peking government in Singapore to listen to the grievances of the more radical elements among the Chinese, who constitute 76 percent of the population of the republic.

The same process continued from 1971 onwards with Thailand, whose Deputy Foreign Minister and Defense Minister in the post-Thanom government visited Peking in unofficial capacities and held talks with the Chinese leaders. The Philippine President sent his brother-in-law, an influential figure in Manila, to Peking to sound out the Chinese leadership on the prospects of normalizing relations, and a state visit by President Ne Win was instrumental in restoring the relationship with Burma that had existed before the disruptions of the Cultural Revolution. Even Indonesia was wooed to some extent. Chi Peng-fei, the Chinese Foreign Minister, had conversations with his counterpart, Malik, at the Paris conference on Vietnam in the beginning of 1973. They were both representing their governments at the conference and took the opportunity to exchange views generally. The Chinese apparently assured Malik that they were not giving military support to the insurgents in Indonesia.

The general picture, therefore, of China's relations with Southeast Asia after the close of the Cultural Revolution is one of friendliness in seeking out contacts and discussions with the representatives of the Southeast Asian governments, while at the same time not completely removing the irritants of radio broadcasts and hospitality to exiles. The attitude to ASEAN also shifted from fierce denunciations when ASEAN was first formed in 1967 to a more sophisticated criticism a few years later that denounced any cover for American or Russian military alliances with the ASEAN governments but conceded that "In the development of their national economies, it accords with the interests of Asian and African countries that they cooperate in supplying each other's needs and develop economic and trade relations on the principle of equality and mutual benefit."[10]

On the more specific question of neutralization, the Chinese have not issued any denunciation of it, responding in a slightly reserved but not impolite and not unsympathetic manner. The Malaysian trade mission that visited Peking in May 1971 was given to understand by Chou En-lai that China was not unsympathetic. When Senator Salvador H. Laurel of the Philippine Congress visited Peking in 1972, he reported afterwards that China would respect the neutralization of Southeast Asia after the military links of the region with the United States were annulled, in other words that it would respect "true" neutralization.[11] A similar message was brought back by Joseph Walding, the Associate Minister for Foreign Affairs of New Zealand, who made an official visit early in 1973. Walding reported after his visit that China did not want to see any part of Asia tied up in a group that could be directed against China, and for this reason the Chinese leaders were ready to give a "hands-off" guarantee and to accept neutralization in the long run.[12] It was also reported by James Cairns, an Australian Minister, that the Chinese leaders in Peking supported the idea of a nuclear-free zone in the Pacific Ocean.[13]

CHOU EN-LAI'S CONDITIONAL APPROVAL

The Southeast Asians received their first direct indication of a more receptive attitude on the part of China toward neutralization in June 1973, when Chen Ji-sheng, Director of Southeast Asian Affairs in the Chinese Foreign Ministry, visited Bangkok accompanying a Chinese table-tennis team. After a conversation with Thai officials, including the Vice-Foreign Minister Chartchai Choonhavan, Pan Wannamethi, the Thai Deputy Under-Secretary of State, said that China had welcomed the ASEAN declaration of peace, freedom, and neutrality for the region. He quoted Chen as saying that the concept was in harmony with Peking's view and that China did not wish to see any power dominating Southeast Asia but rather wished to see the region free of interference. [14]

There were similar assurances given to other Thai leaders during the course of exchanges that took place in 1973-74. The Thai Defense Minister, Air Marshal Dawee Chullasapya, told reporters in Bangkok after returning from a week's visit to Peking at the beginning of 1974 that Prime Minister Chou En-lai had stated to him that China had ceased to support communist insurgents in Thailand, Laos, and other Southeast Asian countries. Chou had argued, Dawee continued, that it was the unfriendly attitude of the Thai military governments dating back to 1958 that had forced China to support rebel activities inside Thailand. But now China wanted to let bygones be bygones and to build up its own country, and Chou was quoted as saying, "China now will not interfere with countries in your region."[15]

Chou En-lai was somewhat cryptic during Razak's visit in 1974. "The Malaysian Government's position," he said, "for the establishment of a zone of peace and neutrality in Southeast Asia gives expression to the desire of the Southeast Asian peoples to shake off foreign interference and has won support from many Third World countries. The Chinese people sincerely wish the Malaysian people still greater victories on their road of advance." The Peking People's Daily made a similar flat statement, neither praising nor condemning.[16] Unofficial reports based on what Malaysian officials said after their return from Peking suggest that Chou privately "accepted and supported" neutralization, "provided foreign bases . . . were dismantled in good time."[17]

It would seem, therefore, that the Chinese view is not necessarily unsympathetic to the neutralization of the region, but that there must be a question about the Chinese capacity to act as guarantor or policeman of such an act of neutralization. As Prime Minister Lee Kuan Yew remarked in Djakarta in 1973, "China has expressed its support but it would first need to develop a blue water fleet to make such a guarantee meaningful."[18] That was before the Chinese naval action in the Hsisha (Paracel) and Nansha (Spratley) islands at the beginning of 1974, which would seem to indicate that there is now a minimal naval capacity by China to venture into oceanic waters. Nevertheless, Chinese naval and air power ranks far below what the Americans and Russians can provide, and for that reason alone there could be difficulties in the way of getting the three powers to come together as joint guarantors of a neutral Southeast Asia.

CHINA'S FOUR GOALS IN THE REGION

China's national interests in Southeast Asia may be summarized under four heads: (1) to minimize the hostility to China on the part of the Southeast Asian states, (2) to prevent an increase in Soviet (or, though less importantly, American) influence in the region, (3) to prevent the Overseas Chinese in the region from swinging to the side of Taiwan, (4) to promote a trade relationship useful to China.

China has always sought a situation where the countries immediately around her borders were led by rulers not hostile to China, and the concept of some kind of cordon sanitaire, which in the Southeast Asian sector might embrace the mainland states as distinct from the archipelago and insular states, has been discussed by observers. The aim of the Chinese would be to secure governments in this cordon sanitaire that were not anti-Chinese in their own policy and did not allow big powers hostile to China (especially the Soviet Union, but also to some extent the United States) to have military bases on their soil. The countries actually bordering China, or in a strategic position to command areas near the Chinese border about which China is particularly sensitive, are Burma, Thailand, Laos, Cambodia, and Vietnam. The list would not, however, include Malaysia, Singapore, the Philippines, or Indonesia, and this breakdown between continental and insular Southeast Asia is beginning to be used by scholars as having diplomatic significance. Alejandro M. Fernandez of the University of the Philippines has predicted that by the end of this century Southeast Asia will have broken up into these two new subregions, of which the continental states will gravitate toward China and "work out policies ranging from uneasy accommodation, or some form of modus vivendi with their giant neighbor to the North, to possible unembarrassed acceptance of satellite status by a few of them," while the insular states, including Malaysia, Singapore, Indonesia, and the Philippines, should remain relatively more independent.[19] A similar point is made by David Mozingo, who argues that the Nixon Doctrine, coupled with the new U.S.-China relationship, implies that the Americans would like to concentrate their economic and military influence mainly on the insular states, "while conceding, over time, mainland Southeast Asia as primarily in the Chinese sphere."[20]

The second Chinese aim of containing Soviet and American influence in Southeast Asia has already been discussed, and was recently well summarized by Doak Barnett:

In Southeast Asia . . . China seems likely, in the aftermath of the Vietnam war, to adopt a more flexible and less threatening overall posture, with emphasis on increased diplomatic activity and regional trade. Peking will probably give some backing to the idea of neutralizing the area, hoping that moves in this direction would enhance China's influence and reduce (not necessarily totally eliminate) U.S. influence and the American military presence without creating a vacuum into which the Soviet Union could somehow move. China will certainly insist on maintaining a viable buffer next to its southern border—in North Vietnam—but barring a serious new security threat in the region, the Chinese seem likely to avoid threatening moves themselves and to oppose sudden or dramatic moves by others (including North Vietnam) that might risk provoking new big power confrontations and conflicts. Over time, China's concerns in Southeast Asia may focus primarily not on the Americans or even the Russians but rather on the Japanese because of their economic dominance. [21]

The point about the Overseas Chinese has also been elaborated above, and the only point that needs to be made here is that if and when Taiwan either ceases to be a credible focus for anti-Communist feeling among the Overseas Chinese in Southeast Asia or becomes in some way reconciled with or affiliated to the People's Republic, then this need for Peking to concern itself about the affiliations of the stateless Overseas Chinese would become reduced. In the long run, therefore, one can perhaps envisage that this particular obstacle to normalization of Chinese-Southeast Asian relations may disappear. [22]

Finally, the commercial goal, although not a high priority for China because of the virtually autarkic nature of the Chinese economy, is to ensure a free supply of the materials of which China is short, notably rubber and to a lesser extent some metals. It should be noted, however, that China has a traditional exchange arrangement with Sri Lanka for rubber and is not dependent on Southeast Asia for this commodity and that in the long run China is likely to increase her own production of synthetic rubber. But for a very long time ahead China will be a customer for many of the raw materials produced in Southeast Asia and will want to sell as many Chinese manufactured products as possible, particularly to Singapore and Malaysia but also to the other states. Already Singapore and Malaysia comprise the second most important market for Chinese manufactures after Hong Kong.

None of these aims of Chinese policy in Southeast Asia require a Chinese domination of the region or a total exclusion of other powers' interests. In this sense the neutralization proposal could be made to appeal to Peking, and this has been the thinking in Kuala Lumpur. If China were to view neutralization as a potential device to neutralize Soviet influence in Southeast Asia, then there would be some advantage to it from the Chinese point of view. Kahin has argued that neutralization of the region would support Peking's basic security interests, and that it would be advantageous to China to be freed from concern over her 2,000-mile frontier with these states.[23] One of the key aides to the Malaysian Prime Minister on this question of neutralization, Zain Azraai, has suggested in a speech in Singapore that "Chinese interest in Southeast Asia will continue to be as it has been in the past; namely to have countries in Southeast Asia, if not subservient at least not hostile to her; to drive out American influence and to stem any Russian attempt to increase her influence; to prevent Japan from asserting herself in the region; and to legitimize China's own role and her interest in Southeast Asia. For China, neutralization could assist in the realization of these objectives."[24] Soedjatmoko, the former Indonesian Ambassador to the United States, has predicted that "with some stretch of the imagination it may not be entirely inconceivable that China at some point will see the advantage to her of a system of interlocking external balances in the region which, in combination with the increased capabilities of the Southeast Asian countries themselves, would amount to an effective neutralization she may not even be asked to guarantee."[25]

This is perhaps to pitch the appeal to China a little too high, and in practice it seems more likely that China would participate in the balancing game between the powers in Southeast Asia rather than join the formal neutralization scheme the Malaysian government would prefer.[26] Perhaps the best that can be said is that China's attitude as expressed so far has been less negative than either the United States' or the Soviet Union's, although it must be repeated that this conclusion must be taken with some caution in view of the Chinese inferiority to the two superpowers in terms of the military and economic strength that can be brought to bear in Southeast Asia.

NOTES

1. Le Monde, 10 November 1972.
2. ND, p. 25.
3. SWB-FE/4616/A3/5, 5 June 1974.
4. People's Daily, Peking, 19 March 1974, as translated in Ta Kung Pao Weekly English Supplement, Hong Kong, 21 March 1974.

5. SWB-FE/4615/A3/1-2, 3 June 1974; New China News Agency, 31 May 1974.

6. SWB-FE/4615/A3/5, 3 June 1974.

7. SWB-FE/4616/A3/5, 5 June 1974.

8. SWB-FE/4613/A3/1, 31 May 1974; see also Harvey Stockwin in FEER, 10 June 1974, p. 15.

9. STK, 16 January 1971.

10. See FEER, 18 September 1971; Peking Review, 18 August 1967 and 18 July 1969; New York Times, 13 August 1967; and Vincent K. Pollard, "South East Asian Regionalism, " Journal of Contemporary Asia, vol. 1, no. 4, Autumn 1971, p. 45.

11. BP, 20 April 1972.

12. STK, 4 April 1973; Canberra Times, 5 April 1973.

13. The Times of India, 19 May 1973.

14. ARB, July 1973, p. 1910.

15. Japan Times, 18 February 1974.

16. New China News Agency, 28 May 1974; SWB-FE/4612/A3/1-2, 30 May 1974, p. 14; People's Daily, Peking, 29 May 1974; SWB-FE/4612/A3/4.

17. M. G. G. Pillai, "Blazing the Peking Trail, " FEER, 10 June 1974; see also Goh Cheng Teik, "Tearing Down the Curtain of Fear, " ibid., p. 28.

18. STK, 28 May 1973; see also Harry Gelbex, Nuclear Weapons and Chinese Policy, Adelphi Paper No. 99 (London: International Institute for Strategic Studies, 1973).

19. "On the Future of Southeast Asia, " in ND, pp. 29 and 31.

20. "China's Future Role in Southeast Asia, " in ND, p. 46.

21. A. Doak Barnett, Uncertain Passage: China's Transition to the Post-Mao Era (Washington, D.C.: The Brookings Institution, 1974), p. 303.

22. The problem of the Overseas Chinese should not in any case be exaggerated. As Soedjatmoko of Indonesia has written, "It . . . would be wrong to underestimate the cosmopolitanism, the self-confidence as well, and even the new sense of a separate Southeast Asian identity that the Overseas Chinese have gained in the past few years. The historical significance of Singapore as an experiment in developing a separate political identity in this connection should not be underrated. " "China's External Policy: Scope and Limitations, " in East Asia and the World System, Part II, Adelphi Paper No. 92 (London: International Institute for Strategic Studies, 1972), p. 18.

23. In ND, p. 80.

24. "Neutralization and Southeast Asia, " in ND, p. 132.

25. "On the Future of Southeast Asia, in ND, p. 19.

26. See Frank Langdon, "China's Policy in South East Asia, " in Mark W. Zacher and R. Stephen Milne, eds., Conflict and Stability in South East Asia (New York: Anchor Press, 1974), p. 325.

14

**THE JAPANESE
POSITION**

"Economically we follow a very aggressive policy in Asia, "
said a Japanese official at the beginning of the 1970s. "Politically, "
he went on, "we are just beginning to put our toe in the water as far
as playing a larger leadership role is concerned. Militarily we are
very reluctant to do more than build up our own self-defense capacity."[1] Japan, already the third-ranking economic power in the
world and the largest to be entirely situated in Asia, is bound to play
an increasingly important role in Southeast Asian affairs. In the
1940s Japan's interest in the region was expressed by military occu-
pation. In the course of this a certain amount was done to prevent
the European colonialists from easily re-establishing their political
hold over their former colonies after the war's end, but local opinion
was also suppressed in a way calculated to earn Japan the hostility of
the region for a very long time. In the postwar era Japan's interest
has assumed a purely economic form. Her trade with the ten countries of Southeast Asia has amounted to some 10 percent of her total
world trade in the past few decades, and the Philippines, Indonesia,
and Malaysia provide Japan with important portions of some of the
principal raw materials she needs to keep her industries going—
minerals, rubber, various tropical agricultural crops, and, more
recently, petroleum. More important, this 10 percent of Japan's
world trade represents 50 percent of Southeast Asia's world trade.

DOMINATING ECONOMIC PRESENCE

Furthermore, the countries of Southeast Asia provide important markets for Japanese manufacturers, their purchase of which
was stimulated by the war reparations program that the Japanese
government initiated in the 1950s and which has gradually merged

into the Japanese economic aid program to Southeast Asia: this now amounts to more than $1.5 billion a year. This figure includes private foreign investment as well as export credits, and the official government assistance, whether in the form of loans or grants, is rather smaller. But whatever the label, this flow of funds from Japan into Southeast Asia has resulted in a steady buildup of local demand for Japanese equipment as well as Japanese consumer goods. This economic role, reinforced by a very heavy flow of Japanese businessmen and tourists, has generated tension of the kind that burst out during the official tour of Prime Minister Kakuei Tanaka to the five ASEAN states in 1974. The Japanese have become highly unpopular, and they are not really sure why. Professor Ajit Singh Rye has described the situation in the following way:

> [Japan has] placed herself in a position of dominance in the area which despite Japanese protestations is patently one-sided and obviously exploitative. The raw material production and supplies have carefully been managed in such a way that each country has been placed in a defensive position. That is, they are made to part with their irreplaceable raw material at a low cost and much of what they earn is eventually repatriated to Japan because of the disproportionately higher cost of the finished industrial goods. The so-called loans and aid to these countries are of such a nature that, by and large, they appear to be investments that tend eventually to improve public works facilities such as transportation, communication, and power in order to help expedite the extraction and transportation of raw materials to Japan and the efficient distribution of consumer and semi-manufactured goods imported from Japan. [2]

Much of the criticism of the Japanese from the region is a little unfair in the sense that the Japanese business activities complained of are activities characteristic of private entrepreneurs in any relatively free economy, not only in Japan but in other Western countries and indeed in Southeast Asia itself. Indonesians are angry, for example, because a Japanese corporation, working anonymously through a local Chinese agent, gradually buys up small plots of land in a village outside Djakarta so that over a period it becomes the owner of a piece of land large enough for it to build a factory. If the Japanese company had approached the Indonesian government directly, it would also have obtained the land, but at far greater cost, since it would have been scheduled as development land. But any risk-taking businessman will do what he can to promote his

133

enterprise and maximize his profits so long as he does not directly contravene the law of the land, and many of the Japanese actions that cause resentment can be put into this category. There is nothing illegal about Japanese travel agencies booking up entire hotels for their clients, or for hundreds of Japanese tourists to pour into them daily from the airport and to live it up in Japanese style with the help of local entertainers and servants. But this kind of activity does irritate local opinion. A Japanese corporation put up a neon sign advertising its name on top of the highest building in Djakarta; it later removed the sign after much public criticism and the harassing of Premier Tanaka by students. This is an example of inadequate public relations, but it hardly qualifies as imperialism.

Much of the bad press the Japanese get in the area derives from the fact that local opinion in Southeast Asia is gradually crystallizing its dislike of substantial foreign intervention in its own society or local economy. This criticism should logically be aimed at the Europeans, the Russians, the Americans, and the Chinese as much as at the Japanese, and indeed it was the local Chinese shopkeepers who bore the brunt of student violence in Djakarta at the time of Tanaka's unfortunate visit. But the "white" faces of the Americans and Europeans have come to be accepted as part of the permanent furniture of Southeast Asia, and it is still counted as a gain that the Europeans and Americans have abdicated from positions of political or administrative power, adjusting to having to live as businessmen or professional men subject to the laws made by the new local nationalist governments. Because no Southeast Asian country fears any resumption of political intervention from Europe or the United States, the presence of a few hundreds or even a few thousands of men and women from the Atlantic areas is not considered provocative, dangerous, or undesirable. To the extent that these Western people have suffered a reduction in their political prestige, they are reasonably diplomatic and aware of the need not to upset local sensitivities, and to the extent that they practice a Western style of behavior in their daily lives, they are seen by a local citizen as models of a Western way of life, which he or she to some degree emulates and seeks to imitate or absorb.

None of these considerations apply to the Japanese, whose sudden access of numbers in the late 1960s and 1970s has often appeared menacing and disturbing. In a sense the Japanese are the nouveau riches, the newcomers to the club of foreign elites on whom the locals take out much of the envy and dislike they nurse against the foreign community generally and against the idea of foreign influence, but from which the more experienced older members of the club have acquired a certain exemption or immunity.

The Japanese economic position in Southeast Asia is bound to grow even larger. The Asian Development Bank, in a study of future trends, has forecast that Japan's share of Southeast Asia's foreign trade will continue to grow to reach a peak of about two-thirds in the 1980s after which it will begin to decline very marginally, but only to be replaced by the higher volume of intraregional trade or commercial exchanges between the countries of Southeast Asia and not by a corresponding growth on the part of any of Japan's competitors outside the region.[3] Japanese investment is certain to continue strongly, whether in enterprises designed to produce or process raw materials for Japan's industries at home or in subsidiary or joint-venture factories where Japanese-brand products can be made more cheaply than in Japan itself, for sale either locally or in Japan or in third-country markets. There is a tacit assumption in international business and aid circles that Japan will acquire a bigger and bigger role in Southeast Asia. Japan already has the position of being the largest single donor to the Inter-Governmental Group on Indonesia, the consortium of donors that coordinates the international aid effort to that country. Japan provides the operational head of the Asian Development Bank in Manila, and the Japanese organize the annual Ministerial Conference on Southeast Asian Economic Development, an organization it is hoped will blossom into a kind of Japanese "Colombo Plan."

LOW POLITICAL PROFILE

What is difficult to predict is the shape the emerging Japanese political interest in Southeast Asia will take. The Japanese have deliberately kept a low profile in their diplomatic relationships with the area, partly to enable their more important economic interests to be consolidated, partly out of the national diffidence that the spectacular military defeat of 1945 had created in the Japanese psychology, partly out of the postwar habit of following the American lead in international affairs, and partly because of the difficulty of identifying Japan's political interests in the region. Under Article 9 of Japan's postwar constitution, the government is prevented from indulging in any military activity of the kind that is taken for granted by such states as the United States, Britain, France, and the USSR. There is no legal possibility of Japanese soldiers being sent abroad, not even for the United Nations, and it seems unlikely that any break with the pacifist constitution will be made in the foreseeable future. Japan has similarly refrained from developing or acquiring nuclear weapons and is obliged to place her security in the hands of the

U.S. alliance. This meant, for example, that Japan played no part in the Vietnam War, and she has no capacity to guarantee any neutralization of Southeast Asia in a meaningful way.

Yet the sealanes of the Southeast Asian archipelago remain vital arteries for Japan's survival as a trading nation: through them Japan receives a very large proportion of vital raw materials and energy supplies, particularly Middle East oil, on which she is dependent to the extent of about 80 percent. It would be a crisis of immense proportions for Japan if these sea routes were closed, interrupted, or harassed, and no Japanese government could simply ignore any event of this kind: Japan has already taken a strong stand against the deinternalization of the Strait of Malacca by Malaysia and Indonesia and is backing the proposed canal across the Kra Isthmus of Thailand. The question is how far any threat of this kind might lead to a greater Japanese military involvement in Southeast Asia. The first context in which such a departure could arise would be the need to give naval protection for shipping routes through Southeast Asia and into the Indian Ocean, and this has occasionally been hinted at or advocated as a present or future need. [4] Premier Lee Kuan Yew of Singapore once proposed in Tokyo that Japan join in an international task force to counter Russian influence in the Indian Ocean. [5] But it is beyond Japan's present military capacity to escort ships even as far as to Singapore or the Malacca Strait, and her defense plans do not envisage enough naval strength to cope with the existing Russian or future Chinese naval offensive forces.

It would seem inevitable, at least for the time being, that aid, investment, and trade must be the substitute for Japan's military capacity to intervene in Southeast Asia. [6] Japan's self-defense forces are very small by comparison with powers of similar economic standing or by comparison with others in the East Asian region. Japan's military forces at present are not only smaller than China's, America's, or Russia's, but also than South Korea's, North Korea's, South Vietnam's, North Vietnam's, Indonesia's, Taiwan's, and India's. As a percentage of gross national product, Japan's military expenditure is much smaller than any of those mentioned, comprising less than 1 percent.

Most observers of Japan are divided on the question whether Japan is likely to undertake a substantial rearmament, possibly including nuclear weapons. Much depends on international developments outside Southeast Asia, notably in the United States, China, and the Soviet Union. Japan certainly has some political ambitions in Southeast Asia, and her participation in the Djakarta Conference on Cambodia in 1970 was a good example of nonmilitary involvement in regional diplomacy. A Japanese was even named as one of the three "ambassadors" for the ten conferring states to tour the capitals

136

of the nations militarily involved in Vietnam in order to canvass for a Cambodian settlement. Japan was welcomed as a participant in that conference, but there was no evidence that the Japanese have any consistent need or determination to take up similar initiatives in the region in the future. Japan's interests will remain primarily economic, and it is in this light that the attitude toward neutralization is likely to be decided.

NONCOMMITTAL ON NEUTRALIZATION

Japan has in fact remained highly noncommittal on the neutralization question, in spite of the occasional indications that Japan might be approached to be a fourth guarantor of the neutralization of Southeast Asia, along with the United States, the USSR, and China.[7] Ghazali explained in an address to the Tokyo Foreign Correspondents' Club why Malaysia had not included Japan as a guarantor: "We are not altogether certain whether, in the light of her own Constitution, Japan herself could be considered for a role, bearing in mind the possibility of diplomatic and military implications which would follow."[8]

Prime Minister Abdul Razak spoke to the then Japanese Prime Minister, Eisaku Sato, a few weeks before the Kuala Lumpur Declaration, in October 1971. He explained his ideas, but Sato took no position on them, and the only result in the official communiqué issued after the visit was that the Japanese Premier had expressed his "appreciation of the Malaysian initiative" on neutralization.[9] Some two and a half years later, when Sato's successor, Kakuei Tanaka, came to Kuala Lumpur on an official visit, he was also highly evasive. He told reporters that it was still premature for Japan to express its definite views on the concept of the neutralization of Southeast Asia, although the idea as such was excellent.[10]

No more concrete opinions have been expressed by any senior Japanese leaders, and it is clear that the Japanese do not wish to be committed one way or the other until either the other powers take a definite stand or the Southeast Asian states themselves advance to the stage of having a concrete proposal to make.

NOTES

1. New York Times, 15 August 1970, as quoted in James W. Morley, ed., Forecast for Japan: Security in the 1970s (Princeton: Princeton University Press, 1972), p. 169.

2. "Japan's Future Role in Southeast Asia, " in NDE, pp. 50-51. See also K. E. Shaw, "Japan's Forces in Southeast Asia: The Problems and the Future, " ibid., p. 80.

3. Asian Development Bank, Southeast Asia's Economy in the 1970's (London: Longman, 1971).

4. The Asian, Hong Kong, 19 March 1972.

5. Japan Times and STS, 12 May 1973.

6. See Frank Langdon, "Japanese Policy towards Southeast Asia, " in Mark W. Zacher and R. Stephen Milne, eds., Conflict and Stability in Southeast Asia (New York: Anchor Press, 1974), pp. 351-54; also Masataka Kosaka, Options for Japan's Foreign Policy, Adelphi Paper No. 97 (London: International Institute for Strategic Studies, 1973), pp. 22-27.

7. STK and Japan Times, 15 October 1971; also New Nation, Singapore, 26 November 1971.

8. FAM, vol. 4, no. 4, December 1971, p. 50.

9. Sunday Times, Kuala Lumpur, 17 October 1971; FAM, vol. 4, no. 4, December 1971, p. 37.

10. Japan Times, 15 January 1974.

It almost went without saying that India would give her immediate and enthusiastic support for the neutralization of Southeast Asia. Not only is India a distinguished pioneer in the prosecution of neutralistic policies in the postwar era but she is also an ardent backer of ASEAN and feels herself to be an important friend, almost patron, of Malaysia, the small Commonwealth country whose path to independence from British rule was hastened by Jawarharlal Nehru. Gaining the seal of Mrs. Gandhi's approval was one of Tun Razak's easiest assignments after launching his diplomatic initiative.

At the Commonwealth Conference in Singapore at the beginning of 1971, Swaran Singh, then India's Foreign Minister, supported the Malaysian plan for neutralization, although he complicated it by adding that "the Western part of the Indian Ocean also" should be brought within the area of neutralization. Sirimavo R. D. Bandaranaike, Prime Minister of Sri Lanka, carried this to its logical conclusion by proposing that the entire Indian Ocean be declared a zone of peace. [1] Swaran Singh did specify later that India would be ready to participate in any moves or consultations that would lead to the realization of Malaysia's neutralization plan. [2] Two years later, when President V. V. Giri of India made a state visit to Malaysia, he declared: "We welcome and support the concept of Southeast Asia as a zone of peace, freedom, and neutrality as stated in the Kuala Lumpur Declaration." [3]

But India's effort to seek a larger role in Southeast Asia, particularly since the creation of Bangladesh, [4] is not welcomed in Southeast Asia itself. Indonesia in particular is somewhat suspicious of India's motives, all the more because India stands as an Asian power that has openly interfered in a neighbor's (that is, Pakinstan's) affairs in order to break it up in favor of a secessionist movement in one part of it (that is, Bangladesh). Since all this was done with vital Soviet support, the disenchantment in Djakarta with the prospect of a greater Indian influence in Southeast Asia is quite strong. But this disenchantment is not to be exaggerated: India retains in general a good image and good relations with many circles in Southeast Asia, including, for example, even the Indonesian navy, in whose early development and training India played an important and helpful part (the two navies thus held joint maneuvers in the Indian Ocean in 1973). But the very mention of the Indian Ocean in the context of Indian-Indonesian relations is a reminder that Indonesia officially refers to it as the Indonesian Ocean and that there is occasional, though unofficial, speculation that the status of the Andaman Islands, inherited by India from British rule but geographically and culturally nearer to the East Indian archipelago than to the Indian subcontinent, is not yet regarded as finally determined. It is in the Andaman Islands that the Indian navy has a base, and there is some fear on the Indonesian side, particularly among the influential army leaders, lest the Indian Ocean become dominated by a combination of the Indian and Soviet fleets, with India giving the Soviet navy bases on the Indian coast. This may be an overdramatized scenario, but from the distance of Djakarta it is one that causes concern.

In any event, India's ambitions for a role in Southeast Asia are not really recognized in Southeast Asian capitals, where the most common view is that India "is not interested in Southeast Asia."[5] Indian diplomacy toward the area is somewhat intermittent, and, not being backed up by any sustained or important economic or military presence, it is not a vital consideration, for the time being at least, in Southeast Asian thinking. India has not been officially proposed as a guarantor for neutralization, and the principal ingredient of any consensus that might be reached in Southeast Asia about policy toward India would be to ensure that Southeast Asia's interests are kept separate from those of India, that Southeast Asia is not identified in world affairs with Indian sponsorship, and that India maintains her present policy of noninterference.

NOTES

1. The Times, London, 22 January 1971.
2. The Hindu, Madras, 23 January 1971.
3. MD, 20 March 1973. But not all Indians are sanguine about the success of the Razak plan; see, for example, A. N. Kakkar, "The Neutralization of South East Asia," The Institute for Defence Studies and Analyses Journal, New Delhi, vol. 5, no. 4, April 1973, p. 543.

4. See Stanley J. Heginbotham, "In the Wake of Bangladesh, " Pacific Affairs, vol. 45, no. 3, Fall 1972, pp. 383-84.

5. See V. T. Sambandan's report of President Giri's state visit to Singapore in The Hindu, 3 October 1971.

16

**THE EUROPEAN AND
AUSTRALASIAN
POSITIONS**

The West European reaction to the plan to neutralize Southeast Asia has been on balance more favorable than the North American, partly because neutralism and neutrality as general concepts have a more respectable pedigree in Europe and therefore strike warmer chords in European ears. The French, it goes without saying, have consistently welcomed the Malaysian plan, and French commentators have written about it with enthusiasm as a vindication of Gaullism in the Far East. When Tun Razak has visited the various capitals of Western Europe, he has almost invariably been able to elicit the support of his hosts for his neutralization plan, albeit expressed sometimes in rather vague and general language. For many countries in Western Europe, a general commitment of this kind is possible precisely because the country concerned has no possibility of influencing events in Southeast Asia, even if it had the will to do so.

SUPPORT FROM BRITAIN

The one country in Western Europe that has to take the proposal more seriously, because in 1974 it still deployed a small military presence in Southeast Asia and has a minimal surviving capacity to influence events in limited parts of it, is Britain, and the British comment has been less enthusiastic than the French and other continental European. When Edward Heath, then the British Prime Minister, visited Singapore at the beginning of 1971 for the Commonwealth Summit Conference there, he told the local press that he believed the neutralization scheme "could in the long term be valuable in helping to ensure the stability of Southeast Asia," but not until there was peace in Vietnam. [1] It was noticeable that the Commonwealth Summits, which, in the absence of an agreement among the other major Commonwealth powers, very often tend to reflect a British view, did not commit themselves enthusiastically to neutralization in spite of its being sponsored by a Commonwealth member.

The first British Minister to visit Malaysia after the Kuala Lumpur Declaration was Anthony Royle, the Under-Secretary of State for Foreign Affairs, who was, so to speak, caught unprepared, since he was in Malaysia only days after the Declaration. In response to reporters' questions, he said that Great Britain supported Malaysia's move but that it was too early to comment on the Kuala Lumpur Declaration. On his departure from Malaysia a day or two later he issued a statement to the press in which he said that the Kuala Lumpur Declaration was

> a most important step on the road to achievement of peace and stability in Southeast Asia, an area in which Britain has so many close ties. As this is also the prime objective of Her Majesty's Government, we are delighted that the leaders of the regional states have been able to reach understanding on how to shape their own destiny, defend their own interests and safeguard their own independence and security. . . . We fully support their determination to achieve an even greater measure of regional cooperation and to ensure that there shall be no outside interference in the internal affairs of the states of the region. [2]

Of course, the wording of the Kuala Lumpur Declaration did not oblige Royle to comment on the specific idea of neutralization under big-power guarantee, but the fact that he did not do so was enough to indicate that Britain held reservations about it.

Another confirmation of this came in a passage in the House of Lords at about the same time, when another Under-Secretary of State for Foreign Affairs, the Marquess of Lothian, was pressed by Lord Brockway to state the British government's attitude toward the invitation given by Malaysia to China, the USSR, and the United States to guarantee Southeast Asian neutrality. Lord Lothian tried to sidestep the question:

> Although we are not aware of any specific invitations, the Malaysian government naturally desire that Southeast Asia should not become an area of conflict between outside powers. Her Majesty's Government support any policies which contribute to the peace and stability of an area with which we have so many ties.

Lord Brockway pressed his point, asking whether it was not undesirable for China and the United States to seek to exert control of Southeast Asia. The noble Under-Secretary replied, still in general terms, that he agreed that Britain would support any initiative, whether from Malaysia or anyone else, that would contribute to the peace and security of Southeast Asia.[3] In 1972 Sir Alec Douglas-Home, the British Foreign Secretary in the Heath government, visited Indonesia and told his hosts that the British government welcomed the "close ties you arc forging with your neighbors and the initiatives you are taking in the Association of Southeast Asian Nations." He told a press conference in Djakarta that Britain supported the activities of ASEAN and would respect the way in which it wished to carry out its activities. Britain wished to see a strong structure to carry on development in the area and welcomed the work of ASEAN in this regard. Despite the continuing public interest in the neutralization proposal at that time, Sir Alec made no reference to it.[4]

It was only in February of 1973 that a senior British Minister spoke directly about neutralization. Lord Carrington, the Defense Secretary in the Heath administration, told reporters in Djakarta that Britain welcomed the concept of a neutral Southeast Asia but thought that it would take a long time to achieve. He noted that the region's neutrality hinged on guarantees from the superpowers, which would take longer to obtain than some people might think. "Your neutrality," he insisted, "depends on whether other people are prepared to recognize it."[5] This British attitude approximated fairly closely to the American, with the difference in presentation that the British could not but be polite and minimally sympathetic to an initiative by a Commonwealth country—whereas the United States had no such inhibition in reacting to the Malaysian suggestion.

EEC VIEW NOT YET FORMED

At one stage of the ASEAN debate about neutralization Indonesia suggested that Britain, France, and West Germany be asked to guarantee Southeast Asian neutralization along with the superpowers, China, and Japan.[6] But it has never been seriously thought in Europe that any European state could in future realistically undertake such a commitment. All the European powers that were formerly strong in Southeast Asia are now either withdrawing or have already withdrawn their military presence in the area and can no longer seek credibly to influence the course of events except through the far less effectual activities of trade, investment, economic assistance, and diplomacy. Insofar as these pressures are operating in Southeast Asia, they can be said to operate, on the whole, in favor of neutralization, but with

144

the rider that the practical difficulties of achieving neutralization should be recognized.

Obviously the Malaysians at one point hoped that the European Economic Community might accelerate its progress toward political unity, which would enable it to take a more credible stance about such questions as the neutralization of Southeast Asia. But this hope was frustrated by the events following the British entry into the European Community and the lack of harmony that came to the surface in the EEC during 1973 and 1974. In general, West European opinion is in favor of the idea of maintaining a balance of big power influence in Southeast Asia.

AUSTRALIA IS INTERESTED

The Australasian attitude to neutralization is in many ways regarded as more important to Southeast Asia than the West European, since Australia and New Zealand, although small powers by international military standards, can wield a more effective defense operation in Southeast Asian waters and skies than any of the West European states are likely to be able to do after another year or two have passed. The Australasian stake and interest in Southeast Asia grows year by year through the natural force of its geopolitical position, whereas Western European influence is inevitably on the wane.

Under the McMahon government, which was in power when the Kuala Lumpur Declaration was made, the Australian attitude was clumsy and vague. When President Suharto of Indonesia visited Canberra at the beginning of 1972 and told his host that Indonesia wished to stay clear of regional defense pacts, such as the Commonwealth Five-Power Agreement, William McMahon was able to claim afterwards that he had agreed with his visitor that they could "cooperate together in a military area when it is in the interest of Indonesia, Australia, and the free world."[7] Of the Kuala Lumpur Declaration, the Foreign Minister, Nigel Bowen, stated in May 1972 that "despite the practical difficulties involved in working for neutrality as a long-term solution for stability in Southeast Asia, Australia welcomes the Declaration as a regional initiative directed toward peace and stability in Asia," and McMahon repeated the sentiment a month later.[8] But the state of perception of a leader like McMahon was indicated by the fact that when welcoming President Suharto he committed the error of saying "India" instead of "Indonesia," a mistake that might be forgiven in a European, African, or Latin American capital but hardly in Canberra.[9]

When Gough Whitlam took over the Premiership, he gave Australian foreign policy toward Southeast Asia a better informed and more ambitious, though not necessarily less abrasive, touch. On visiting Indonesia early in 1973, he said that he "looked toward the eventual emergence of a comprehensive regional organization without ideological overtones to help free the Asian-Pacific area of great power intervention and rivalries."[10] Although this set of goals corresponded closely with those of the ASEAN Foreign Ministers in the Kuala Lumpur Declaration, Australia's hope of insinuating itself into the regional action was rebuffed by the Indonesians. Indeed, the lack of interest shown by Indonesian leaders in his ideas for a larger grouping in East Asia and the Western Pacific placed Whitlam in an embarrassing position. President Suharto finally expressed his welcome of the new Australian government's idea but went on record as saying that it was unlikely to be achieved in the short term, although he "recognized its potential value in the longer term."[11]

Since then the Australian efforts to collaborate with ASEAN in a more meaningful way have borne some fruit, and there is a sense in which one can talk about a collaboration of interests and activities between Indonesia and Australia if for no other reasons than their common interest in the economic and political development of the island of New Guinea, which they used to share between them (the eastern half has now become an independent state). That is to place this new development at its narrowest. At its widest extent, it might be seen as the germ of a wider forum in which not only Australia but New Zealand as well would play a role, together with the other ASEAN nations. When the late Dr. Ismail, then Malaysia's Deputy Premier, went to Canberra in March 1973 for talks with Whitlam, he voiced "Malaysia's profound appreciation of the unqualified support of the Prime Minister on the neutralization of Southeast Asia."[12]

Neutralization as a concept certainly appeals to the Whitlam government, although there is also some anxiety about the possibility of the area's being beguiled by protestations of nonintervention that the big powers do not really mean to carry out. Whatever the fluctuations in Australian policy, it is likely that there will be a greater degree of consultation and collaboration between the Australasians on the one hand and the ASEAN states on the other about the general direction in which Southeast Asia wishes to go.

NEW ZEALAND APPROVES

New Zealand's attitude is broadly similar. When Ismail visited Wellington in 1973, Norman E. Kirk, the Prime Minister, stated that New Zealand "had every sympathy with the desire of the ASEAN

146

countries to limit outside interference in their affairs and expressed New Zealand's good wishes for the success of the proposal" (in the Kuala Lumpur Declaration). [13]

NOTES

1. STK, 23 January 1971.
2. STK, 28 and 30 November 1971.
3. Hansard (Lords), vol. 325, pp. 898-99.
4. SWB-FE/4033, 6 July 1972; The Times, London, 5 July 1972.
5. Ibid., 9 February 1973.
6. See S. M. Ali and V. K. Chin in New Nation, Singapore, 26 November 1971.
7. New York Times, 13 February 1972.
8. Current Notes on International Affairs, Canberra, October 1972, pp. 503-4.
9. The Hindu, Madras, 8 February 1972.
10. New York Times, 25 February 1973.
11. The Guardian, Manchester, 26 February 1973.
12. Australian Foreign Affairs Record, March 1973, p. 182; MD, 20 March 1973.
13. FAM, vol. 6, no. 1, March 1973, p. 29.

Southeast Asia's indigenous defense capacity is strong in terms of land forces, but it is virtually helpless in terms of strength at sea or in the air. Some of the national armies are formidable, not only those of North and South Vietnam, which amount to about half a million men each, but also those of Indonesia and even Thailand. But the total strength of the combined navies and air forces of the ten Southeast Asian states hardly exceeds 300,000 men, sharing only five warships, ten submarines, and a thousand combat aircraft for the entire region. It should be added that those five warships are the former Soviet cruiser and four Soviet destroyers that were given to Indonesia under the Sukarno regime prior to 1965 and whose operational capacity is dubious; the same goes for the submarines. The cruiser is in any case being sold. Apart from Indonesia, none of the countries boasts an armed ship larger than a frigate, escort ship, or patrol boat.[1] It is clear, therefore, that not only are the Southeast Asian states justly nervous about the ease with which any external power could interfere by sea or air but also that the majority of these states must and do entertain some reservations about their possible future position should Indonesia begin to attempt any kind of dominating role in the region, since Indonesia is the only one so far to have attempted a naval buildup.

The reason why no fewer than six of the ten countries in Southeast Asia have standing armies of more than 100,000 men is, of course, that they are all in one way or another fighting armed insurgency or civil wars. These have been endemic to the region since the Second World War, when anti-Japanese or resistance movements tended to be led by Communists or left-wing Socialists. After the peace these leaders continued their campaigns against their more moderate compatriots and against the Western powers that supported the latter as inheritors of the powers of government after the colonial withdrawal. The various insurgencies are often competing; a notable example of this is in Burma, where the government has had to defend itself against attack from rival factions of the Communist Party fighting separately and from tribal and secessionist movements in the minority areas, as well as having to deal with some Chinese Kuomintang remnants left over from the Chinese civil war and operating partly in Burmese territory. Thailand also faces indigenous Communist, tribal, and secessionist guerillas as well as the Malay Communist insurgents under Chin Peng who make their base on the Thai side of the border. The Malaysian "emergency" has long been over, but sporadic raids still take place, and in the past two or three years there has been a slight upsurge in the number of Communist terrorist incursions into Western Malaysia, quite apart from the continuing Communist insurgency in Sarawak. The Indonesian army is fighting Communist-backed rebels in Kalimantan, and the Philippine government is attempting to defeat not only ideological insurgents (some of whom call themselves Maoist or Communist) but also Muslim dissidents in the southern islands.

In the four states of Indochina, civil war has taken on an international dimension with the involvement of the United States and the open support on the other side of China and the Soviet Union. The Americans have now withdrawn their forces from Indochina, but the possibility of bombing from other neighboring countries, notably Thailand, continues, and there is little prospect of an early end to the internal fighting, which the big powers are unable to stop. The Southeast Asian governments have therefore been led to bolster their military security by alliances with better-equipped foreign powers. As a Communist state, North Vietnam is assured of Soviet and Chinese assistance, and there have been a large number of Chinese engineering and construction servicemen working in North Vietnam, mainly on railway rehabilitation to help the transporting of supplies from China.

THE ROLE OF SEATO

On the other side of the ideological fence, there is the Southeast Asian Treaty Organization, or SEATO, set up at American instigation in 1954 to cope with the consequences of the Communist military successes in Indochina. Thailand and the Philippines are the only Southeast Asian countries belonging to SEATO, the other members of which are the United States, Britain, France, Australia, and New Zealand. Pakistan withdrew in 1972, and France has been a sleeping member for some time. SEATO has hardly been an efficient military instrument on the model of NATO, and it was pretty ineffectual in the crisis in Laos and Vietnam in the early 1960s. In fact, the most important aspect of SEATO has been the American commitment, and the U.S. government has taken the position that its obligation to its allies in Southeast Asia under SEATO does not depend on the prior agreement of other signatories since the treaty obligation is individual as well as collective. Now that the Indochina war has been brought down to a local scale again, the crucial theater so far as SEATO is concerned is Thailand, and it looks as if SEATO will remain for a time as a cover for the U.S. commitment to help and retain a modest military presence in Thailand in order to assist its defenses against insurgency and subversion.

COMMONWEALTH DEFENSE PACT

It was always somewhat anomalous that Singapore and Malaysia did not join SEATO when they became independent. Instead they preferred to rely on their traditional defense relationship with Great Britain, extending that to include the friendly assistance of two nearer Commonwealth states, Australia and New Zealand. The Anglo-Malaysian Defense Agreement expired in 1971 but was immediately succeeded by a five-power agreement between Malaysia, Singapore, Britain, Australia, and New Zealand. This is not a formal treaty, but an arrangement spelled out in a public communique and exchange of letters between the governments. It merely commits those governments to "immediately consult together" in order to decide, in the event of any external threat to Malaysia or Singapore, what measures should be taken. On paper this may sound like a very loose arrangement, but it is buttressed by the presence in Malaysia and Singapore of a small combined force, known as ANZUK, supplied by the three external powers. At its peak ANZUK had three battalions, eight frigates and a submarine, two squadrons of Mirage III interceptor fighters, some maritime reconnaissance aircraft, and a few other supporting aircraft. In other words, it was a foreign presence of more psychological than combat significance.

The five-power arrangement made sense in Commonwealth terms, but it was difficult to explain in the Southeast Asian and ASEAN context, which for Malaysia and Singapore has now become more important. Carlos P. Romulo, the Philippine Foreign Minister, questioned publicly the rationale of the five-power arrangement, which he saw as conflicting with SEATO and which he therefore considered a farce. If the arrangement was aimed to deter external aggression, "why was this not sought to be undertaken by simply enrolling Malaysia and Singapore in SEATO?"[2] The answer was, of course, that Malaysia and Singapore were critical of the pro-American and anti-Chinese nature of SEATO; they did not wish to join the ranks of American camp followers, nor did they wish to reduce their options in foreign policy by joining what was to some extent a discredited anti-Communist bandwagon—although their anti-Communism was, if anything, more deeply felt in domestic terms than that of some other SEATO members.

In fact the five-power arrangement also has an uncertain future. It became clear soon after it started that the two local states had different motives for seeking the military help of their non-Asian Commonwealth friends. Malaysia saw it as a deterrent to the threat that would be created by a revived Indonesian claim to the Borneo states or by the reactivated Philippine claim to Sabah as a former part of the Sulu Sultanate. The fact that the Philippines is one of the potential aggressors in this scenario helps to explain why Malaysia was not attracted by SEATO. For Singapore, picturing its possible fate as a Chinese nut in a Malaysian-Indonesian nutcracker, the ANZUK force serves as a deterrent to Malaysian or Indonesian ultranationalism; the Commonwealth forces are also useful to Singapore economically and technologically. But the three external powers are now withdrawing even this modest presence. The process was begun by Australia when Whitlam's government decided to withdraw; it is likely to be followed by the British Labour government of 1974, acting under the pressure of the need to economize yet further on overseas defense expenditure. The five-power arrangement is therefore a transitional one to provide some measures of defense cooperation among its members for a limited period. It was not envisaged as a permanent arrangement and is not likely to evolve into anything long-lasting. In the period since it was inaugurated, both Singapore and Malaysia have built up their own defense forces, and so the five-power arrangement provided an umbrella under which they could acquire credible defense forces of their own. [3]

These are the only formal international defense arrangements in Southeast Asia, but there is a good measure of bilateral defense cooperation within the region. The armed forces of Malaysia and Indonesia collaborate in Sarawak against the Communist insurgents on their mutual border, and the same goes for the armies of Malaysia and Thailand on the northern Malaysian border. But these two examples of collaboration are somewhat weak as forerunners of regional defense cooperation. The Thai assistance to Malaysia on their mutual border is inhibited, whatever the contrary protestations in public, by the fact that Thailand fears that the Muslim provinces in the southernmost part of the Thai kingdom may ultimately opt for or be encouraged to join the Malaysian Federation on religious and cultural grounds and by Thai resentment at the incorporation into Malaysia during the colonial period of provinces that had at an earlier time been under Thai rule. In Borneo the military collaboration between Malaysia and Indonesia is slightly overshadowed by the feelings of uncertainty some Malaysians have over the long-term Indonesian intentions toward Sarawak and Sabah.

WILL ASEAN ASSUME A MILITARY ROLE?

What about ASEAN? Some observers see this regional organization as a potential security system, or as a loose political grouping that may gradually develop military overtones. These include some American leaders who would like to use such a development in the region. There are also leading Indonesians who advocate it, notably General Maraden Panggabean, the Commander-in-Chief of the Indonesian armed forces. Panggabean said at the end of 1970 that Indonesia would come to its neighbors' help if they were attacked (a remark immediately softened by Foreign Minister Malik, who claimed that it was moral and not material help that had been meant). A few weeks later Panggabean told the National Defense Institute, "More than just agreeing to it, I will arrange for a joint defense of ASEAN countries. Among other things, visits have been arranged and students exchanged but we have not yet come to an arms exchange."[4] The Chairman of the Philippines Senate, on a visit to Djakarta at the time, said that there was a "chance" of ASEAN's making a joint defense arrangement. Again Malik came in swiftly to qualify the impression that had been left: The idea was only "theoretically . . . under consideration, . . . it is by no means certain that it will be realized." The Foreign Minister added, significantly, the opinion that the idea did not conflict with the People's Assembly decision that Indonesia should not join military pacts.[5] But Malik stated a few weeks later, "Indonesia is against any form of military pacts," and in 1972 went on record as asserting that it would be impossible for ASEAN to become a military pact.[6]

An Indonesian scholar, Sutomo Roesnadi, has put this wavering Indonesian position in the following terms:

> It cannot be denied that certain groups exist in every ASEAN member country which want to convert ASEAN into a military alliance. Basically ASEAN is for promoting regional cooperation in the economic and cultural fields. Indonesian civilian and military leaders do not believe in the effectiveness of such a military pact. They are of the opinion that a military alliance is obsolete in the light of the emergence of guerrilla warfare and subversion. Military pacts certainly are

not an effective form of defense for they may weaken
national defense and identity. Apart from that, military pacts may provoke other countries to strengthen
their armaments and form counter-military pacts. [7]

Governments of the other countries of ASEAN have made the same
point. When the Foreign Ministers of ASEAN gathered in Kuala
Lumpur in November 1971 to consider how they should react to the
Chinese entry into the United Nations and to discuss Malaysia's
neutralization plan, and when it transpired that many delegations
were bringing with them military advisers and leaders of their
armed forces, Utusan Melayu, the newspaper reflecting the opinion
of the Malaysian ruling party, insisted that neutralization was a
"nonmilitary political plan" and that ASEAN was only a "loose" pact
and not a military or defense alliance. [8]

BILATERAL DEFENSE COOPERATION

But if there is still an official reluctance to enter into a regional defense pact or to inject a security element into ASEAN,
there are no such inhibitions about bilateral cooperation between
the armed forces within the region. As Foreign Minister Malik
said, after he had made clear that Indonesia did not approve of a
military pact, "But this does not mean we cannot have military cooperation in maintaining our national security, such as the one we
have with Malaysia on the Sarawak border to keep out Communist
guerrillas. "[9] And Sutomo Roesnadi, in the same paper where he
described how Indonesia did not believe in the validity or relevance
of military pacts, offered the following addition: "It should not,
however, be interpreted as a complete rejection of the idea of military cooperation. The Indonesian-Indian military cooperation in the
1950s and the recent Malaysian-Indonesian border security agreement are examples of Indonesia's willingness to involve herself in
joint military exercises, as well as joint campaigns to eliminate the
common enemy on her borders. " Indonesia was willing to share her
experience in dealing with Communist subversion and other insurgencies, and it would enhance the defense capability of ASEAN or other
neighboring countries if military information and training were exchanged. "It is the considered opinion of the Indonesian government, "
he concluded, "that the possibility of a foreign military invasion of
Indonesia or of any ASEAN member country, which will lead to an
open war, is still remote. "[10]

And it goes without saying that bilateral military cooperation
between the individual members of ASEAN can logically lead to a

degree of multilateral cooperation, even if it is not within the formal scope of the rules of the Association. The Indonesian naval Chief-of-Staff, Admiral R. Sudomo, has offered the opinion that military cooperation among ASEAN countries would be acceptable provided that it did not involve either regional ties or any interference in internal affairs.[11] The Philippine Deputy Foreign Minister, Jose Ingles, has said that the Philippines would support military cooperation among ASEAN members, even outside the framework of SEATO, to promote regional security.[12] And in Bangkok the Nation, the outspoken Bangkok newspaper, argued in 1972 that since President Suharto had agreed during his visits to the Philippines and Australia to hold joint military exercises with those countries, "the next logical step is to bring about military cooperation among ASEAN countries, strictly among themselves with no foreign forces involved."[13] This view was attributed to diplomatic forces in Bangkok, and although it was subsequently denied,[14] there is little doubt that there are a number of national figures within ASEAN who would go along with it. It remains to be seen how far this will go in practice. One should perhaps add that there is a degree of naval cooperation between Malaysia and Indonesia arising out of their joint deinternationalization of the Straits of Malacca, and that there is similarly a fairly strong connection between the Philippine and Indonesian armed services. Indonesia has given military training of various kinds to officers from a number of countries, including Malaysia, Cambodia, and the Philippines.

The November 1971 meeting of Foreign Ministers, the one that issued the Kuala Lumpur Declaration, was important in military terms. It was attended, among others, by the Philippine Deputy Chief-of-Staff General Fidel Ramos, General Charis Suhud of Indonesia, and General Lek Neomali of Thailand. It was argued by the Indonesians and Filipinos that it was no longer possible to separate questions of defense and security from questions of political policy, especially where relations with China were concerned.[15] The Thai delegation had no need to make any explanation, since it represented a government that was overtly a military dictatorship.

Finally, one must consider the extent to which governments in the region conceive themselves as owing a moral duty, in the absence of any legal obligation, to assist a neighbor against the unlikely event of aggression. The smaller countries have not made any authentic or considered statement on this, but Foreign Minister Malik recently said on behalf of Indonesia: "If Singapore or Malaysia is attacked and they ask Indonesia for help, we certainly cannot remain idle as we are morally bound to help them."[16] Indonesia is, of course, the country best placed to provide military help to one of the smaller countries. But it is widely agreed that this eventuality is so unlikely that it does not have to be seriously considered.

THE MODEL OF ARMED NEUTRALITY

In the end, whatever arrangements, informal or otherwise, are arrived at for the collaboration of the military forces of Southeast Asia, their effectiveness will depend on the efficiency of each national force and the domestic will to defend the nation against attack. Tun Razak was particularly impressed by this factor after his visit to Switzerland and other small European countries concerned for their neutrality. "It is important for Malaysia," he said to Malaysian reporters in Europe in 1972, "to have some kind of internal defense based on the Swiss system where every citizen gets military training. It is thought important for the people themselves to have the collective will to survive as a nation and to be prepared to defend the country."[17] But the comment next day in the Straits Times that it was "improbable that Malaysia will wish to emulate the Swiss exactly"[18] was well put, and it is indeed hard to see that this degree of defense enthusiasm could be achieved in Malaysia or in any other ASEAN country with the possible exception of Singapore, where there is already the infrastructure for the self-image of a siege state and where Chinese discipline lends itself to this kind of development.

One of the Western commentators on the Malaysian neutralization plan has pointed out to Southeast Asia that the successful examples of neutrality in Europe are dependent on being heavily armed, and that Sweden spends more per head on defense than any other country in the world.[19] Thanat Khoman, the former Foreign Minister of Thailand, in an influential article widely publicized in the region in 1973, argued that neutrality involved the prohibition of foreign bases but that this did not mean that "the neutral nations should allow themselves to be caught militarily unprepared." He urged the necessity of "armed neutrality" so that they could protect themselves, initially at least, against a conventional armed attack.[20] But in spite of the unimpressive figures on the military balance in the region (see Appendix B), such a state of affairs is far from being achieved in Southeast Asia.

It is to be presumed that as the search for regional protection from big power conflict proceeds in the years to come, the national forces within Southeast Asia will progressively improve, arm, and train themselves to the point where they genuinely constitute a credible deterrent. The only risk, perhaps, is that in this process the weight of military opinion in the political affairs of each state will be enhanced to the point where military dictatorship could become an even graver threat than it is now in those countries that have so far escaped it. It is perhaps not accidental that the neutralization proposal came from one of the Southeast Asian states that has never had to face that particular threat.

The military implications of the neutralization proposal for the Southeast Asian states have not been spelled out in detail, and this was one of the most delicate subjects of the secret discussions by senior ASEAN officials during the period of 1972-74. They must presumably involve some degree of multilateral collaboration on security matters, if only effectively to ensure the successful peaceful settlement of intraregional disputes without external interference. The Malaysian philosophy underlying neutralization is that an outright attack on any part of Southeast Asia by an external power could only occur in the event of a general world war in which the area would be supported by other powers and would in any case be ineffectual in keeping the powers out. At the same time, insurgency is an internal problem, in Tun Razak's view, and one that has to be resolved domestically. On these premises there is obviously no need for any of the Southeast Asian states to seek the protection of an outside power.[21] Tun Razak's colleague, Ghazali bin Shafie, has argued that the arrangements which have so far been tried in Southeast Asia for international help against subversion and infiltration across borders have not proved effective: "The alternative security arrangements in terms of a balance of power with offshore American air power, or a purely Asian balance of power on an Asian collective security pact, are unlikely to prove effective or credible, even if in fact one or other variation could be constituted."[22]

This view would not be accepted by some other Southeast Asian leaders. For the immediate future, albeit for a temporary period, the Thai, Philippine, and Singapore governments are certainly pinning their faith on offshore American air and sea power as a deterrent against both Soviet and potential Chinese interference in the region. Indonesia would sympathize with this latter view, although she would not say so in public. As with other aspects of the neutralization proposal, the essential conflict of opinion within Southeast Asia is between those who put the short-term future first and those who place more importance on the longer term. All are agreed, however, on the need to build up their own individual defenses and, with some reservations and within limits, to encourage the habit of working together in regional military circles rather in the same way that cooperation is being encouraged in diplomatic and business circles.

NOTES

1. See The Military Balance 1973-1974 (London: International Institute of Strategic Studies, 1974), especially pp. 51-52; see also Appendix B below.

2. New Nation, Singapore, 4 May 1971; Manila Chronicle, 2 May 1971.

3. See T. B. Millar, "The Five-Power Defence Agreement and South East Asian Security," Pacific Community, vol. 3, no. 2, January 1972, p. 341.

4. See O. G. Roeder in FEER, 13 February 1971; also T. B. Millar, "Prospects for Regional Security Cooperation in Southeast Asia," in Mark W. Zacher and R. Stephen Milne, eds., Conflict and Stability in Southeast Asia (New York: Anchor Press, 1974), p. 464; and K. K. Nair, "Balancing Interests in ASEAN," STK, 28 June 1973.

5. Roeder, op. cit.

6. BP, 9 March 1971; and New Nation, Singapore, 15 March 1972.

7. In Yong Mun Cheong, ed., Trends in Indonesia (Singapore: Institute of South East Asian Studies, 1972), p. 67.

8. Utusan Melayu, Kuala Lumpur, 24 November 1971.

9. BP, 9 March 1971.

10. In Yong Mun Cheong, ed., op. cit., p. 68.

11. New Nation, Singapore, 24 April 1972.

12. BP, 20 April 1972.

13. See STK, 25 February 1972.

14. See STK editorial, 3 March 1972.

15. New Nation, Singapore, 26 November 1971.

16. STK, 14 February 1973.

17. STK, 2 October 1972.

18. STK, 3 October 1972.

19. Brian Crozier, "Neutral Dreams in South East Asia," Daily Telegraph, London, 5 July 1972.

20. Japan Times, 22 April 1973.

21. See Goh Cheng Teik's article in STK, 23 February 1973.

22. FEER, 27 August 1972.

18

Southeast Asia has great economic potential. It is richly en-
dowed by nature, its resources are easily accessible because of the
proximity of most of its important agricultural and mineral areas
to seaports, and those resources have for the most part a long history of exploitation (albeit under colonial auspices) for world markets. Although the region embraces only 3 percent of the world's
total land area and 8 percent of its population, it produces 98 percent of its abaca, 80 percent of its natural rubber, well over 50 percent of its coconuts and tin, 33 percent of its palm oil, and 20 percent of its rice and pineapples. The list of the region's plantation
crops extends to cocoa, tobacco, tea, coffee, and spices, not to
mention the timber industry. More recently its mineral riches have
come into the limelight, with major new oil, nickel, copper, and
bauxite extraction projects concentrated in Indonesia, the Philippines, and Malaysia. Indonesia is already the eleventh largest oil
producing nation in the world.

The average level of national income per head in Southeast
Asia is about U.S. $180. This is not to be compared with the
$3,600 average national income per head of the industrialized na-
tions of Western Europe, North America, Japan, and Australasia.
Nor can it be compared with the figures for Latin America and the
Middle East, where oil is such an artificial contributor to this sta-
tistic. Its true comparison is with the $140 which is the average
for the whole of the rest of Asia, including the vast millions of India
and China, though not Japan. Singapore, indeed, has the highest
standard of living on the Asian continent after Japan, while Malaysia
and the Philippines also enjoy a far higher average standard of
living than the larger countries of their continent.

161

TWO ECONOMIC MODELS IN THE REGION

There are two economic models in the region. North Vietnam, Burma, and to a lesser extent Cambodia have taken a socialistic path that attaches more importance to the spirit of self-reliance and to social justice than to production or economic growth. The other states have chosen the conventional Western pattern, leaving development primarily to private enterprise (domestic and foreign) and regarding inequality as a price worth paying temporarily for the creation of an economic development base. Indeed Malaysia is hailed, particularly by Americans, as one of the Third World's success stories for the free-enterprise open-economy system. In the mid-1960s Indonesia moved from the socialist to the capitalist group, which in the late 1960s and early 1970s was scoring annual real growth in GNP in the 6 percent to 8 percent range, or double the average growth rate for the Third World as a whole. But there would be immense difficulty in realizing any significant economic collaboration between Burma and North Vietnam on the one hand and the remaining Southeast Asian states on the other.

Even the "capitalist" countries of the region fall into two categories whose economic policies are diverging. Indonesia and the Philippines, with large populations pressing on limited land, have chosen a controlled economy in order to shake themselves free from their colonial legacy of dependence on land-based exports. Malaysia and Thailand, by contrast, with an abundance of natural resources easing the pressure of the population on the land, have seen no need to break with the past and have gone on pursuing noninterventionist policies designed to encourage the export of primary products. Now the former countries are striving for agricultural self-sufficiency, while Malaysia and Thailand are going for self-sufficiency in manufactures. So sharp is this distinction that two economists have concluded that it "precludes the evolution of a meaningful basis for intraregional trade integration."[1]

A survey of Southeast Asia's economic prospects during the 1970s and 1980s, recently carried out by the Asian Development Bank, sets out the evidence for continued optimism for the region.[2] While agriculture is likely to remain the weak link in the economic chain, and population growth is expected to maintain its current annual rate of about 2.7 percent, big developments are forecast for minerals, manufacturing industry, tourism, and trade. Exports of metallic minerals are likely to expand fivefold between 1971 and 1990, and there seem to be good chances of new oil strikes both underground and offshore. The volume of foreign trade should treble by 1990, and manufacturing should score annual growth of between 8 percent and 11 percent (especially chemicals and fertilizer, wood processing, cement, shipbuilding, mineral refining, textiles, and simple light engineering or electronic articles such as transistor radios). Singapore is already used by several Western corporations, including Rollei, the German camera maker; Phillips, the Dutch electrical giant; and Beecham, the British pharmaceutical firm, as a manufacturing base for export to world markets.

The region as a whole has extended a warm invitation to foreign capital, offering tax privileges and other inducements. Only recently has a more wary and selective approach toward the foreign investor become apparent, partly because of the rising self-confidence of indigenous enterprise and partly because of the political backlash that a too powerful foreign economic presence can release. The student demonstrations against Kakuei Tanaka, the Japanese Prime Minister, during his tour of the ASEAN states in January 1974 were an indicator of the intensity of feeling against foreign commercial influences.

It can thus be said that the Southeast Asian countries are better placed for the foreseeable future than many others in the world with regard to their potential for economic development and therefore for economic collaboration. There traditionally has been a considerable degree of economic cooperation among the Indochina states, reflecting their common heritage of development under the French colonial aegis, although their involvement in hostilities of one kind or another throughout the post-World War II period has hindered their development along these lines. Burma has stayed out of regional cooperation projects, and so the burden of initiative has been left with the five ASEAN countries, which have for many years now been building up the habit of working and consulting together.

"For the present," the Singaporean Prime Minister declared in 1972, "ASEAN does not aim at integrating a regional economy."[3] Although the idea of a Southeast Asian common market is frequently bandied about in the region, by politicians rather than economists, even the politicians have now begun to realize that there is simply no chance in the near future of realizing such a project. Adam Malik, the Foreign Minister of Indonesia, once joked that it was difficult enough for Indonesia to establish a common market within its own borders (because of the autonomous instincts of the various islands and their ruling elites), let alone attempt anything so ambitious as a common market stretching across national frontiers.[4]

THE UNITED NATIONS RECOMMENDATIONS

Nevertheless the initial groundwork is beginning to be laid for a gradual movement toward commercial and industrial collaboration. In 1968 ASEAN concluded an agreement with the United Nations—

principally with ECAFE in Bangkok, United Nations Conference on Trade and Development (UNCTAD) in Geneva, and Food and Agriculture Organization (FAO) in Rome—for an expert study to be made on the possibilities for economic cooperation. The U.N. team, led by G. Kansu of UNCTAD and advised among others by the distinguished Cambridge Professor of Economics E. A. G. Robinson, worked from 1970 to 1972 and produced more than 40 papers on various aspects of the economic collaboration possibilities for ASEAN. The principal recommendations were brought together in a report that was eventually printed by the Malaysian government in 1973 and whose 147 pages provided an excellent summary of the possibilities.[5]

The analysis of the U.N. experts' report began by pointing out that although these five countries include only 5 percent of the world population, they enjoy a gross domestic product per head that is twice as large as that of India, and if Indonesia is left aside, it reaches approximately U.S. $250, which is much higher than Egypt or Morocco. Their average annual rate of economic growth was 4.5 percent in the first half of the 1960s but rose to 6 percent in the second half of that decade, and the U.N. experts estimated the growth rate for the 1970s at 6.5 percent, "among the highest in any part of the world."

These five countries are now conducting foreign trade that aggregates approximately U.S. $20 billion a year, although only 15 percent of that trade is among themselves. Even this proportion is exaggerated by the inclusion of Singapore, the traditional entrepot port; if the other four countries are considered alone the proportion of their intratrade falls to 6 percent. The likely growth of imports into the ASEAN region in the years to come is in manufactured goods, for which the market is worth around $5 billion.

So far, little more than 3 percent of this valuable market is met from within the region because its export industries are either in their infancy or else geared to more distant markets. Import substitution manufacturing of the simpler consumer goods for domestic national markets has taken place. But the next stage of industrialization should be the making of more complex products that are already mass-produced in large-scale plants in the West and Japan. Only by collaboration among themselves can the ASEAN countries hope to become efficient and competitive producers of these goods.

A newsprint mill, to take only one example, would have to produce at least half a million tons a year to be competitive in prices with the rest of the world. Total ASEAN consumption will only reach that level in about 1980. To take another example, an economically viable automobile factory should have an annual run of over half a million vehicles, while the present annual demand in the five ASEAN countries together is less than 200,000. The same applies to chemical fertilizer, steel, and a number of other products.

As the work of the U.N. team progressed during 1970 and 1972, the experts became aware that the governments were not ready for close industrial integration. The report was not, therefore, naive enough to press the arguments for a common market, customs union, or free trade area. It did urge limited trade liberalization in carefully selected commodities, and it recommended "a limited scheme for cooperation in the development of new industrial projects," supplemented by specific measures of collaboration in the monetary and financial fields as well as in shipping and tourism.

One method of achieving these goals would be to cut tariffs within the ASEAN group, but this is politically unacceptable because it would lead to a polarization of industrial growth that would favor those countries (particularly Singapore) that are already better equipped to be the host for new industry. It is also acknowledged that the countries within ASEAN might become too interdependent, particularly for basic key commodities, for comfort.

The U.N. report therefore concentrated on a selective program of liberalization of trade, carefully balanced to allow each of the five nations to benefit more or less equally and thus to keep pace with one another.

For the purpose of gaining international acceptance and qualifying under Part 4 of the General Agreement on Tariff and Trade (GATT), the ASEAN governments were asked to declare their intention "to create by a date sufficiently far ahead to give ample time for adjustment . . . an ASEAN Free Trade Area." This would involve a commitment to remove all tariffs and quota restrictions, and the U.N. team suggested that 1990 should be the target date. In the interim period a series of tariff-cutting negotiations should be held every year or even more frequently, covering initially those products that are manufactured competitively in one ASEAN country but are still supplied from more distant sources in others. Textiles, footwear, processed foodstuff, household appliances, pharmaceuticals, and cement are possible products on this list.

On Industrial Collaboration

The most controversial element in any report of this kind concerns industrial cooperation. The U.N. team suggested to ASEAN two quite different techniques. One of these was for private industrialists to concoct complementarity agreements in their own sectors and then to seek government approval that would facilitate the elimination of intra-ASEAN tariffs and the substitution of a common external tariff on these goods, as well as fiscal or financial incentives to make them for the regional market.

But the second and more important U.N. proposal was to allocate major industrial projects to the five countries, on the basis of a preagreed "package deal." A number of projects were identified that could be viable economically only if they served the regional market rather than the five small national markets. The U.N. team suggested ways of distributing these projects fairly on the basis of each country giving unidirectional tariff preferences for each product only to the ASEAN country of manufacture.

The thirteen projects recommended for this package were nitrogenous fertilizer, phosphate fertilizer, carbon black (mainly used to stiffer rubber tires), soda ash (used in glass, paper, soap, and chemical manufacture), caprolactam (the raw material for nylon), DMT (dimethyl terephthalate, a raw material for polyester synthetic fiber), ethylene glycol (the other raw material for polyester, also used in explosives, etc.), newsprint, sheet glass, small internal combustion engines, compressors (for refrigerators and air-conditioners), typewriters, and steel billets. [6]

The total capital investment needed for these thirteen projects was some $750 million between now and 1980, and the estimated capital saving of building for the ASEAN market (instead of constructing smaller national plants of the same aggregate capacity) would be $240 million or 25 percent. Average operating costs would be 20 percent lower for these projects than for the comparable sets of smaller national plants.

It would still be necessary to provide some tariff protection, although not on the scale that the smaller national plants would require. The caprolactam plant, for example, would need about 15 percent protection, but the typewriter factory should be fully competitive by 1980, and many of the others would not need even temporary protection.

To "go regional" on these thirteen projects would not signify a dramatic move into economic integration, since they would represent less than 2 percent of all manufacturing output within ASEAN and would absorb only 1.2 percent of all capital formation (3 percent of capital formation in manufacturing industry).

The allocation problem is the most delicate one, and so the U.N. team suggested not only detailed criteria but also seven possible "package deals." In one of these, for instance, Singapore gets the steel mill; Indonesia nitrogenous fertilizer and caprolactam; Malaysia compressors, typewriters, and engines; the Philippines carbon black and newsprint; and Thailand phosphate fertilizer, glass, and the other chemical materials. Other ways of dealing the cards, with the net balance of advantage and disadvantage, were carefully set out.

Adam Malik, the Indonesian Foreign Minister, may have had this page of the report in mind when he told reporters after the

Ministerial consideration of the U.N. report in Singapore in April 1972 that the steel mill should be allocated to Singapore because of its geographical advantages. But he was speaking as a diplomat rather than as a Minister responsible for national development, and U.N. officials have gained the private impression that Indonesia, potentially the dominant member of ASEAN but with a long lead to make up after the economic neglect of the Sukarno era, is not really ready to cooperate on industry.

The recommendations of the U.N. team went beyond manufacturing industries. They ranged over the whole gamut of economic life. They envisaged some coordination in economic planning compatible with national autonomy. They looked to the standardization of trade procedures, administration, and documentation, and indeed to common standards of all kinds between these five countries.

On Agriculture and Forestry

In agriculture it was suggested that there was room for joint action in the fields of chemical fertilizer and insecticide production and distribution and in agricultural research (especially research on maize, the Pakchong Center in Thailand being considerably behind the longer established International Rice Research Institute in the Philippines or the Malaysian Rubber Research Institute). But the report admitted that "it is not yet clear how far in the future ASEAN countries may wish to open their markets for foodstuffs to each other."

Forestry is a different matter. Timber exports from the ASEAN region amounted to $550 million in 1969, the second most important export line after rubber. Only about one-third of log production, however, is processed at home. There are problems of transportation, and the total value of the freights paid on tropical log exports from the ASEAN countries has been put at $250 million, the equivalent of an additional 60 percent over and above the value of the logs themselves. It was therefore recommended that the ASEAN countries acquire a fleet of log carriers, although the U.N. experts hastened to point out that high shipping rates are not wholly a consequence of the monopoly position of the Conference Lines but are also due to inadequate port facilities, low storage factors, and inefficient handling. The loading rates at many ASEAN outports are reported to be in some cases only one-fifth or one-tenth of the rates achieved in Korea or Taiwan. A Central Freight Booking Center and standard formats of contract would assist this trade, as would a Trade Promotion Center with offices in most of the larger timber buying countries stocked with samples, leaflets, and grading rules. It was considered important to extend to other countries the

Malaysian practice of enforcing strict grading rules for logs, sawn wood, and plywood.

An all-ASEAN Timber Export Board should ensure that the interests of this trade are kept in mind internationally. The report pointed out that the European market for ASEAN sawn timber, for example, is limited to some half-dozen commercial timbers. And yet 2, 500 timber-producing species have been identified in the forests of Sarawak, although data on their properties are available for fewer than one hundred. It would be important to standardize the nomenclature, among other things. In the long run, since forestry is shifting from the lowlands to the hills, with consequential problems of erosion and reforestation, it would be advantageous to develop intensively managed forest reserves that would take the form of vertical industry comprising sawmills, manufacturing shops, plywood factories and pulp mills, and suitable infrastructure.

On Shipping Developments

This leads to the shipping sector. It seems that the total net overseas payment by ASEAN countries for shipping is certainly $350 million a year and may be considerably higher. Although the inward and outward movements in liner vessels and movements of liquid bulk are reasonably well balanced, the dry cargo shipped in bulk is very unbalanced, with exports running at about six times imports into the ASEAN countries. If ASEAN wishes to reduce its heavy expenditure on shipping, it should increase the efficiency of the whole system of sea transport at each stage and should increase its participation in the operation of ships.

One economy is to use large ships rather than small, another is to speed up loading and discharging, and a third is to ship in bulk. A study of the rubber export trade from Malaysia showed that about 80 percent of exports were shipped in consignments under one thousand tons, while less than 1 percent were shipped in consignments of over two thousand tons. There could be considerable savings on the basis of cooperative improvements in shipping using a Central ASEAN Freight Booking Center.

Containerization will play an important role in this but will, of course, as the report noted, "involve agreed decisions as to which of the possible deep-water ports in the region should be developed as central container ports." Singapore may be at odds with Indonesia and Malaysia on this matter. The anticipated growth in dry cargoes moving in intra-ASEAN trade is likely to "require complete rethinking of the shipping policies." Effective competition could be provided with Conference Lines by bulking cargoes wherever

possible and using ASEAN resources to operate bulk carriers. The
possibility of multinational cooperation in shipping could take the form
of pooling, joint operating, or joint shipowning. The United Nations
invited the ASEAN governments to take their choice.

As for the financing of development, the United Nations recommended that a regional development corporation be set up, and it suggested that the proportion contributed by each government should be
35 percent from Indonesia, 29 percent from the Philippines, 18 percent from Thailand, 12 percent from Malaysia, and 6 percent from
Singapore. The U.N. experts noted that intra-ASEAN payments are
made almost wholly in sterling or U.S. dollars, with the final payments being effected in London or New York. They urged that an
ASEAN Clearing Union be established to clear payments between the
five countries. The total value of internal trade within ASEAN was estimated as $1.4 billion in 1968, of which about $900 million would theoretically have been capable of being compensated by bookkeeping trans-
actions without the actual use of foreign exchange. If one discounts
the requirements of the oil companies and multinationals and of some
trades, like rice, that are conducted on credit terms, the actual trade
flows that could have been handled by an ASEAN clearing mechanism
might have been only $400 million. But by 1980 this figure could well
rise to $1 billion. A regional reinsurance pool to redistribute business
among companies in the ASEAN area was recommended, and proposals
were made for cooperation in export credit finance and insurance.

The report concluded by requesting its public approval in
principle by the ASEAN Foreign Minister. It then suggested that a
group to coordinate economic policy be set up, composed of the most
senior officials responsible for economic planning and the chairmen
of the Investment Boards of the various ASEAN countries; it also
recommended the establishment of a Steering Committee for Trade
and Industrial Negotiations. The experts noted that the preconcep-
tions within ASEAN "include a very healthy skepticism of the results
to be expected from excessive government control and from over-
large bureaucratic organizations." It identified the problem as one
of reaching the right compromise between overloading too small a
central organization and creating an excessively large bureaucracy
that could frustrate decision making.

RELUCTANCE OF GOVERNMENTS

But one comes back again and again to the industrial proposals
as the most controversial and significant. Two kinds of apprehen-
sion were noted and rebutted in the U.N. report. The first of these
was the fear that industrial development might become concentrated
in certain countries or that growth might be polarized. "It is feared

that if certain industries are encouraged and assisted to grow up in one country, other countries will have permanently to surrender the opportunity of entering that industry. " The fear is legitimate and real, but the experts argued that what they were proposing was a means of ensuring that there should be a number of nexuses of growth spread all over the countries of ASEAN in such a way that no one country should seriously or permanently fall behind. At the rate at which ASEAN is developing there should be scope after a few years for at least one additional unit in the same industry, and for many industries the second units could be established in a different country from the one that hosted the first unit.

The second area of anxiety concerned balance of payments. It was feared that the cooperation proposals would involve each government in a commitment to import products from other ASEAN countries more expensive than similar goods available elsewhere, and that this could imperil the country's balance of payments. Singapore, still largely a free port, is especially anxious on this score. Detailed arguments were put out to minimize these fears. It was pointed out that "a small country cannot escape a higher measure of dependence." If there is going to be cooperation in ASEAN then the individual countries implicitly agree to increase their dependence on each other, but it is a limited dependence. For all the products under consideration there are alternative sources of supply outside ASEAN. Suppose Malaysia is supplying ASEAN with chemical fertilizer and the Philippines are supplying it with typewriters; in the unlikely event of a war or some other crisis causing a trade stoppage between Malaysia and the Philippines, Malaysia could temporarily get its typewriters from Japan or the United States and the Philippines could get its fertilizers from Japan or India. Each of the individual projects set up on a regional basis could explicitly include training facilities available to all the other ASEAN countries to enable them to develop that industry as quickly as possible when the time comes. But these anxieties have prevented the ASEAN Foreign Ministers from taking any real action on the U.N. report.

It was possible for Goh Cheng Teik, a lecturer at the University of Malaysia, to argue in 1971 that it was "futile" to talk about a common market for Southeast Asia but that it was "no sin for the rich Southeast Asian states to gang up." Goh added that "the capital resources and the purchasing power of their populations can effect change in a Brunei-Malaysia-Singapore context but they will become diluted, if placed in a Southeast Asian context, to such an extent as to be of little use."[7] This is by no means an official view, but it reflects some of the inequalities within ASEAN that act as a hindrance to cooperation. Indonesia in particular is jealous of her own economic potential, and to that extent is unwilling to cooperate with the industrialization of her neighbors.

Another factor that is sometimes overlooked is the growing desire by the Southeast Asian intelligentsia to rid itself of the economic dominance of the Overseas Chinese community. Economic growth, especially industrial, is very often seen to benefit the local Chinese business community more than the indigenous people, and regional development holds out the same risks. As the Indonesian writer and editor Mochtar Lubis put it in 1973, "The development of easier movement of capital, technology, investments and the breaking down of the impediments which bar the way to close cooperation should not mean the perpetuation of the present unbalanced economic strength between foreign minorities and indigenous majorities. "[8]

Apart from all this, the individual governments find it difficult enough to prosecute energetically their own national development, let alone find surplus energy for integrating them with their neighbors. Not only are skilled personnel in short supply, but the entire infrastructure for development is weak, and this reinforces the sentiment that priority should go to national rather than international development. A final handicap faced by those who would like to see a movement toward economic integration in ASEAN is the wealth of duplication and overlapping of regional development plans, programs, proposals, and projects.

DUPLICATION OF EFFORTS

The Asian and Pacific Council (ASPAC) has an Economic and Social Center called ECOCEN, whose founding director, Ammuay Virivan, is one of Thailand's most energetic economic officials. ECOCEN's province excludes Indonesia and Singapore, which are not members, but includes South Korea and Taiwan and indeed Australia and New Zealand as well. In practice ECOCEN cooperates with Indonesia and Singapore, but the presence of Korea and particularly of Taiwan makes it difficult for ECOCEN to gear itself to a genuine ASEAN effort. [9] ECOCEN has taken much of the initiative in promoting the automobile developments whereby international corporations like Ford, General Motors, and even Mitsubishi are producing relatively cheap automobiles in Southeast Asia in the hope that they will penetrate the regional market on the basis of complementation of production. [10] Ford Asian Pacific, for example, envisages fitting together engines from Taiwan, electronic and plastic components from Singapore, diesel engines from South Korea, gasoline engines from Thailand, and axles and transmission equipment from Indonesia for assembly in Malaysia of automobiles to be sold throughout the region. [11] The defect of this kind of scheme from the ASEAN point of view is that some stages of assembly and production are envisaged outside ASEAN—especially in Korea, Australia, and Taiwan.

Another organization that contributes greatly to regional economic developments in Southeast Asia is the Asian Industrial Development Council (AIDC), which is studying schemes for joint ventures involving both ASEAN and non-ASEAN countries. One scheme, prepared by ECAFE, is for a $265 million petrochemical plant to serve the Philippine, Malaysian, Singaporean, and Indonesian markets, to be located in either the Philippines or Singapore. [12]

AIDC also has sent a mission of Japanese experts to survey a project for a regional steel billet plant to integrate with existing steel mills not only in the ASEAN countries but also in Taiwan. AIDC includes not only the ASEAN countries but also Australia, New Zealand, India, Iran, and Pakistan and, to the northeast, Japan, South Korea, South Vietnam, Hong Kong, Cambodia, and Laos. It has launched its own Asian Industrial Survey under H. C. Vos, Director of the Netherlands Economic Institute, to study the potential for industrialization in the larger area of Southeast Asia including but not limited to ASEAN. [13] Even the Food and Agricultural Organization has produced a newsprint survey for Asia by a firm of Finnish consultants that recommends five new mills to be set up between 1975 and 1983, three of them in India and Pakistan, one on the west coast of Malaysia, and one in West Java. [14]

Further complicating these overlappings are private bodies like the Southeast Asian Businessmen's Council (SEABEC), which was formed in Bangkok at the beginning of 1971 with the help of the Stanford Research Institute, the body that had also helped to launch the Pacific Basin Economic Consultative Committee (PBECC), comprising New Zealand, Australia, the United States, Canada, and Japan. But at least ASEAN has now started a confederation of its own Chambers of Commerce and Industry, ASEAN-CCI; it had its inaugural meeting in Djakarta in April 1972. ECAFE provides a number of competing initiatives including the Asian Clearing Union and the Asian Reserve Bank. [15] In the field of insurance there is the Asian Reinsurance Pool, set up at the beginning of 1972, which includes most of the ASEAN countries but also Taiwan and South Korea. [16] The Asian Coconut Community also embraces most of the ASEAN countries, but along with Sri Lanka and India. SEACEN, the Southeast Asian Group of Central Banks, is another competing body; it was founded by Malaysia and Thailand but has not extended its empire to embrace Sri Lanka, Laos, South Vietnam, Nepal, and Cambodia as well as the other ASEAN nations. It has been active in starting training and research centers and in concerting international diplomacy at the International Monetary Fund. [17] It is to be noted, however, that there is now a Committee of ASEAN Central Banks and Monetary Authorities, which held its inaugural meeting in Singapore in the middle of 1972.

HOPES FOR AN ASEAN INITIATIVE

All this shows that the desire for regional cooperation is strong but that it is somewhat diffused and disorganized. Eventually ASEAN is likely to emerge as the strongest framework for the most important of these economic collaboration ventures, if only because it has the best record so far for political coexistence. It is a matter of regret that the ASEAN governments have not felt able so far to endorse unambiguously the surprisingly limited and practical recommendations of the United Nations. The advisory committee of senior officials unanimously approved these in principle at a meeting in Bali in July 1972, and it was hoped at the time that there might be an ASEAN Declaration on the lines suggested by the U.N. experts, to be made by the Foreign Ministers at their Pattaya conference in 1973. [18]

But neither the Pattaya meeting nor the following one in 1974 responded to the challenge, and it was left to subsequent meetings to take a firm stand on the U.N. report. Meanwhile the ASEAN Permanent Committee on Commerce and Industry, meeting in Singapore in August 1972, set in motion the long and arduous process of working toward cooperation. It was agreed to establish a study group to begin work early in 1973 in Indonesia toward establishing uniformity of trade and tariff classifications—a sine qua non of any kind of economic cooperation.

This is perhaps a reminder of the length of the path ASEAN has to tread before it can begin to prosecute its economic collaboration in any meaningful way. Something a little more dramatic than the positions taken so far at the annual meetings of Foreign Ministers will, however, be needed if the economic self-reliance of the ASEAN region is to be convincingly presented as a factor in world diplomacy. There has never yet been a meeting of the five ministers responsible for economic development within each of the five governments. Only when this meeting occurs could one begin to say that economic cooperation in ASEAN has made a significant start.

NOTES

1. John C. H. Fei and Douglas S. Paauw, "International Economic Aspects of Southeast Asian Development, " NDE, p. 40.

2. Asian Development Bank, Southeast Asia's Economy in the 1970s (London: Longman, 1971).

3. STS, 14 April 1972.

4. The Economist, 23 March 1968.

5. Economic Co-operation for ASEAN: Report of a United Nations Team (no date).

6. For details, see Dick Wilson, "Economic Co-operation within ASEAN, " Pacific Community, vol. 5, no. 1, October 1973.

7. STS, 14 June 1971.

8. New Nation, Singapore, 8 February 1973.

9. See Anthony Haas's articles in New Nation, Singapore, 3 February and 21 June 1972.

10. See Sixto Roxas in The Times, London, 8 August 1972; also Sunday Times, Singapore, 31 October 1972.

11. Japan Times, 23 July 1971; The Asian, Hong Kong, 14 January 1973.

12. The Asian, Hong Kong, 6 February 1972.

13. See Anthony Haas in New Nation, Singapore, 11 May 1971.

14. Sunday Times, Singapore, 20 February 1972.

15. See the articles by N. K. Sarkar, Phuey Ungphakorn, and Benito Legarda, Jr. in FEER, 1 April 1972.

16. Financial Times, 12 July 1972.

17. STS, 15 May 1971.

18. The Nation, Bangkok, 12 July 1972; The Asian, Hong Kong, 16 July 1972.

19

POLITICAL UNITY
AND DISUNITY

"Our vision for the future, " declared the Malaysian Prime Minister at the time his neutralization proposal was being discussed, "is that of a Community of Southeast Asia. "[1] Since there has been no progress toward the integration of the sovereign states of Southeast Asia, such an ideal is obviously held in the long term. Razak's deputy subsequently speculated that it might be possible to forge such a community by "the close of the century if not earlier. "[2] It is important meanwhile to examine how far the present bilateral relationships between the various states of Southeast Asia hold out hopes of moving toward a sinking of national differences in a regional community. The catalog of quarrels hardly allows for optimism.

POLITICAL DISPUTES OVER ISLANDS

The bitterest disputes between the region's governments have concerned the sovereignty of territory in the border regions. The worst of these center on the island of Borneo, or Kalimantan, which was never fully absorbed into the colonial administrative systems of either the British or the Dutch, and which became something of an awkward ragbag as the decolonization process drew to its conclusion in the late 1950s. The British did not wish to stay in Sarawak and Sabah once they had left the Malayan peninsula and once they had decided to surrender political power in Singapore. Yet these two states in northern Borneo were too weak to be viable as independent sovereign nations, nor was there any clear desire on the part of the local leadership for such independence. They were therefore in 1963 affiliated to Malaya in the new Federation of Malaysia. Unfortunately the circumstances in which it was done led to suspicions on the part of both the Indonesian and Philippine governments as to whether this adhesion to the Malaysian Federation genuinely reflected the wishes of the inhabitants. Indonesia had never claimed sovereignty herself in these two states, and the matter was eventually settled.

But the Philippine claim to Sabah was in a different order. The pedigree by which the British had obtained sovereignty there from the Sultan of Sulu derived ultimately from a legal document which is differently interpreted, regarded by the British and the Malaysians as an act of cession but regarded by the Philippine government, which has inherited the Sultan's rights, as merely a revocable lease. The bad feeling over the accession of Sabah to the Federation of Malaysia in 1963 revived the Philippine claim and has involved the two governments in angry exchanges ever since, despite their mutual membership of ASEAN and their cooperation in a number of other fields. The Philippines would like the issue to go to the World Court for settlement, but the Malaysians feel that it would be an act of weakness on their part to agree to any such reference and that it would lessen the confidence of the Sabahan population in the Federal government.

The Malaysians have a good argument that would almost certainly prevail if there were any international adjudication on the matter, namely that there have been elections based on universal suffrage in the state of Sabah since 1963, all of which have resulted in the formulation of parliamentary governments committed to the state's inclusion in the Malaysian Federation. The fact that the Chief Minister of Sabah has become something of a local potentate, in whose administration even the federal government in Kuala Lumpur is not always able to interfere, does not alter this constitutional factor in Malaysia's favor. Efforts have been made to mediate this dispute, and both the Thai and Indonesian governments have made attempts to patch up the quarrel, but without success. From time to time there are unofficial calls in Manila for a force of "volunteers" to invade Sabah and "liberate" it from Malaysian rule, and until the question is resolved it will remain an important irritant in Malaysian-Philippine relations.

Meanwhile the Malaysians have not forgotten that the Indonesian government under President Sukarno actually invaded Sarawak and challenged Malaysia's sovereignty in both Sarawak and Sabah. And the Indonesians, in their turn, do not overlook the fact that if the old claim of the Sulu Sultanate is revived in its entirety it would involve a small amount of what is now Indonesian territory in Kalimantan as well as the state of Sabah, although this has never become an issue between the Philippine and Indonesian governments.

DISPUTES OVER LAND BORDERS

There are potential differences and rivalries on the land frontiers on the mainland itself. In the southern part of Thailand bordering on Malaysia there are Muslim provinces whose ancient ties lie more to the south with the Malaysian states than to the Buddhist north. On the other side of the present frontier, just inside the north of Malaysia, there are also provinces that were in the past governed from Bangkok and were indeed temporarily transferred to Thai sovereignty under Japanese rule during the Second World War. There is thus reason for the Malaysians to fear a revival of the Thai claim to their northern provinces, as well as reason for Thai fears lest the Malaysians lend support to the secessionist tendencies of some of the leaders in their southern provinces.

Between Thailand and Cambodia there are similar irredentist problems, and the vexed question of which country should own the Phreah Vihar temple was referred to the International Court of Justice in the 1950s. The Court decided in favor of Cambodia; the Thais conceded to their neighbors, but with less than good grace, and there are still tensions arising from this problem—both locally, in the area of the temple itself, and in the respective capitals. Again, there are parts of western Cambodia that have been ruled by Thailand in the past and that were "restored" to Thailand by the Japanese in the early 1940s, so the same hostility presents itself as over the Thai-Malaysian border. Cambodia also has ambivalent feelings about its border with Vietnam, since there are a large number of people living just across the border in the southern part of Vietnam who are Cambodian by ethnic origin and language. Similar ambiguities could arise in the future between almost all the smaller continental states of Southeast Asia, if only because their border regions are inhabited by minority peoples and tribes whose location tends to shift and whose loyalties to any one of the established governments is often nonexistent. [3]

These tensions even spread into the continental shelf and offshore seas. The matter was not very important until the 1950s, when geologists declared the existence of important potential oil fields and other mineral deposits in these waters (for example, tin in the Straits of Malacca); since then each coastal nation has staked its maximum claim to obtain the most benefit from these offshore resources. There has been a bilateral agreement demarcating both the seabed and territorial waters between, for example, Malaysia and Indonesia, and there have been similar agreements between neighboring countries (for example, between Malaysia and Thailand) on the exact line their frontier should pursue when taken out to sea. But there are still some parts of the offshore oil concessions that have not been diplomatically settled or adjudicated, and these could lead to trouble in the future. [4]

OTHER CONFLICTS IN SOUTHEAST ASIA

The existence of ethnic and religious minorities fuels international disputes in the archipelago as well as on the mainland. Antagonism between Indonesia and the Philippines reached considerable heights in 1972-74 when there was a dramatic flare-up in the fighting between Christians and Muslims in the southern Philippine province of Mindanao. Both Indonesia and Malaysia were indignant at the apparent suppression of the Muslim minority by Christian authorities in this area, and it developed into an international incident.

Finally, there are economic divisions, which chiefly affect Singapore. Singapore is regarded with suspicion by both of its neighbors, Indonesia and Malaysia, as a Chinese city and as a base for Chinese "economic imperialism." What in Singapore is seen as free trading can be interpreted in Djakarta as smuggling with official acquiescence on the part of the Singapore government. There were even discussions at one stage as to whether the bad feeling created by this divergence of interpretation of an economic fact of life (whereby a genuine Indonesian demand for goods was met by Singapore traders) could be minimized through a voluntary remission by Singapore to Indonesia of a proportion of the estimated foreign exchange involved—but the two governments could not agree on the proportion. In the past five years or so, both Malaysia and Indonesia have begun to press more realistically along the path of economic development, and there has in consequence been less envy and resentment of Singapore's role. Good diplomacy on the part of Singapore should avoid any significant disputes arising out of this in future. The capacity of the Singapore government to be diplomatic was demonstrated by Lee Kuan Yew when he scattered petals on the graves of two Indonesian marines whom his government had executed six years before for their outrages against Singapore civilians during the confrontation war of 1963-65. In the longer run there will be the possibility of economic domination by some countries in the region over others which would create tensions, but their state of economic advance is too similar for this to be a realistic factor in the near future. [5]

THE VIABILITY OF ASEAN

Given this sad inventory of regional disputes, it is perhaps rather creditable that ASEAN has got as far as it has. It has done so because it meets a very genuine need of the five countries involved. In terms of legitimacy and credibility, ASEAN possesses tremendous advantages as a regional grouping. "It does not, " said Ghazali bin Shafie to the Malaysian Parliament a few years ago, "have any outside powers in any capacity even as donor countries. It is entirely intraregional. . . . ASEAN cannot be regarded as being in any way offensive to any of the superpowers. "[6] And President Suharto has made it clear that Indonesia regards ASEAN as the major organization for the region. "The most important thing, " he said in 1973, "is to consolidate ASEAN as a regional force. " The Indonesian leader went on to make it clear that ASEAN would not seek any links with external powers: "There is no point linking it with larger Asian lands like India and Pakistan or China and Soviet Russia. That would merely embroil the area in new contradictions. "[7]

ASEAN's Potential Membership

Before ASEAN can become completely representative of Southeast Asia as a whole, it must, of course, extend its membership to include the smaller countries of the region. President Suharto told the Philippine Congress in 1972 that "a strong and cohesive ASEAN, I hope, can become the nucleus for a wider regional organization which encompasses all nations of Southeast Asia, irrespective of differences in political systems, on the basis of mutual respect, equality, noninterference, mutual cooperation, and national integrity. "[8] It is on this reasoning that, on another occasion, Suharto said specifically that Indonesia would "welcome as members Southeast Asian nations like Burma, Laos, Cambodia, and, should they so desire, both South and North Vietnam. "[9] And Ghazali has observed that if these five states of Southeast Asia were to join ASEAN, and if as a regional organization ASEAN could begin to "replace foreign aid, " then a big step would have been taken toward the exclusion of external influence over the region. [10]

Burma and Indochina

There is agreement on the general desirability of extending ASEAN membership to at least these five states of Burma and

Indochina. But Burma will not join until the Indochina states have joined, and the Indochina states present ticklish problems of protocol. When the ASEAN Foreign Ministers were to meet in the Philippines early in 1971, the Indonesian Foreign Minister suggested that an invitation be extended to Hanoi, and the Deputy Foreign Minister of Thailand at the time was reported to have agreed.[11] In fact the invitation, if it was ever issued, was spurned. After the Kuala Lumpur Declaration by the ASEAN Foreign Ministers at the end of 1971, President Marcos of the Philippines was keen to invite the other five Southeast Asian states to a summit in Manila to endorse the Declaration, but Malaysia, probably wisely, would not consent.[12] Again, it was North Vietnam from which difficulty was anticipated.

The following year there was some crystallization of the Indochinese attitude to ASEAN when it was reported that three of the Indochina governments, those of Cambodia, Laos, and South Vietnam, were anxious to join ASEAN in a collective approach to the European Economic Community on commercial matters, and it was said that ASEAN had agreed in principle to admit these three to the special Committee dealing with this subject.[13] But no word came from Hanoi on this question. At their meeting in Kuala Lumpur in February 1973, the ASEAN Foreign Ministers actually agreed in principle that they would enlarge their Association to include the other five nations, who would be invited "at the appropriate time."[14] The Thai delegate declared that he hoped this would encourage those "Southeast Asian countries not yet members of ASEAN to participate in a joint endeavor which will serve the long-term interests of the entire region."[15] But when the same delegate asked Indonesia (at that time the only ASEAN member enjoying diplomatic relations with North Vietnam) to invite North Vietnamese observers to attend the ASEAN Foreign Ministers' Conference at Pattaya in April 1973,[16] the North Vietnamese refused on the grounds of Thai participation in the war in Vietnam.

The Foreign Ministers at Pattaya endorsed the call for an all-Southeast Asian meeting on regional security at the appropriate time. But again, it was only Cambodia and Laos that sent observers to the Pattaya Conference, and the Straits Times was probably reflecting official Malaysian opinion when it commented editorially that the Thai policy of inviting observers to that meeting "may have been a mistake."[17] There was, of course, the additional problem by that time of the role of the Viet Cong, or Provisional Revolutionary Government (PRG) of South Vietnam. The Thai government explained its position of not having invited the PRG by arguing that it was "only a political party at the present time."[18] Obviously the question of gaining North Vietnamese collaboration in ASEAN would depend on a movement toward a genuine ceasefire in Vietnam and an end to the wars in Laos and Cambodia as well.

Other Candidates

Australia. ASEAN also had to face questions of extending its coverage and membership in other directions—southwards toward Australasia and westwards toward the Indian subcontinent. When Gough Whitlam became the Prime Minister of Australia, he initiated a new policy of seeking to set up some kind of Asian-Pacific regional forum that would include not only the ASEAN countries but also Australia and New Zealand on the one hand and even China and Japan on the other. President Suharto made it clear that there could be no question of diluting ASEAN in this way, [19] and there is little possibility of Australia's canvassing in future for admission to ASEAN.

Sri Lanka. Sri Lanka has always had an ambiguous geopolitical place between the Indian subcontinent, to which it is attached geographically and ethnically, and Southeast Asia, where its shipping and emigration links lead its interests. [20] It is the right size for belonging to a Southeast Asia grouping, and needs membership in such a grouping in order more effectively to resist the pressure of absorption into the Indian political and economic system. Notions that Ceylon, as it was then called, might become a member of the predecessors of ASEAN were lent credibility by the attachment which Tunku Abdul Rahman, then the Prime Minister of Malaysia, had to Ceylon as the nearest Commonwealth peer to find itself facing similar problems. Foreign Minister Malik of Indonesia once conceded that neutralization of Southeast Asia could eventually cover Ceylon, [21] and this comment perhaps was triggered by Prime Minister Bandaranaike's advocacy of a neutral or nuclear-free zone in the Indian Ocean. But in practice the Southeast Asian states are not likely to welcome the prospect of having to work with Sri Lanka as a full member of ASEAN, if only because they would risk entanglement in subcontinental affairs.

Bangladesh. The same perhaps goes for Bangladesh, which at the time of its creation would have liked to have strengthened its options and reduced the obviousness of its dependence on India by having membership in a wider grouping. [22] Pakistan in fact carried out an active campaign of diplomacy designed to ensure that Bangladesh should not be allowed to join ASEAN, [23] and this was countered to some extent by Indian diplomacy in the contrary direction. At the beginning of 1973 a report in a leading Malaysian newspaper included Bangladesh as one of the six countries expected to be invited to join

ASEAN if a general enlargement of that body were to be agreed upon. [24] But it is extremely doubtful whether this represented anything more than some private hopes among some of the Malaysians. Indonesia, despite the link of Islam, was extremely suspicious of Bangladesh at the beginning because of the precedents its creation through civil war with Pakistan could have for the future unity of Indonesia. It is safer to assume that no countries on the Indian subcontinent will gain membership in ASEAN.

Internal Divisiveness: Maphilindo

But one must return to the question whether ASEAN will succeed in extending its coverage to Indochina and by the same token to Burma, since even this is far from certain. Some observers agree with the Philippine scholar Alejandro M. Fernandes that "the future of continental Southeast Asia is Chinese, " whereas insular and archipelagic Southeast Asia has a better prospect of retaining independence from the big powers. [25] This is because each of the continental states either has land frontiers with China (Burma, Laos, and North Vietnam) or else is very close and vulnerable to the Chinese frontier (Thailand, Cambodia, and South Vietnam), so that China represents for them their nearest big power. Since Chinese strength is certain to be enlarged in the years and decades to come, it would seem inevitable that these smaller states on China's fringe would feel impelled to work out policies of accommodation or modus vivendi with China as a first priority. The insular and archipelagic countries, by contrast, do not need to do this.

There is another factor tending to draw the insular-archipelagic countries together as a subgrouping within Southeast Asia, namely what one might loosely call the "greater Malay" or "Maphilindo" idea. Maphilindo, a product of the Sukarno age in Southeast Asia, was a short-lived grouping between Malaya (as it then was), the Philippines, and Indonesia—hence its name. It was based, intellectually, on a harking back to precolonial eras in which the various peoples of "Malay" stock supposedly had influence spreading from Madagascar in the west to Easter Island in the east. The same Philippine scholar who predicts that the mainland states of Southeast Asia will tend to revolve around China also argues that the insular-archipelagic countries will come together under a Maphilindo label. Maphilindo, he argues, "as a novel experiment in interstate formation . . . died prematurely, but not for the reason that the grandiose idea was not viable. Maphilindo was based on an ideal or regional organization toward which, for the past three or four decades, leaders of great vision in Southeast Asia had been leading their peoples across

barriers of geography, race and tradition." There is, Fernandes
goes on, "much to commend Maphilindo"; it could be the answer to
"the problem of rival imperialisms threatening the area, . . . the
perfect vehicle for solving common economic problems, and for
cultural and social cooperation." It could be much more than a diplomatic contrivance, enjoying the vitality and resilience that comes
from having been formed by "the creative effort of human will out
of three kindred nations with the common underlying culture."
Fernandes notes that without Thailand, "but with a place for Singapore and for Brunei," ASEAN would in effect become "a resurrec-
tion of Maphilindo."[26]

It is certainly true that there is a difference in quality between
the kind of cooperation practiced between the three ASEAN states of
Malaysia, Indonesia, and Singapore and the kind of cooperation that
prevails when Thailand or the Philippines are involved. And it is
indeed possible that Thailand may become so absorbed in the demands
of her new post-Shanghai diplomacy, involving delicate accommoda-
tions with both Hanoi and Peking, that she will increasingly swim
free of her Southeast Asian involvements. But this is speculative,
and it is enough for our purposes to have established that the diplomatic harmony of the states of Southeast Asia is not to be taken for
granted. At this point we can begin to examine ASEAN's actual
record of coordinating diplomacy.

Diplomatic Achievements

The Question of China Detente

The five ASEAN partners have now had some experience of
attempting to harmonize their diplomatic actions in the arena of the
outside world. One of the most obvious cases for this kind of collaboration concerns the occasions when an act of international diplomatic recognition is called for by some or all of the ASEAN states.
The best example of this came when China entered the United Nations
toward the end of 1971. The meeting of Foreign Ministers at Kuala
Lumpur in November of that year was largely designed to see if
there was a possibility of a common stand on this position, and the
Singapore Foreign Minister went so far as to tell his Parliament
subsequently, "There is an agreement that before any member country enters into diplomatic relations with China, we must consult and
coordinate actions."[27] The Indonesian Foreign Minister later confirmed this, [28] but the ranks were broken, as on the neutralization
issue itself, by Malaysia. Tun Razak was keen to exchange diplomatic relations with China as soon as possible, and was not happy

at holding back in order to allow the more skeptical Indonesians to keep in step.

The Malaysians said that the ASEAN governments had merely agreed on the general goal of normalizing relations with China and had agreed to keep each other informed but were left to make their own final decisions, [29] and Kuala Lumpur pushed ahead with its negotiations with China, largely through the respective missions at the U.N. headquarters in New York. A little later, when it appeared that the Malaysian approach to Peking had been stalled because of China's reluctance to abandon its ties with those Chinese residents who were not citizens of Malaysia, there were stories that Malaysia was coming round to the view of coordinating a collective or simultaneous ASEAN approach to China[30]—a move that would obviously bear more weight and would give ASEAN more bargaining power, although it would not allow any one country to get more credit in Chinese eyes or in international circles than the others. In the end Malaysia did go it alone, and the others were left to make the best of the situation.

The position was well reflected outside the strictly diplomatic field when delegations to the Asian Games Federation Council divided at the end of 1973 on the question of admitting China to the exclusion of Taiwan. The Malaysian and Singapore delegates voted for this, but Indonesia and the Philippines voted against, while Thailand managed not to be present after having protested against the exclusion of a motion admitting both China and Taiwan. [31] Such was the confusion in public opinion in Southeast Asia that the efforts of the five Foreign Ministers at their ASEAN summit were not able to resolve it.

Recognition of North Vietnam
and Bangladesh

A similar issue was what attitude to adopt toward North Vietnam. When ASEAN was founded, only Indonesia had relations with Hanoi, but Malaysia was keen to follow step, for reasons similar to those that had prompted her to move toward China. It was agreed that the ASEAN governments would keep each other informed on their views about recognizing Hanoi, and, indeed, on the activities of North Vietnam in their respective countries after recognition. [32] But in the end Malaysia went ahead of Thailand, Singapore, and the Philippines by exchanging recognition with North Vietnam in early 1973, declaring that this was a step to "forging a cohesive regional identity within Southeast Asia."[33]

Finally, the civil war that ended in the declaration of Bangladesh as an independent republic provided another occasion for ASEAN to act collectively. Once the division of the former two wings of

184

Pakistan had become an incontrovertible reality, the two Commonwealth members of ASEAN—Malaysia and Singapore—wanted to
recognize Bangladesh. But up to the last minute, and even beyond,
Indonesia was endeavoring to mediate between Pakistan and Bangladesh and did not in any case wish to be associated with too hurried
a recognition of Bangladesh before Pakistan agreed to it. Inferences
might otherwise be drawn about the legitimacy of future secessionist
movements within Indonesia itself. In deference to this feeling,
Malaysia, as a fellow Muslim country, also held back, so that Thailand, presented by this joint pressure from Kuala Lumpur and
Djakarta, postponed its own recognition, which it had prepared for
early in 1972.[34] Singapore did likewise, although there were mur-
murs in the Singapore press that Indonesian special interests in
this situation were threatening to strain the unity of ASEAN.[35] The
Philippines at this time was about to play host to President Suharto
and did not wish to embarrass him on the eve of his visit, so Thailand was left isolated. The final result was that Thailand recognized
Bangladesh unilaterally, followed by Singapore, leaving the others to
straggle in much later, after the international recognition of Bangladesh had consolidated.[36]

It can hardly be said that these three specific cases, where
recognition presented itself as a common problem to the ASEAN
membership, served to strengthen the international image of ASEAN.

The Vietnam Ceasefire

The same can be said of ASEAN's faltering attempts to maximize its role in the Indochina ceasefire. In the middle of 1972 the
five ASEAN governments drafted their own proposals for a settlement in Vietnam, embracing a ceasefire, the withdrawal of foreign
troops and release of prisoners of war, a political solution to the
conflict, and a free general election. But the proposal was rejected
both by Hanoi and by Saigon (as well as by the Viet Cong), and the
North Vietnamese denounced it for not distinguishing between the
"aggressor" and the "victims."[37] Undeterred, the five ASEAN Foreign Ministers went on to attempt to cash in on the Vietnam reconstruction bandwagon. Meeting at Kuala Lumpur at the beginning of
1973 they said they would participate "meaningfully" in this, and an
ASEAN Coordinating Committee for Rehabilitation and Reconstruction of Indochina was set up to meet at the end of March 1973.[38]

The Indonesians said that they felt that Japan's offer of U.S.
$7.5 billion should be channeled via the ASEAN Committee,[39] but
reports in Japan suggested that the ASEAN countries were merely
trying to deflect Western aid for Indochinese reconstruction so that
it would be spent on ASEAN materials and products.[40] Foreign

Secretary Romulo insisted, "We have recognized our responsibilities toward Indochina by exerting greater efforts to achieve genuine peace in the peninsula, and by contributing to the reconstruction and rehabilitation of war-torn countries which after all belong to our region."[41] But Malik had to report to his colleagues, after canvassing the idea among the parties concerned, that the war-torn combatants did not appear interested in the idea of multilateral aid, preferring to take their reconstruction funds and materials in the privacy of bilateral agreements with the big powers. As Malik admitted, ASEAN had not proved itself effective enough to influence either the big powers or the flow of aid.[42]

Dealing with the U.N. and the EEC

Where the common problems were less controversial, however, ASEAN did have some success in forging a common front. The best example is probably in the United Nations itself, certainly after the debacle of ASEAN's divided vote on the Chinese entry. It goes without saying that the five states vote collectively on the election of any one of their representatives standing for U.N. office. They all rallied behind Malik's candidacy for President of the General Assembly in 1971. As a result of this tendency to vote on candidates as a group, ASEAN has become something of a nucleus for the smaller countries of Asia in several international settings. A similar cohesion has been achieved where ASEAN has had to deal with other international organizations and bodies.

Perhaps the outstanding case here is the European Economic Community. When it became clear what problems were created for Southeast Asia by the common tariff policies of the founding EEC Six and later by the enlargement of the Community to embrace Great Britain, a Special Coordinating Committee of ASEAN Nations was formed under the initiative of Sumitro, who was then the Indonesian Trade Minister and enjoyed good connections in the Hague as well as in Brussels.[43] This committee sat in Southeast Asia, but there was an ASEAN Brussels Committee, comprising the five Ambassadors accredited to the EEC, that met frequently to discuss the progress of the Commonwealth negotiations with the EEC on various commodities and of their own representations to the Community about palm oil, spices, coconut products, and other exports whose earnings in the enlarged EEC seemed to be threatened.

On similar lines an ASEAN Geneva Committee was later formed, comprising the senior representatives of the five governments accredited to the international organizations in that city, the two most important of which are UNCTAD and GATT. When GATT held its ministerial conference in Tokyo in 1973 in order to declare the opening of the new round of multilateral tariff negotiations, the five ASEAN countries negotiated a common stand to which they adhered during the discussions in Tokyo and later in Geneva.[44] The five countries also managed to put together a common stand at the second United Nations Sugar Conference in 1973,[45] and held collective talks with the Japanese, at ASEAN's request, about competition between Southeast Asian natural rubber and Japanese synthetic rubber.[46] On economic issues, particularly where there is no conflict of interest within Southeast Asia or within the ASEAN group, there is a possibility of substantial coordination of diplomacy.

Even on some political issues the capacity of the region to maximize its own unity vis-a-vis the outside world was shown during the crisis that developed in 1973 over the clashes between Muslims and Christians in the southern Philippine province of Mindanao. These clashes naturally disturbed public opinion and political leaders in Malaysia and Indonesia, the two Muslim countries in ASEAN, as well as the Islamic nations farther away. The Philippine Foreign Ministry devoted special attention to keeping the other ASEAN governments informed of its actions and the background to the dispute, making little secret of the fact that it regarded the Muslim rebels in Mindanao and Sulu as deriving assistance from Libya, via the Malaysian state of Sabah whose Chief Minister, Tun Mustapha, was born in the Philippines and ruled his state patriarchally with little interference from Kuala Lumpur. The conference of Islamic Foreign Ministers discussed the Mindanao problem and sent a delegation to investigate it, requesting the Indonesian and Malaysian governments to use their good offices to assist the investigation within the framework of ASEAN.

But as a well-known regional commentator observed at the time:

> The two Muslim nations of the region adopted a position which was in marked contrast to the general Arab attitude. Both pointed to the dangers of attempting to interfere in the internal affairs of a sovereign state, and thereby helped the Libya conference to adopt a more moderate tone than had been sought by the host government. The illustration of Asian common sense may not ultimately enlighten the more emotional elements in the Arab world, but it should be the watchword for this region.[47]

In other words, within the ASEAN framework, Indonesia and Malaysia were at pains to encourage the Philippine government to give the best possible deal to its Muslim dissidents in the south. But when it came to a confrontation between the Philippines on the one hand

and the more powerful and wealthy Muslims of North Africa and Western Asia on the other hand, the two Muslim states in ASEAN spent more energy persuading the Arabs to remain calm and not to make the situation in the Philippines worse. Their regional loyalties were stronger than their universal ties of religious brotherhood.

NOTES

1. Speech to Parliament, in STK, 27 July 1971. The word "community" suggests the EEC model.

2. Sunday Times, Kuala Lumpur, 16 April 1972.

3. Jerry M. Silverman presents an excellent summary of these disputes in "Historic National Rivalries and Interstate Conflict in Mainland Southeast Asia, " in Mark W. Zacher and R. Stephen Milne, eds., Conflict and Stability in Southeast Asia (New York: Anchor Press, 1974), p. 45.

4. See Petroleum News South East Asia, Annual Contract Number, 1973 (Hong Kong).

5. See Lee Soo Ann in NDE, p. xii.

6. STK, 24 March 1971.

7. New York Times, 18 March 1973.

8. STK, 15 February 1972.

9. New York Times, 18 March 1973.

10. STK, 24 March 1971.

11. BP, 9 March 1971.

12. STK, 3 December 1971.

13. Manit Jeer, in The Nation, Bangkok, 24 February 1972.

14. The Times, London, 16 February 1973; STK, 16 and 17 February 1973.

15. BP, 14 February 1973.

16. Japan Times, 8 April 1973.

17. STK, 21 February 1973.

18. ARB, May 1973, p. 1761.

19. STK, 22 February 1973.

20. When the term "Southeast Asia" was first invented, Ceylon was included in it, providing the headquarters of Mountbatten's South-East Asian Command in 1943.

21. STK, 11 March 1972.

22. Dawn, Karachi, 24 February 1973. But see also Dawn, 13 July 1973, quoting the Bangladesh Foreign Minister as saying there was no intention for the time being to approach ASEAN.

23. The Times of India, 6 July 1973.

24. STK, 11 February 1973.

25. Alejandro M. Fernandes, "On the Future of Southeast Asia, " ND, p. 29.

26. Ibid., pp. 33-35. See Peter Lyon, War and Peace in South-East Asia (London: Oxford University Press, 1969), pp. 156-58.

27. STS, 18 March 1972.

28. STK, 30 March 1973.

29. STK, 30 April 1973.

30. The Hindu, Madras, 9 November 1973.

31. ARB, December 1973, p. 2283.

32. BP, 25 February 1973.

33. ARB, April 1973, p. 1696.

34. New Nation, Singapore, 11 February 1972.

35. Ibid., 12 February 1972.

36. Ibid., 18 February 1972.

37. ARB, September 1972, p. 1163; Daily Telegraph, London, 28 August 1972.

38. BP, 7 March 1973.

39. BP, 16 February 1973.

40. Japan Times, 3 April 1973.

41. Sunday Times, Kuala Lumpur, 22 April 1973.

42. Report by Pran Chopra in the Japan Times, 11 May 1973.

43. Harvey Stockwin in the Financial Times, 3 May 1973.

44. Musa Hitam in the Japan Times, 14 September 1973.

45. STK, 24 August 1973.

46. Japan Times, 22 September 1973.

47. T. J. S. George in FEER, 2 April 1973; ARB, April 1973, p. 1700.

20

The most skeptical view of the neutralization proposal is that it was launched essentially to gain domestic prestige for the Razak government—"as a kite displayed for domestic viewing, flown to gauge international currents of air and wearing respectable but as yet transparent colors," to use Tom Millar's colorful image. [1] It is perfectly true that the Malaysian government has extracted from neutralization the fullest mileage in terms of internal politics, hoping thereby to blunt the appeal of the Communist insurgents in Sarawak and on the Thai border, to reassure its Chinese minority that it was set on behaving properly to the Chinese government, and to show its Malay constituency how foreign governments were impressed by Tun Razak and his United Malay National Organization (UMNO) colleagues. But it is not possible to dismiss so easily the international significance of the proposal. Neutralization has been heatedly argued with Malaysia's four partners in ASEAN, strenuously lobbied in Burma and Indochina, and exhaustively explained to external powers big and small. It is not to be taken merely as a public relations exercise on the domestic front and would not have been treated with the same seriousness internationally if it had. What is more to the point is to decide how far the proposal became watered down as it met with criticism after criticism, and whether it is still possible to describe it as neutralization at all. The Kuala Lumpur Declaration, after all, speaks of a zone of neutrality, not a zone of neutralized states.

NEUTRALIZATION, OR A NEUTRAL ZONE?

This is a vital difference, since neutrality does not involve the paraphernalia of international treaties, guarantees, and onerous obligations on both neutralizor and neutralizee. Neutralization is a more complex and burdensome institution than the mere profession of neutrality or a profession to respect the neutrality of others. But it is not quite as dauntingly rigid as some of Razak's detractors have claimed; history shows how successful and how flexible both the concept and the practice of neutralization can be. [2] It is not enough for the purposes of criticism to say that Belgium fell to the German army in two world wars. Neutralization is no protection against total war and has never been realistically claimed as such. Belgian neutralization lasted 80 years, from 1839 to 1919, and Luxembourg's lasted 52 years, from 1867 to 1919. Both of these small nations survived a major war between France and Germany in 1870-71, as well as half a century of intense national rivalry on the part of their guarantors. They succumbed only in the course of a major world war that marked a dramatic reorientation of relations between the principal European nations. "It would be extravagant," the leading manual on neutralization comments, "to expect that treaties neutralizing states by international guarantee would survive a period in which the guarantor states were prepared to seek fulfilment of their national interests by means of total war." [3]

It is not essential to the case for neutralization that it should be shown to be successful in perpetuity (even if that were logically possible). Switzerland's neutralization has lasted for 159 years (since 1815), Belgium's lasted for 80 years, Luxembourg's for 52 years, the Vatican City's for 45 years (since 1929), Cracow's for 31 years (1815-46), the Congo's for 23 years (1885-1907), and Honduras's for 16 years (1907-23). "A neutralization that resolves a difficult problem for a period of twenty to fifty years may well constitute a vital contribution to the maintenance of peace." [4] To which one might add that twenty years at nineteenth-century speeds may be taken as equivalent to a decade in the fast-moving world of today. To secure a decade's peace, a decade's noninvolvement, is surely better than nothing at all. Let us concede from the very start, therefore, that it is the relative and not absolute success of neutralization that is the goal, and that neutralization can be eminently varied in its actual application.

BIG POWER GUARANTEES UNACCEPTABLE

It nevertheless appears that neutralization under big power guarantee, as elaborated by Malaysia since April 1970, is acceptable neither to the majority of Southeast Asian states nor to the external powers that count. Malaysia's neighbors are reluctant to accept the limitations of action which the status of neutralizee would impose upon them—particularly the odium of having to appear in international affairs as a weakling, requiring special treatment and disqualified from such manly pursuits as "showing the flag" (even the U.N. flag, in the form of providing contingents for U.N. peace-keeping forces). Cyril E. Black and his Princeton associates have convincingly shown that this particular self-restraint may not be absolutely necessary for a neutralizee. [5] But even the indignity of having to prove it unnecessary is enough to deter a country like Indonesia—the fifth largest in the world by population—which sees itself eventually as playing a diplomatic role almost comparable to that of India, certainly of Brazil or Iran, even possibly of China or Japan. As Black conceded, "Neutralization seems potentially attractive only for relatively minor states that, by reason of strategic position or symbolic political value, have become or threaten to become the focal point of contests for control or dominant influence between principal regional or global rivals."[6] Indonesia rejects it because it sees itself as too grand for such a demeaning status. A united Vietnam might in the long run come to the same view, although there could be an initial period during which it might regard neutralization as a useful device for effecting the transition from wartime dependence on external allies to peaceful re-establishment of an independent regional or subregional role. That must remain speculative. Cambodia and Laos would welcome reneutralization, if only because its larger context—assuming it were Southeast Asian in scope—would reinforce their existing and somewhat battered neutralizations of 1954 and 1962. But Thailand, the Philippines, and Singapore would prefer to prolong their bilateral alliances (with the United States, United Kingdom, Australia, and New Zealand), Burma hopes to maintain its unique status of neutrality undiluted by a regional coverage, and only Malaysia is left officially committed to neutralization. Indeed, one scholar[7] has argued that Malaysia might opt for neutralization on her own, leaving her neighbors to follow their different courses, although it is hard to see Malaysia's neighbors coguaranteeing her neutralization—or Malaysia's accepting that status without their participation. A more logical candidate for simple, as distinct from multiple, neutralization is Malaysia's immediate neighbor to the south. Peter Lyon has speculated "whether an international agreement to neutralize Singapore might serve both to mollify some of Singapore's understandable fears of her larger neighbors and, by associating these neighbors with interested outside powers, perhaps might thereby provide some guarantee of an established international status for this Chinese city-state within the Maphilindo realm."[8]

But it is, of course, this unprecedented multiple character of the neutralization proposed by Razak that creates further difficulty. Even if, with the passage of time, Malaysia's ASEAN partners prove ready to do without their American air bases and token

ANZUK Commonwealth units, and even supposing that Indonesia in an access of statesmanship agreed to forego the trappings of a great power, it would still be necessary to ensure peace among the ten neutralized states without recourse to the guaranteeing powers. We have seen in the previous chapter how intractable some of the intra-regional disputes are, and the political order within each state is hardly encouraging for the construction of a complex network of intraregional pledges, verification, conciliation machinery, and the like.[9]

The ASEAN governments seemed to recognize their propensity to quarrel with each other when they defined "neutrality" as requiring them to refrain from involvement in international conflict of any kind "particularly between powers outside the zone"[10]—as if intraregional conflict were something else and impossible to shake free of. One factor in this attitude is that neutralization would tend to freeze the relations within the region along with the region's external relations. There are Southeast Asian states that still hope to aggrandize themselves at their neighbors' expense, as is the case with the Philippines regarding Sabah and could become the case with the various irredentist claims in Thailand, Cambodia, and Malaysia, leaving aside such disputes as that between Vietnam and the Philippines over the Spratley islands. It would be fatal to such unsatisfied claims to sign a pledge to respect existing borders.

PERPETUATING THE POWER BALANCE

And this cold-storage effect of neutralization applies to the external guaranteeing powers also, in what Coral Bell calls the double balance of power in Southeast Asia—the balance between the regional states and the balance between the interested external powers.[11] All three of Malaysia's proposed guarantors have proved unresponsive to the Razak initiative. China, the least able to back up any guarantee it might give (can one imagine this side of 1980 a Chinese force arriving in Malaysia to help repel a Soviet invasion?), has given informal but noncommittal support to the Malaysian proposal, but in Moscow and Washington the disinterest and skepticism has not even been sugared with politeness.

As Peter Lyon has observed of Southeast Asian neutralization, it would mean perpetuating the balance of forces that produced the agreement to neutralize,[12] which is not in the interest of those participants who expect to increase their relative involvement in the region over its present level (that would include Indonesia and a united Vietnam among the regional states, and Russia, Japan, and possibly China among the external powers). Of the four external powers with a capability of intervention in Southeast Asia, one (the United States) is retrenching since the Guam Doctrine, one (China) is consolidating its position in the region following an earlier period of brittle hostility during the Cultural Revolution, and the other two (the USSR and Japan) are in the process of extending their power in the region. If there is now any "balance of power" between these four in Southeast Asia it must inevitably be a temporary balance, liable to be broken when their relative weights shift significantly. [13] It is possible, of course, that there is not actually a balance of power of this kind at all. T. B. Millar believes that "there is not really a quadrilateral balance of exerted power, although there may be, to an extent, a balance of restraint or of inertia among the four." [14]

Southeast Asia has proved to be the "graveyard for single power hegemony"; [15] enough of the big powers have learned this (Britain and Holland in the nineteenth century, Japan in the 1940s, the United States in the 1960s) for all of them to be wary of seeking out- right dominance, especially in an era of the acquisition of power by the indigenous regional states themselves. Their apprehensions re- garding Southeast Asia are primarily negative, in the sense that none of them wants more power than it already wields there, pro- vided the others refrain from building up theirs. It is a game of "competitive containment," [16] in which China's interest is to re- strain the growth of Soviet or Japanese power, the Soviet interest is to restrain the growth of Chinese power, and the American inter- est is to see that neither Soviet nor Chinese power expands in the region to such a point that one begins to render the other ineffective. (Similarly, the interest of each Southeast Asian state is to keep the interest of the big powers so balanced that no one of them becomes dominant in the region, and their majority collective interest re- garding each other is likewise to prevent any one of their number from becoming the local bully-boy.) In the long run the Americans would seem to have the most to gain and the Chinese the most to lose from an early neutralization of the region, and it is ironical that their respective initial responses to Tun Razak have gone, if anything, the contrary way.

But it can be objected that this entire line of argument is flawed by its assumption that the fate from which Southeast Asia needs delivery is outright aggression or conquest from the outside. One of the reasons for the air of unreality that has appeared to over- hang the ASEAN Senior Officials in their discussions of neutraliza- tion is the fact that most of the ASEAN governments now agree that Hitlerite annexation is the least likely of their worries. Only Singa- pore is so compact and so well governed that its leaders' night- mares star foreign generals in the villains' roles. Razak, Suharto,

Marcos, Ne Win, and Sanya have their sleep broken by domestic opponents and by their own organizational weakness. By this logic neutralization is like taking out an insurance policy only against thunderbolts and not against the usual and more frequent hazards of daily life.[17]

Thus the conclusion is that neutralization, even liberally defined, does not stand a good chance of acceptance and implementation. But that is by no means the end of the story. At the less formal level of neutrality, or at a midway level between neutrality and neutralization, the Razak plan looks far more healthy. Noordin Sopiee of Malaysia has argued that informal assurances by the great powers to respect Southeast Asian neutrality would be enough to get the desired result,[18] at least for the immediate future, and the ASEAN Senior Officials have discussed sympathetically the idea, backed by Dr. Ismail, Tun Razak's former deputy, of calling on the powers (in company with all the other nations of the world) to make such a declaration at the United Nations. This would not commit them to intervene against violations of Southeast Asian neutrality, although it would give them a moral responsibility to avoid—and, short of war, to oppose—such violations. In practice, if external aggression is not seriously feared, even this would in strict logic be unnecessary, but it would nevertheless be comforting.[19] At this early stage of Southeast Asia's indigenous international diplomacy, West Europeans and Americans may profess skepticism at such naivete, but Asians still attach importance to the written word and the public pledge.[20]

One of the traditional functions of neutralization is to transform a military stalemate into a political stalemate.[21] Much of the intellectual energy that went into the debate in the mid-1960s about neutralizing Indochina was derived from the intense desire to achieve just such a transformation in Vietnam. That transformation has already been consummated so far as the United States is concerned, but there is as yet no shared desire on the part of the indigenous belligerents to do the same. If and when they weary of the sword then neutralization would be a helpful device for their purposes, as the U.S. Senate study of 1966 spelled out in some detail. But the rest of Southeast Asia does not face military stalemate in any international sense.

Neutralization of Southeast Asia would mean a dramatic shift in the traditional international stance of the region. In a sense it has been proposed too late, in that Vietnam is universally agreed to be the last use of the region as a convenient site for big power fights. It is more appropriate in the mid-1970s for Southeast Asia to pursue its slow transition from outer-directed to inner-directed development—an inexorable process that has the result of progressively reducing the incentive for (and effectiveness of) external intervention as indigenous society builds up its own strength and momentum. The "vacuum" left by neocolonial withdrawal is filled by the local element.

A CHALLENGING EXPERIENCE

What Razak and his Malaysian colleagues have done is to make the other Southeast Asians more aware of these dimensions to their dilemma and of their collectivity in facing it. As a result of the questions posed by the neutralization proposal, the ASEAN governments are much clearer in their minds about their foreign policy options. For once, instead of discussing generalities—or particularities like China or the Malacca Straits—the ASEAN Ministers and officials have had to explore the utility of a European device— neutralization—for their own collective global situation, and the exercise was not only salutary and stimulating, it cemented the common bond between them in a new and important way. Beyond this, Razak's insistence has weaned the hawks of Djakarta, Bangkok, and Manila away from their unthinking rejection of neutralism as a pillar of foreign policy. That in itself is no mean achievement, and it may be that Razak will be most remembered by the region's historians for this reason.

Neutralization in the strict sense will remain a realistic option, certainly for Laos and Cambodia, probably for Vietnam, and possibly for Malaysia and Singapore. Its usefulness has not yet been outlived for specific national situations now and in the future. As for the ambitious concept of multiple neutralization, that died somewhere along the journey from the Non-Aligned Summit at Lusaka in 1970 to the Kuala Lumpur Declaration of November 1971.

NOTES

1. T. B. Millar, "Prospects for Regional Security Cooperation in Southeast Asia," in Mark W. Zacher and R. Stephen Milne, eds., Conflict and Stability in Southeast Asia (New York: Anchor Press, 1974), p. 463.
2. See Black et al., Neutralization in World Politics (Princeton: Princeton University Press, 1968); also U.S. Senate Foreign Relations Committee, Neutralization in South East Asia: Problems and Prospects (Washington, D.C.: Government Printing Office, 1966).

3. Black et al., op. cit., p. 41.

4. Ibid., p. 42.

5. Ibid., pp. 51-56, 165-66.

6. Ibid., pp. v-vi.

7. M. Pathmanathan, unpublished paper.

8. Peter Lyon, War and Peace in South East Asia (London: Oxford University Press, 1969), p. 175. Lyon goes on to comment that the only modern precedent for city-state neutralization, that of Cracow, is hardly a "happy" one because it was swallowed up by Austria, one of its guarantors, 31 years later. Yet, given the propensity of powers like nineteenth-century Austria to annex vulnerable adjoining small states, 31 years of separate existence would seem worth striving for.

9. Michael Leifer, Dilemmas of Statehood in Southeast Asia (Vancouver: University of British Columbia Press, 1972).

10. See Chapter 2 above. Emphasis added.

11. The Asian Balance of Power: A Comparison with European Precedents, Adelphi Paper No. 48 (London: International Institute of Strategic Studies, 1968).

12. "Reorientations in South East Asia, " in Round Table, No. 246, April 1972, p. 237.

13. See T. B. Millar, "The 'Asian Quadrilateral': An Australian View, " Australian Outlook, vol. 27, no. 2, August 1973, p. 134.

14. Ibid., p. 138.

15. Peter Lyon, speaking in Kuala Lumpur, STK, 14 July 1973.

16. The phrase is Coral Bell's, in "Security Preoccupations and Power Balances After Vietnam, " in Zacher and Milne, eds., op. cit., p. 471.

17. The metaphor is taken from Bell, in Zacher and Milne, eds., op. cit., p. 488.

18. "The Neutralisation of Southeast Asia, " a paper presented at a Conference on Asia and the Western Pacific of the Australian Institute of International Affairs, Canberra, 14-17 April 1973, pp. 11-12.

19. Bell, in Zacher and Milne, eds., op. cit., pp. 488-89.

20. See, however, Michael Leifer, "Great Power Intervention and Regional Order, " ibid., p. 181.

21. Black et al., op. cit., p. vi.

THE KUALA LUMPUR DECLARATION

27 November 1971

We the Foreign Ministers of Indonesia, Malaysia, The Philippines, Singapore, and the Special Envoy of the National Executive Council of Thailand:

Firmly believing in the merits of regional co-operation which has drawn our countries to co-operate together in the economic, social and cultural fields in the Association of Southeast Asian Nations;

Desirous of bringing about a relaxation of international tension and of achieving a lasting peace in Southeast Asia;

Inspired by the worthy aims and objectives of the United Nations, in particular by the principles of respect for the sovereignty and territorial integrity of all States, abstention from the threat or use of force, peaceful settlement of international disputes, equal rights and self-determination and non-interference in the internal affairs of States;

Believing in the continuing validity of the "Declaration on the Promotion of World Peace and Co-operation" of the Bandung Conference of 1955, which among others, enunciates the principles by which States may co-exist peacefully;

Recognising the right of every State, large or small to lead its national existence free from outside interference in its internal affairs as this interference will adversely affect its freedom, independence and integrity;

Dedicated to the maintenance of peace, freedom and independence unimpaired;

Believing in the need to meet present challenges and new developments by co-operating with all peace and freedom loving nations, both within and outside the region, in the furtherance of world peace, stability and harmony;

Cognizant of the significant trend towards establishing nuclear-free zones as in the "Treaty for the Prohibition of Nuclear Weapons in Latin America" and the Lusaka Declaration proclaiming Africa a nuclear-free zone, for the purpose of promoting world peace and security by reducing the areas of international conflicts and tensions;

Reiterating our commitment to the principle in the Bangkok Declaration which established ASEAN in 1967, "that the countries of Southeast Asia share a primary responsibility for strengthening the economic and social stability of the region and ensuring their peaceful and progressive national development, and that they are determined to ensure their stability and security from external interference in any form or manifestation in order to preserve their national identities in accordance with the ideals and aspirations of their peoples";

Agreeing that the neutralization of Southeast Asia is a desirable objective and that we should explore ways and means of bringing about its realization, and

Convinced that the time is propitious for joint action to give effective expression to the deeply felt desire of the peoples of Southeast Asia to ensure the conditions of peace and stability indispensable to their independence and their economic and social well-being;

Do hereby state:

(1) that Indonesia, Malaysia, the Philippines, Singapore and Thailand are determined to exert initially necessary efforts to secure the recognition of, and respect for, Southeast Asia as a Zone of Peace, Freedom and Neutrality, free from any form or manner of interference by outside Powers;

(2) that Southeast Asian countries should make concerted efforts to broaden the areas of co-operation which would contribute to their strength, solidarity and closer relationship.

SOUTHEAST ASIAN ARMED FORCES

Country	Men in Arms (thousands)				Defense Budget (U.S. $ millions)	Warships	Submarines	Combat Aircraft
	Army	Navy	Air Force	Total				
Burma	135	7	7	149	91	--	--	19
Cambodia	180	3	4	187	98	--	--	40
Indonesia	250	39	33	322	287	5	10	89
Laos	72	1	2	74	17	--	--	73
Malaysia	46	5	5	56	287	--	--	38
Philippines	19	12	11	43	95	--	--	62
Singapore	19	1	1	21	249	--	--	48
Thailand	125	20	35	180	293	--	--	160
S. Vietnam	460	62	50	572	379	--	--	309
N. Vietnam	565	3	10	578	584	--	--	178
Total	1,871	153	158	2,182	2,380	5	10	1,016
By comparison:								
China	2,500	180	220	2,900	7,000	6	43	3,800
Japan	180	41	45	266	3,530	29	13	386
India	826	31	92	948	2,386	4	4	842
United States	801	760	691	2,253	85,200	125	84	6,300
USSR	2,050	475	550	3,425	85,000	106	285	8,250
Australia	33	17	23	73	1,575	8	4	210

Note: Figures are rounded and simplified to facilitate quick comparisons; they should not be used as the basis of further calculations. Some (especially for China and USSR) are intelligent foreign estimates only. Defense budget is latest available (range: 1971 to 1973/74). Warships include aircraft-carriers, cruisers and destroyers.

Source: The Military Balance 1973-74 (London: International Institute for Strategic Studies, 1974).

66-67, 112-13. (See also
Sabah.)
Malaysian-Singapore Airways
(MSA), 80
Malaysian Digest, 30
Malik, Adam, 23, 28, 30, 42-
43, 47, 51, 52, 57, 80, 82,
89, 95, 111, 122, 126, 155,
156, 166, 181, 186
Malta, 37
Mao Tse-tung, 118-19
Maphilindo, 182-83
Marcos, President Ferdinand,
68-70, 180
Marcos, Imelda, 110
Matak, Sirik, 92
Matveyev, V. V., 110
Maung Maung, 38
Merdeka, 29
military bases, 13, 16, 40, 57,
66, 70
Millar, Tom B., 190, 194
Ministerial Conference on Eco-
nomic Development of
South East Asia, 24, 135
Monde, Le, 56, 92
Mongolia, 42
Mozingo, David, 10, 128
Mustapha, Tun, 187

Nation, 29, 157
national resilience, 56-57
Napoleon, 37
Nasser, Gamal A., 36
Ne Win, 86, 88-89, 125
Nehru, Jawaharlal, 6, 36, 37,
139
Nepal, 42
Nepszava, 112
Nesterenko, A. E., 112
neutralism, 26
neutrality, 25-26
neutralization, definition, 16,
25-26, 190-91; models of,
36-38, 191; multiple or
regional, 38, 192

New Nation, 82-83
New Zealand, 16, 40, 42, 51,
126, 146-47, 152, 153, 171-
72, 181
New York Times, 32, 41, 97
Ng, John, 30
Nixon, Richard M., 25, 55, 73,
95, 96, 104
Nixon Doctrine, 65, 104, 128
Nkrumah, Kwame, 36
nonaligned group of nations, 22,
23, 64; Algiers Conference,
1973, 23; Dar-es-Salaam
meeting, 1970, 8; George-
town Conference 1972, 23;
Lusaka Conference 1970, 23,
51, 65, 196
Norway, 18, 37
Nu, U., 86
Nugroho, 59

Observer, 111
Orn, Korn, 92

Pacific Basin Economic Consul-
tative Committee, 172
Pacific Community, 5, 57
Pakistan, 41, 42, 111, 113, 139,
152, 181-82
Pan Wannamethi, 127
Pancha Shila, 38
Panggabean, General Maraden,
155
Paracel Islands, 127
Pathet Lao, 72
Pavlovsky, V., 113
peaceful settlement of disputes,
17, 193
People's Daily (Peking), 119,
120, 127
Pertamina, 52
Philippines, 42, 125, 176, 178,
187; foreign policy, 68-69;
and neutralization, 68-70.
(See also Sabah.)
Phreah Vihar Temple, 177

ABOUT THE AUTHOR

DICK WILSON is editor of the China Quarterly and writes and lectures about East and Southeast Asian affairs.

Mr. Wilson is a former editor of the Far Eastern Economic Review, and a former financial editor of the Straits Times. He has published a number of books on Asia, including Asia Awakes and The Long March 1935.

Mr. Wilson graduated from Oxford University, and took his LLM at the University of California at Berkeley.

CHINA AND THE GREAT POWERS: Relations
with the U.S., the USSR, and Japan
edited by Francis O. Wilcox

CHINA AND SOUTHEAST ASIA: Peking's
Relations with Revolutionary Movements
John J. Taylor

THE POLITICS OF MODERN ASIA
Edmund S. Wehrle
and Donald F. Lach

SINO-AMERICAN DETENTE AND ITS POLICY
IMPLICATIONS*
edited by Gene T. Hsiao

SOUTHEAST ASIA UNDER THE NEW BALANCE
OF POWER*
edited by Sudershan Chawla,
Melvin Gurtov, and
Alain-Gerard Marsot

*Also available in paperback as a PSS Student Edition.